Confessions of the Post-Modern:
The Political Awakening of a Freedom Fighter

> Karen,
>
> No matter how much time passes, no matter how old we get, no matter how much our lives change — never stop learning. Never stop questioning. Never stop looking for answers as to how to improve the lives of our fellow human brothers and sisters around the globe. Never stop fighting for freedom. Liberty is beautiful and worth fighting for. Never let anyone tell you you can't be whoever you want to be.

I dedicate this book to the American working class, and to all individuals struggling for economic and social justice. Thank you for all of your activist work and for fighting to restore the American Dream. Together, we will succeed. Another world is possible.

With special thanks to:
David Jacobsen, Jake Hatch, Eric Landry, Amanda Gagnon, María-Isabel Carrasquillo, Maureen Raubach, Cory "Raphael" Hayward, Aaron Guyett; all of my friends from the University of New Hampshire in Durham who helped me grow and learn; my family, for having to deal with my budding radicalism at the dinner table; political science and philosophy Professors Matthew Dowd, Susan Siggilakis, and Duane Whittier; biology and chemistry Professors Donald Chandler, Andrew Ladauno, Laurie Westover, John Burger, Jessica Bolker, Rudolph "Rudi" Seitz, Gary Weisman, and Thomas Harris; the staff and leadership of *The New Hampshire* university newspaper; and my fellow progressive activists, academics, and voters, who helped provide me with constantly stimulating conversation, and who bravely advance the causes of Democracy and Liberty each and every day.

The tree of liberty must be refreshed, from time to time, with the blood of patriots and tyrants. It is its natural manure."
Thomas Jefferson

Labour is prior to, and independent of, Capital. Capital is only the fruit of Labour, and could never have existed if Labour had not first existed. Labour is the superior of Capital, and deserves much higher consideration.
Abraham Lincoln

Poverty is not an accident. Like slavery and apartheid, is it man-made and can be removed by the actions of human beings.
Nelson Mandela

No man talks more passionately about his rights than he, who, in the depths of his soul, doubts whether he even has any.
Friedrich Nietzsche

There are more things in Heaven and Earth, Horatio, than are dreamt of in your philosophy.
Hamlet

Table of Contents

Preface   **Page 11**

Introduction   **Page 14**

Section One: Treatises on the Revolutionary Left   **Page 23**
Musings on the Market
Non-Violent Existential Revolution?
Random Thoughts on the Revolution
On the Theory of the Vanguard Party
"An Advocate of Social Violence"
Theoretic First Steps
Thoughts on Parliamentarianism
On "Left" and "Libertarian" Marxism
Thoughts on the Vanguard Party
On the Historicism of Bourgeois-Democratic Revolutions
On Councilism, and Potentially Bourgeois Binaries
On "State-Capital" and Fascist "Justice"
On "Socialist" Co-Operatives and the State's "Withering Away"
On the Transitional Period, and the Initiation of Planning
On Purist Decentralization, and "Market" Socialism

Section Two: University Newspaper Articles   **Page 93**
Democracy Endangered
Romney is Not a Working-Class Hero
Obama Re-Elected
American Foreign Policy Gone Wrong
Obamacare, and Other "Evil" Socialist Ideas
The End of Reaganism
Capitalism is Killing our Humanity
Legalizing Marijuana is Only Step One
Let's Not Forget the 'T' in LGBT
The Sequester: Another Attempt by the Corporate Élite to Crush Labor
The American Republic has become the American Empire
Proposed Immigration Reform Doesn't Go Far Enough
Recent UNH Transgender Conference a Wild Success
US-UN Sanctions Created the North Korea Disaster

Americans Should Support New Venezuelan Leader
America Needs Political Change to Restore Liberty
Is Our Education System an Indoctrination System?
No War but Class War
Do Not Accept the Police State
Partisan House GOP vs the Working Class
A Co-Op Economy Can Effectively Replace Wall Street
Democrat, GOP "Reforms" Don't Go Far Enough
Two-Party System is Anti-Worker to the Core
"Liberty" is More than Just a Word
Amnesty for "Illegal" Immigrants is Step One
Fascism is Becoming Mainstream
Jesus, Socialist Extraordinaire
Living Wage, not Minimum Wage, is the Answer

Section Three: Exegetical and Thematic Papers   Page 179
Republic Revisited: A Marxian Critique of Platonic Justice
Socialist Economics: The Cure for Capitalist Estrangement
What is Freedom?: An Inquiry into the Possibility of Absolute Freedom
State and Polity: Man and His Relation to the Political Ultimate
Nietzsche, and the Intersectionality of Continental Philosophy and Radical Humanity
Marx vs Marcuse: Aesthetic Theory and the Campaign for "Revolutionary" Art
Existential Subjectivity as Radical Humanity

Section Four: Hermeneutics, Notes, and Thoughts   Page 265
On the Existentialism of Political Vanguardism
On Sartre's "The Ghost of Stalin"
On Luxemburg's "Reform and Revolution"
On Social Intersectionality and Base-Superstructure Theory
On Derrida's "Violence and Metaphysics"

Section Five: Early Works and Pre-College Essays   Page 303
The Importance of Property
The Alleviation of Poverty: Refocusing and Readjusting our Social Consciousness
Lincoln: Anti-Liberty and Necessary Imperialism
In Defense of the Progressive Presidency

Radical Westernism: Imperialism, Consumerism, and the Abuse of the American System
"Right to Work" Not Right for New Hampshire
The Realpolitik of Socialism
Collective Bargaining
Keynesian vs Austrian: Two Names for Bourgeois Exploitation

Preface

Daniel Fournier is a man I have known personally for the majority of my life, from a very early age. From early own, Dan showed his quintessential life trait: his ability to think more critically about political issues than most others. This ability set him apart from his peers, where they fumbled through monotony - Dan opened his eyes and questioned his surroundings constantly and fully.

Dan quests not only to find solace within himself, but also for the continued benefit of mankind. Politically, Dan stands in a space that is far to the left of any modern political party in America, often clashing with liberals and progressives in the process. However, this is not because he is an disenfranchised zealot or radical idealist, but rather because it is, in fact, the product of Dan's holistic nature of critical thinking. Dan has a profoundly Nietzschean view of morality, and his view that it is a social construct has put him at odds with moral conservatives and structuralists. Despite of the utilitarianism that I see running through his works, one has to admit that his ideas of both genuine socialism and libertarian freedom seem a lot more plausible and appetizing when place yourself in a futuristic culture with community-based altruism, not present-day America.

A point Dan makes, one echoed constantly throughout history, is that a correct and "moral" human society is one that best cares for all of its people. Dan is incredibly politically active, but his vocal discontent with the current political system is based on the core of his philosophic and political beliefs: a sort of so-called libertarian socialism that draws from both Marxian socialism and anti-establishment anarchism. When mixed with his firm existentialist views, it paints an interesting picture about the nature of mankind and its politics.

He argues - rightly - that the globalized economy that currently operates across the face of the earth is the root of many of the horrific problems we as a species face on a constant basis. War, hunger, and poverty are all caused by governments full of bureaucratic, upper-class élites who are in turn influenced (if not outright controlled) by corporate interests domestically and abroad. The moments of crisis in various parts of the world spur the cogs in our massive global-industrial machine. Supply and demand can be reworked in ways where prices for even simple domestic goods like, food, oil, and medicine are such that they are completely accessible by the majority of the working population. The current structure of the global economy did not come about by mere chance - there is an élite agenda being pushed, an agenda that does not take the interests of middle-class American citizens into consideration. This needs to change.

The modern economies' vicious cycle of destruction and poverty - this is what Dan is most actively addressing, and he does so boldly by offering solutions that others wouldn't normally think about. Human rights such as the access to reliable healthcare, affordable housing, and nutritional food are denied to so many millions of people living in the United States of America, a nation which boasts to have one of the highest standards of living, vast wealth, and a strong economy, but which refuses to step up to the plate and provide for the populace which makes the country work every day.

The worker, the student, the children, the elderly - every demographic of humanity on our planet needs to come together and think critically about the problems that we are facing. When people work together, they can overcome amazing challenges. History is full of examples of popular movements, from the rise and fall of empires to the wars that changed that world. Only together can the world population tackle and overcome the problems that we face today: wasteful and bureaucratic globalization, domestic poverty and mass-hunger, and the largest wealth disparity in our country's history since the Great Depression.

In this book, Dan does his best to document his political and philosophic awakening through his years of newspaper articles, essays, and lectures. His message is clear: our freedom is slipping away and we need fundamental change to bring it back. He draws on Sartre, Nietzsche, Marx, Judith Butler, and Noam Chomsky to do so. Dan weaves their ideologies with his personal experiences and outlooks on life to create a picture of society could be. This society may not be possible to achieve in this life time, but he presents a rough framework for future generations to follow. I hope you enjoy his works as much as I do, and I hope they make you question your political views.

Eric Landry
16 December, 2013
Durham, NH

Introduction

When I first started working on this book towards the beginning of my university career, I never expected it to be anything more than a dozen pages or so. I've started other books in the past, but they've all fallen to the wayside as other, more important things have arisen and required my attention - family matters, school and university classes, work and money, and so on. Maybe in the future I'll be able to get around and finish them. At this point, though, it looks as if this will be the first one, and possibly the only one that I'll be able to finish in the immediate and foreseeable future.

I've been meaning to get around and put several of my works together for some time now, if for nothing else other than to document my own political growth. I was a young teenager when I first started reading about politics, and most of it was confined to the liberal wing of the Democratic Party. I read things that were mainstream - the *New York Times*, the *Nation*, the *Progressive*, the *Washington Blade*, the mainstream CNN-FOX-MSNBC complex, and a handful of newsletters that were sponsored by local Democratic and progressive organizations. Having grown up in a working-class family with two struggling divorced parents, I was acutely aware that the system was not geared in the direct interests of the Average Joe. There was something missing - I was aware that the system was vaguely anti-worker and pro-corporate, but I wasn't old enough to properly understand the struggles that my parents each went through as they were forced to live paycheck to paycheck and stretch every dollar to put food on the table. I didn't understand what it was like to lay in bed and be unable to fall asleep from the sheer stress and anxiety of wondering if there'd be enough money to pay the bills the next month. I was far too young and naïve to understand the structural problems in our society and how close to home those problems hit. I was blissfully ignorant for most of my childhood while my parents secretly (and sometimes not-so-secretly) hid their borderline financial catastrophes from me.

It wasn't until I began studying at the University of New Hampshire that I developed a more sophisticated outlook on the world. My biology and chemistry teachers taught me how to analyze the material world around me, but they taught me *what* to think and not *how* to think. It wasn't until I had my first political theory class my freshman year that I was exposed to alternative ways of thinking. Capitalism, socialism, fascism, Marxism, liberalism, Naziism - these words are thrown around far too often and carelessly in mainstream American political discourse, and I didn't have much clue about what they really meant until going to the University. I had my first encounters with non-capitalist theory there, and I don't think I every properly expressed my thanks to the University's political science professors at the time for opening those academic doors for me.

During my freshman year, I joined my University's local College Democrats chapter in order to get civically involved. I already knew that I was a liberal by the time that I got there, and I expected the rest of the Democrats to be just as, if not more, liberal than me because they'd had the opportunity to take more classes, read more, mature with age, and so on. It was there that I met my close friend David Jacobsen, someone who would be instrumental in molding my politics into what they are today. He did so not just through our conversations over lunch regarding immigration, healthcare, economics, and social justice, but by giving me my first Noam Chomsky book at the time of his graduation. It was, as he said, supposed to open doors to explicitly radical politics and teach me that the information that I hear on the mainstream media (generally, what most of my liberal tendencies were informed by) served corporate interests by, as Chomsky has famously put it, manufacturing consent among the general populace. From the first page I was captured. There was something in Chomsky's book that impacted me in a way that mainstream liberal newspapers weren't able to. He offered a scathing, honest, thought-provoking analysis of everything in society that I'd taken for granted for the first eighteen or so years of my life.

From that moment on, I couldn't get my hands on enough books; I couldn't read fast enough to sate my voracious appetite. Even though I was still studying evolutionary biology and ecology at the University, my hobbies shifted dramatically. Politics replaced science-fiction novels, and philosophy replaced fantasy stories. I spent less time re-reading Harry Potter and Lord of the Rings and more time reading Rousseau, Plato, Marx, and Hegel. I'd set the *New York Times* down and picked up Sartre's *Existentialism is a Humanism*. From that moment on, my eyes were open and I saw the world in a whole new way. I've never been able to close them since.

My own political stance became increasingly concrete as time went on. Originally, I was a liberal Democrat; after a while, when I knew that I was more progressive than mainstream liberals, I made a joke to my father wherein I called myself a "radical liberal", for lack of a better word, because I wasn't as familiar with the different technical "-isms" at the time as I later became. I later self-identified as a social democrat, inspired by the Keynesian, reformist progressivism associated with the Nordic model. Toward the middle of my University career, I finally decided to abandon capitalist dogma altogether and embrace a democratic socialism reminiscent of Eduard Bernstein's gradualist "evolutionary socialism", mingled with a sort of non-violent civil disobedience. In the last two years at the University, I came out as a socialist with explicitly Marxist tendencies, tendencies which have only solidified as I've grown and have had to face to adult "real world". Coming face-to-face with working-class "real world" problems has only convinced me that there are systemic, structural problems that plague our society, and they have further opened my eyes by bluntly teaching me that the economy is not geared in the interests of the working-class majority.

Since, my politics have become increasingly tinged with elements of continental philosophy. Phenomenology, existentialism, nihilism - these and more have contributed to my political growth and have led me into a rough political framework that I can foresee myself occupying for the rest of my life. However, if the material conditions of my life change and I have the opportunity to engage in new educational endeavors, then I am more than open-minded enough to re-adjust and tweak the political-philosophic framework that I have inside my head.

For now, though, I sit comfortably on the libertarian Left, surrounded by my fellow anti-statist socialist comrades. My own brand of existential Marxism is becoming increasingly mature and comprehensive as time goes on, and I am excited to see what philosophic impacts the future has in store for me, particularly as I leave the hyper-academic environment of the University classrooms and step into real-world science laboratories and put my degree to use.

I have tried to break this book down into several distinct sections to show the different phases that I have gone through. The first section, "Treatises on the Revolutionary Left", includes the various essays and letters that I've written while formulating a cohesive socialist framework while communicating with explicitly revolutionary individuals around the world - be they anarchists, Marxist-Leninists, eco-socialists, or obscure far-left tendencies that are too academic to go into in any proper detail here. This may be some of the more theoretically substantive material presented in this book, if for nothing else than to illustrate how profound person-to-person Left-wing political debate has been for me. If one is looking for explicitly theoretic works on Leftist issues, this is probably some of the most substantive section of the book.

The second section is titled "University Newspaper Articles" and includes the articles that I wrote for my University's *The New Hampshire* paper under my column "From the Left". This was the first opportunity that I had to engage with the public on a relatively large scale, and it gave me the chance to see how my own views would be felt by the campus community at large. Some of them (such as "Let's Not Forget the 'T' in LGBT") were met with wild approval and explicit public support, while others (such as "No War but Class War") were not as popular, and received credit from those in academia but scorn from the political non-Left.

The third section, ""Exegetical and Thematic Papers" constitutes a collection of essays and response papers that I submitted to my professors during my social and political philosophy classes. The fourth section is titled "Hermeneutics, Notes, and Thoughts" and is a collection of the random thoughts that I have had while formulating my own existential Marxism, sometimes vis-à-vis books that I've read in the past. Given that my own political philosophy is still developing, there may be additional essays - and perhaps even books, or at least revised editions - written about it in the future. If there are sentences, ideas, and paragraphs that are repeated in more than one entry in this book, it is because I thought that they were pertinent enough to repeat. As the book is organized in chronological order, the ideas will become increasingly cohesive and formulated as you reach the back cover.

The fifth and final section, "Early Works and Pre-College Essays", encapsulates the progressive and social democratic space that I occupied early in my life, while some ("The Importance of Property") show the influence that classical liberalism had on me while I just starting to read and how radically my views have shifted during my time studying at the University.

I hope that this book serves as effective documentation for my philosophic development during my University career. But, more so than that, I hope that it is thought-provoking enough for the reader that it causes them to question the structural integrity of the system under which we live, similar to what Chomsky's book did for me several years ago. That is my greatest hope for this book: not that it will sit unread on a bookshelf, gathering dust and sitting unused, but rather that it will serve as the means through which critical thought is stimulated, thorough analysis is inspired, and rigorous debate is initiated.

If there is one thing that readers can take from this book, it is that any discourse that we have regarding a post-capitalist society needs to tackle the issue of climate change. It's not a joke - even some of the conservative estimates put out by the U.N.'s International Panel on Climate Change show that we are perilously close to the point wherein the aggregate impact of capitalism on the earth's ecology may initiate a feedback cycle, a domino cascade wherein the collapse of important ecologic keystone species will result in an unfathomable ripple effect across the entire planet. Any revolutionary mass party is going to need to be dedicated to a fundamentally eco-socialist programme that does not view *Homo sapien* as being radically independent of other organisms. The proletarian party is going to need a comprehensive, radically green programme that views mankind as *part* of the ecosystem, not above and distinct from it.

Given that we combat climate change and are able to have a realistic conversation about the possibility of building socialism without irreparably damaging the earth via the necessary industrialization beforehand, we should be mindful of several things. Firstly, we socialists must not shy away from the Soviet experience that, for better or worse, has tainted the word socialism for - arguably - the rest of human history, and honestly discuss the historical and economic impacts that the USSR had on the greater socialist movement. Secondly, we must not be afraid to have intense, critical discussions wherein we deconstruct and debate the most fundamental elements of Marxism, socialism, and anarchism without falling into complacent reformism. We need to re-read Marx, Lenin, Luxemburg, Bernstein, and the host of other Left theorists that came about both before and after the October and February Revolutions in Russia, and be unafraid to update their works in the wake of nuclear development, ecologic crises, globalization, neoliberalism, and neocolonial occupations without compromising our principals. We need to be able to have an honest discussion about the historical role - and indeed, the future - of socialism since the early-industrial era of Marx and Engels, and how the material conditions of the world have changed since.

All of this needs to be done without being dogmatic purists. We need to abandon the more-revolutionary-er-than-thou sentiments that consistently plague the Left and fragment it into unrealistic, hyper-radicalized sectarian groups. The conditions of our nation's working class, and of the whole global proletariat, need to be taken into consideration so that we can do whatever is needed to ameliorate the systemic immiseration that they are facing each and every day. Whether this involves reform or revolution, we need to be willing to do both with an open and willing mind in order to elevate the proletariat to the position of political supremacy.

I hope that this books serves to stimulate conversation amongst its readers and, in some small way, encourages the development of a consciousness conducive for fundamental social and economic change, and for the improvement of the conditions of the working class. If nothing else, I hope that it at least opens people's eyes so that they can look at the world in a new and different way, so that they can go about their lives mindful of political and economic reality. But do not take what I, or what anyone else, says to be the Gospel truth. Read every side of every issue, and do not be afraid to thoroughly deconstruct them and question their legitimacy.

The future of our planet, and of the workers' movement, is in your hands. Do not shy away from this awesome responsibility - rise up, seize the moment, and do what you can to make this world a better place. I think that you'll be very surprised how much political impact a single individual can make - and then step back and think about what a massive, public, populist movement could do if it went global. The world does not have to be this way. Another world is possible.

In solidarity,
Dan Fournier
26 December, 2013
Manchester, NH

Section One
Treatises on the Revolutionary Left

Musings on the Market

I'll admit that I used to be a huge fan of capitalism, back before I did any reading or critical thinking on my own. Now that I've decided to actually get around to educating myself, I've been growing increasingly skeptical of it. I dislike it now and consider it economic planning to be superior.

I'm siding with Marx when he confessed that he was in awe of the productive powers of the market. I'm as much an anti-capitalist as anyone else on the Left, but you have to give the market credit where it's due - it's wily, adaptable, tricky, and has an incredible reach. The system exploitation, surplus-value, wage-slavery, etc are far less appealing

I don't like the capitalist marketplace (be it national or global) but what about if we created a sort of "socialist marketplace"? Be it either in the post-revolutionary socialism or the evolved-from-capitalism-through-social-democracy-and-into-real-socialism gradualist approach, what if we were able to tame the market such that we could make a sort of partially planned / partially market-based system?

Now, I'm not talking about social democratic economics. I'm not trying to describe a Scandinavian or Keynesian "soft" capitalism, a mixed market, a regulated capitalist economy, etc.

What if we were able to establish an economy based on worker-owned cooperatives that compete with one another?

This would induce some competition and make the cooperatives work to make the best products at better prices, despite the fact that I am invoking market fundamentalist rhetoric. The means of production would be owned by the workers themselves, and any and all profit that's generated in the 'market' would be either split up and divided equally amongst the worker-owners, or be invested into the community as a form of public financing.

Maybe some people would condemn my idea of market socialism because they think that the market is inherently bad, but I'd argue that the *capitalist* market is what's wrong, and if there's a way that we can harness market forces for a *socialist* cause, it might be something that we could conceivably do while we're transitioning from capitalism.

It might be a good idea to have regional federations of worker's councils set up too, so that we can do our best to prevent these worker-owned competing co-ops from duplicating products and services too much and draining unnecessary resources for unnecessary production. A little bit of regional economic planning might be a nice idea, so long as it sets some boundaries and a general direction on the way that the economy should move.

The ones that are part of the planning process need to be democratically elected; if we're going to have some economic democracy, need to have *complete* economic democracy. Anything less than that is a disservice to the proletariat

Maybe if we had representatives from each regional workers council (elected from the council itself, with input from both the council members and the members of the community) meet and form *larger* regional areas workers councils, and have the same for larger regions, and for larger regions, until we have a *national* workers council.

I'd like there to be a government too, but one that's stripped of all class influence so that's its not a tool for the bourgeoisie, etc and so that it's only around for administrative purposes to keep everything running smoothly. Like city hall - my town's city hall is purely administrative and there aren't really much politics to it. If we could set up government so that it's apolitical, that would be nice.

Anyone who is in the government would have to have gotten there through the democratic process, of course. No nepotism, appointments, etc should take place. If the administrative local, regional, and national governments worked with the local, regional, and national workers councils, it might be able to have their activities synced so that the system runs a bit smoother.

To prevent the various factions in the workers councils and governments from breaking up into factions (which might eventually develop into all-out political parties), an idea might be to have a single-party state. But that might lead to some sort of democratic centralism, which I feel like leads to a bureaucratic, dictatorial rule by the leader(s) of the party, wherein one imposes his political viewpoint on the entire party without there being the possibility for free speech, critique, dissent, etc. So maybe it might be better to have a "party-less" state, so that that sort of bureaucracy and sectarianism wouldn't become a reality.

That's not to say that vague, loose alliances of workers inside the workers councils couldn't happen, or between administrative officials in the governments - but they just shouldn't become legitimate political parties. A party-less, democratic body would probably be a good idea.

If we're going to have a marketplace built up of competing worker-owned co-ops, there has to be *some* profit motive to motivate and inspire the workers to develop and create new things, tools, procedures, etc. Maybe legalizing free enterprise on a small scale (allowing workers to open up and start their own businesses) would be a good idea too, so long as that enterprise's actions don't effect the region's (socialist) market too much and / or too negatively. In a marketplace that is overwhelmingly dominated by co-ops, a very small percentage of the institutions being private probably wouldn't be *that* bad.

I'm just trying to be flexible and think up of a sort of market-based scenario that could feasibly work as we transition from social democracy into real socialism. Given time, I'm sure that more planning would take place, and more and more of the institutions would be public rather than private.

But it seems like this process is reasonable if it's a temporary phase in the historical evolution.

Non-Violent Existential Revolution?

To those who have attempted to discredit my Leftist credentials by arguing that synthesizing continental philosophy with Marxism dilutes and sterilizes both, I would reply with emphatic disagreement. The merger of the two traditions enriches both.

I identify as a revolutionary democratic socialist and Sartrean Marxist, but when I use the prefix "revolutionary" in front of democratic socialism, I don't just mean "an advocate of the proletarian revolution". There are two reasons for this.

Firstly: don't get me wrong - I'm all for the proletariat rising up, the seizing of control of the means of production, the socialist revolution, etc as preached by other revolutionaries. I'm just a little skeptical about the *timing* of the revolution. I'm a big fan of the dialectic process - and I feel as if we'll never be sure about exactly *when* the right time is to have the revolution. That's the primary concern that I have with Leninism: I don't think it's wise to surgically insert one's self into the historical process and try to instigate the revolution; rather, it should happen naturally and the proletariat should rise up together, on their own, as a whole, rather than be lead by a group of self-nominated élitist Communist Party members. I'm not going to pretend that I have all the answers about the revolution, but I'm pretty skeptical about anyone saying that "this is the time to have it", because we'll never know if the revolution would have been better historically situated a decade or a generation later. But if a revolution does come along, I'll be there

Secondly: when I say "revolutionary democratic socialism", I'm not just referring to the aforementioned points, but also "revolutionary" as a synonym for "bold, dramatic, thorough, comprehensive". I guess my own little brand of proletarian-revolution-sympathizing socialism brought about through the democratic process requires extraordinarily bold proposals to be continuously introduced. If we just create a slow gradualist approach, we'll probably end up at best with social democracy and the proletariat will be really complacent and won't fight for anything better. I'm all for the gradualist approach cause I'm not a fan of violence, but I recognize it's shortcomings. If we're going to get things done through the parliamentary process, we can't let ourselves become stagnant and content. We have to hold on to the vision of socialism and never let it out of our sight and never settle for anything less.

Hopefully this has clarified issues that others have thought vague. I'm a proponent of establishing a socialist mode of production, but I'd like to see that happen through a democratic and non-violent process, and seeing as working through the electoral process often ends up with a sort of progressive social democracy at best, we need a forceful, bold, unapologetic, openly socialist presence to continuously fight for it.

I mentioned Sartre above. I'm not going to spend the next couple minutes outlining everything that he said while politically active, but I think that it's important to make this point: he says that people gain definition from the choices, conflicts, struggles, etc in their lives, and every choice that we make helps define us a little bit more.

I'd like to see the transition from capitalism to socialism be a gradualist one, and I think that the extra time it takes to do so (rather than a short and immediate revolution, I mean) helps peoples, parties, classes, etc gain better definition.

Just as people gain definition through choices and conflicts, so does the extended democratic process and all its parliamentary actions help define the proletariat. Nothing is going to be won without a bit of conflict, and the electoral struggle *for* socialism will define and prepare the proletariat for life *under* socialism.

I'd like to see us move from capitalism to social democracy, from social democracy to some form of decentralized mostly-planned market socialism, to actual socialism - and I think that a bold, non-sectarian but also non-vanguardist socialist presence that doesn't stop when we hit social democracy might do the trick. If there's a revolution and we hop from capitalism to socialism, awesome - but if we evolve gradually over time, I think that's preferable.

Random Thoughts on the Revolution

Recently, I spoke about the possibility of a non-violent revolution. As I've indicated before quite explicitly, I would prefer a gradualist approach (as long as it's bold and forceful enough that it won't end up with some social democratic proletarian complacency, *and has the energy to actually move from capitalism to socialism*), but I'm starting to lean a bit more towards the necessity of a revolution to get to socialism, rather than doing so exclusively via democratic reform.

I'd love a non-violent capitalist-to-socialist evolution, but I'm starting to think that it might not be possible to get to socialism that way. That is, I think that democratic socialism is viable *as long as the socialist organization / party that's helping lead the system-wide reform doesn't loose sight of its socialist goal and ends up sitting in some social democratic limbo phase forever.*

I don't want to end up with some vaguely Nordic, social democratic, Keynesian welfare state - but I'd much rather take an extra couple years and slowly float through it on the way to full socialism than have a blood-red revolution that might accidentally end up with some weird authoritarianism.

I feel like there might actually be a need for a legitimate revolution. I'm aware - I've been pretty skeptical about the need for an actual revolution, but I'm starting to think that the democratic process shouldn't be *the* means through which we go about establishing socialism - that is, it should be a tactic of the proletariat, *but it shouldn't invest all of our energy in it*. We can't just depend on democracy to get us to socialism, we need to make it a multi-front action: we should encourage democratic reform, sure, because raising political awareness, getting people involved, etc may raise some proletarian consciousness, *but we should also encourage the revolution as well.*

So I'm thinking of instead of pursuing a purely democratic approach, we should approach *both* a democratic one and a revolutionary one.

This may not be a huge epiphany for my comrades on the Left, but it's a significant step Leftward for me. I don't want to say that I'm "anti-revolutionary". I'm much more "anti-violence" and pacifistic, so I'm just opposed to a violent revolution, I suppose, but I'm starting to see the folly in thinking that an entire system-wide reform might not be entirely possible through the democratic process and might involve a little bit of revolution here and there.

I'd rather have a peaceful revolution, but I can't really see capitalism being overthrown without a little bit of damage here and there. I'd like to keep that damage to a minimum, but there might be a bit of a need to have it once in a while.

Although, I think that I should point out that I'm not really a fan of a vanguard party surgically inserting itself into the historical process and instigating a revolution ... maybe I'm not as comfortable with Leninist theory as several of our other comrades, but I feel like a Communist Party (or whatever the group wants to call itself) that tries to rush the historical process by making us jump from capitalism to socialism/communism. I feel like the revolution needs to come on its own, and we should support it when it does, rather than try and make one when we're not ready.

On the Theory of the Vanguard Party

Comrades, let me re-state what I've said before. First and foremost, I'm a gradualist, and I would love to see capitalism evolve into socialism as the result of the bold, democratic action of a class-conscious proletariat. I'm a democratic socialist, *not a social democrat*: I want to abolish the capitalist mode of production, but I want to do so in a non-violent and preferably evolutionary manner. However, I'm also not naïve: I realize that the bourgeois may cave to some of the proletariat's demands so as to pacify them, and we may end up with a sort of progressive, social democratic system instead. The whole problem of trade union consciousness might come into play and, once the proletariat gets a couple of its immediate reform that it wanted (healthcare, better hours, social security programs, etc) it could quite possibly get very complacent and give up the push towards complete socialism .... hence why I've come around to the idea of a vanguardist organization to help educate and organize the proletariat so that will actually have the will and power completely abolish capitalism.

Therefore, there are several things that I should say to you.

I would prefer to see the vanguard party be non-revolutionary. I know that that sounds bizarre, so let me explain: *I want a peaceful, non-violent, evolutionary approach to socialism* (yes, I'll admit that I have my revisionist tendencies, but I think that it is necessary to view and apply Marx's theories in accordance with the current material conditions ... perhaps as I learn more this may change) *wherein the vanguard party to educate and organize the proletariat so that it will not loose vision of actual socialism, so that it will hold fast the idea of what they are really fighting for - of there democratic reforms being a means to socialism, not being and end in and of themselves.*

And thus is the crux of my problem: I want socialism, but I want it done through gradualist and reformist means. There is a distinct possibility of proletarian complacency with its achieved democratic reforms ending up in mere social democracy, yes, but I think that a proactive political party (the vanguard party) could organize them to keep pushing forward and never letting go of the vision of their final goal.

But I recognize that this may be rather idealistic, so I think that it is far more likely that there will be a revolutionary transformation to socialism than a evolutionary one. I'm still a pacifist and love the famous quote "peacefully if we may, forcibly if we must" because it sums up what I'm thinking so eloquently.

A revolution is going to have to be lead by a vanguard party - not only am I skeptical in thinking that the proletariat may obtain class consciousness (I think Lenin's idea of trade union consciousness is *far* more accurate) and that it may require vanguardism to inspire a mass movement, but the (very probable) existence of bourgeois, bourgeois-sympathizing, and anti-revolutionary forces will attempt to quell the revolution, and a centralized organization will be needed to repel them.

However, my support for a vanguard party is tamed by two lingering questions.

Firstly: I subscribe to the argument that I often hear other Marxists say regarding the Russian Revolution - that the reason that it did not successfully reach socialism is because the vanguard party attempted to surgically insert itself into the historical process, rush the not-yet-fully-developed Russian proletariat from agrarian-feudalism into socialism without passing through capitalism and developing the necessary productive forces to overcome scarcity. *So my first question is how do we ever know when we are at the right historical moment in the dialectic process to commit the revolution?*

Secondly: I am not authoritarian, I am libertarian (not in the sense of contemporary libertarianism vis-à-vis classical liberalism, but instead as a general opposition to determinist authoritarity). I do not like authoritarian, totalitarian, or oppressive institutions. Part of my awakening to socialist consciousness is the realization of the inherent oppression in capitalist sociology and the desire to abolish it. I do not, though, want to have the vanguard party that is leading the proletariat into socialism to become the *de facto* ruling class in the new society. I do not want to exchange bourgeois oppressors for party-élite oppressors. *My second question then is whether or not the vanguard party may establish itself as a authoritarian regime and institute new conditions of oppression and sociologic determinism.*

Perhaps a temporary, short-term vanguard party-run "state" is necessary to centralize the means of production and prepare them for socialist democratization, protect the developing society from bourgeois retaliation, and so on. I accept that. However, what I do not accept is vanguardism that may result in a Stalinist dictatorship, and I do not want a party-run "state" to last in the long term. If it is a means to socialism, so be it; if it is the end in itself, then I'm not so keen on it.

I wonder if (with the State having been abolished in the proletarian revolution and it fundamentally transforming from an institution of class-rule to purely administrative matters) the party might not exist at all. I mean this: political parties are interest groups inside the system, and, if the system is gone, then that party is no longer a "party". It's entire purpose - changing, controlling, altering, etc the system - is gone because there is no system for it left to change.

I'm also *not* a fan of democratic centralism - if anything, the vanguard party needs to be democratically-run. If the party is not completely democratic, then I think that it's doing a disservice to the proletariat ... I don't think that it's appropriate for the party élite to adopt a "more righteous than thou" or a "we're more enlightened so we know what's best for you" mentality and dictate the orders for the party from the top-down. It should be bottom-up and people-run.

It seems that I'm coming around to vanguardism, so long as it is done in the right historical moment and does not lead towards a new vanguard-élite oppression.

"An Advocate of Social Violence"

Comrades, there are several issues that need to be addressed in regards to Sartrean Marxism.

Sartre only flirted with the PCF (Partie Communiste Française), as he decided that they were too reactionary. He began to lend his name and support to various militant far-Left groups instead, and he ended up being something of an unofficial Maoist; as his life went on, his views became increasingly tinged with anarchism. He was often associated with the Maoist-inspired Proletarian Left and with the Revolutionary Democratic Rally.

Sartre was described as an "advocate of social violence" because he thought that the State was an enemy to personal liberty and that it should be fought against. As I've mentioned before in preceding discourse (and those who read this that are already familiar with existentialism should be aware of this), Sartre believed that his own brand of existentialism was a philosophy of action, that the decisions and choices that people make throughout their lives constitute their character. We gain definition based on our choices, he argued, and that we had ultimate responsibility for who and what we are because we chose to become that, over the course of many years. Towards the end of his life, Sartre became increasingly aware of the concept of economic determinism, and wanted to overthrow the State and the capitalist mode of production because he believed that, with them, we are determined and influenced, rather than having the free will to define ourselves.

I agree with Sartre. The economy and capitalism does go a long way in determining how society is structured and how people act, but we do have a little bit of wiggle room. Sartre was a playwright, and a theatre-loving friend of mine once described Sartre's beliefs as "capitalist production sets the stage for what your life is, but you have the power to write the script".

Sartre realized that the capitalist mode of production takes freedom away from people and that the government enacts laws and policies that legitimize that oppression. In order to be free, one needs to abolish capitalism, and to abolish capitalism, one needs to abolish the State. This is logical. But here's where I start thinking - Sartre was saying that strikes, lock-out, clashes with the police, both violent and non-violent protest, workers expropriating the workplace from its capitalist owners, and such things (what people would call his "social violence") suited his existential beliefs *because they provided a series of choices, opportunities, decisions, actions, etc wherein people could gain existential definition.* I agree - part of what's been driving my personal evolution from a reformist to a revolutionary are the arguments that Sartre makes. A peaceful, gradual approach is all well and good because it gives you a series of choices and decisions, but a *revolutionary approach gives you bigger, bolder, more character-defining choices.*

What I'm not so sure about is Sartre's advocacy for "social violence". He says that it creates miniature, isolated, microcosmic events that provide choices and opportunities similar to a proletarian revolution. Union strikes, protests, workers' uprisings, etc not only provide people with an opportunity to gain bold existential definition, but they serve a *secondary tactic*: *they goad the State into small, isolated conflicts*. These small conflicts bait the State and test its strength, similar to poking a hornets' nest with a stick - you won't destroy it, but you'll agitate it. Sartre postulated that having such isolated people-vs-State conflicts allow the proletariat to see how the State would react to the threat of an uprising, that it would be a way to expose the State's violently anti-revolutionary reaction, and be an effective way of rallying proletarian support.

Here's my ambivalence with Sartre's "social violence" (for the record, I think that referring to them as "isolated revolutions" are a better way of putting it, because they serve as a small-scale examples of what may happen in an all-out proletarian revolution): they do provide bold, dynamic circumstances through which we can gain existential definition and do indeed goad and test the State, but they may also serve as something that the State could paint as "terrorism". Any action that we take against the State could be branded as terrorism and, if the State utilizes its propaganda machine effectively enough (which I'm also certain that it would), it could portray us in such poor lighting that it would turn others off from joining the revolution and make people afraid to question that State.

That would make our actions awfully counter-productive, because all we're trying to do is expose the violence of the State and *we* could come across as the ones who are the radical terrorists! If we're going to stage a revolutionary overthrow of the State, having *us* look like the bad guys certainly wouldn't help our cause.I'm not saying that we should sit here in a sort of pessimistic quietism and be afraid of doing anything against the State because of a potential bad reputation we get - I'm just thinking about the consequences of such "isolated revolutions". Discussing the immediate political implications of our actions during the proletarian revolution is a conversation that the Left needs to have.

Theoretic First Steps

Comrades, if we're going to have a revolution, we can't just wake up and decide to do it one day. It will be the culmination of a series of political and economic struggles, not a single, spontaneous event. If we want that revolution and we want to get rid of capitalism, we have to take some steps now to construct a political climate that will foster a revolutionary mindset and be sympathetic to our socialist cause.

I think that we need to come at the capitalist establishment from all fronts - launch a political attack on it from the inside and a revolutionary uprising from the outside. I know that bringing about socialism is going to be a long and tough battle, and it will be full of plenty of surprises and unforeseen material circumstances. That being said, I think that there are a couple things that we can do right now ... given that we're discussing an industrialized and capitalist nation with a thriving proletariat like the United States, not a backwards pre-capitalist Third World country. Then again, I'm making a huge assumption about future material conditions, so maybe everything I'm saying will end up being totally wrong!

Firstly, we need to get rid of the Supreme Court's *Citizens' United* decision and replace it with a publicly-financed campaign system.. I've heard others around revleft say that too, and I absolutely agree. Capital is always going to be involved in politics, but if we can get rid of *Citizens' United*, we'd be making progress. If we get a public campaign system, we'd be able to run more progressive, socialist, and communist candidates and inject a bit of new dialogue into the electoral process.

So here's a rough map of what I think our immediate program should look like in regards to immediate reforms that we, via democratic socialism, should call for.

Firstly, Have as many liberals, progressives, socialists, communists, anarchists, and anyone else that is left-of-centre or anti-establishment as possible to register as a member of the Democratic Party. I think that it's better to capitalize on the Democrats' national party infrastructure rather than have to build up a brand new one on our own, given that we can work from inside and swing the Party Leftward rather than leave it the way that it is. At least it gives us ballot access and a path inside the system, if nothing else. *We need to be open, bold, not be afraid to state our aims publicly, and preach them in a populist manner so that we can get mass support.* Once we get *Citizens' United* gone, we can ditch this tactic - it should be only a temporary, short-term approach I think.

  Secondly, elect a progressive president, a progressive majority to both chambers of Congress, and and a progressive majority to state legislatures and governor seats around the country. Once they're in office, they'll be able to use the media to get their messages heard better, and the result will have a positive feedback. It doesn't matter if they're progressive Democrats or part of the Socialist Party, Green Party, of local or state parties, etc - *as long as we can get solid, unabashed, fiery progressives in, we can start to work on a massive, system-wide reform agenda.* I'm not sure how we'd deal with reactionary politics, other than make our message more populist so that we come across as more sympathetic to the working class. I realize that electing a progressive majority around the entire country would be difficult to accomplish, but if it can be done, it would be a small step that could be in our favor.

  Thirdly, while in power, we should rapidly do the following: overturn *Citizens' United* and establish a publicly-financed campaign system so that we would be able to run radicals without relying on the Democratic ticket. We should have all of our elected agents cooperating and working together, though, rather than fall apart into a sectarian, multi-party legislature. *We should also work to abolish, limit, restrict, or repeal as much bourgeois police and military power as possible* - if we can work to weaken the State from within, it will make our revolution a little easier, I think. If we withdraw from NATO and the UN too, that might limit external bourgeois influence.

  Fourthly, while we're at it, our inside-the-system agents could also work to push the Supreme Court as far Left as possible, pass the single-payer healthcare bill H.R. 676, push the Supreme Court to enact marriage equality, end the war on drugs by (at the very least!) nationally decriminalizing cannabis (if nothing else, this cuts back on some community police involvement), grant undocumented citizens amnesty, end all wars abroad, bring the troops home, and close all foreign military bases, make deep cuts to the Defense budget and invest in a pro-socialist education system and green energy, enact a *real* war on poverty, pass major infrastructure repair bills, expropriate private land for common use, forgive foreign and student debt, pass a modern-day Lenin-like New Economic Policy to nationalize the commanding heights of the economy, democratize corporations, advocate global nuclear disarmament, support the establishment and expansion of worker-owned cooperatives, and tweak the laws so that they do not favor private property or bourgeois dominance. *In order to do this, we could continuously hold their feet to the fire and threaten them with being kicked out of office and being replaced by more left-wing candidates - plus, as this may take a generation or more to bring about, we'll have more and more younger, more liberal people able to vote, and that would help us a little. As they pass, one by one, people will see the changes in society and slowly gain a modicum of class consciousness* ... all this reformism won't bring about socialism, but we can chip away at the bourgeois establishment a bit.

    Fifthly, *while all that is being done legislatively across the country, there needs to be work done outside the system, too. Parallel institutions should be set us that increasingly make the State obsolete.* Labour unions should sync their efforts together and plan mass strikes, expropriate the workplace, enact workplace democracy, and stage indefinite walk-outs and non-violent sit-ins. We shouldn't be afraid to support the workers when their conflicts get militant, either - we should always stand with the workers, regardless of the circumstance. We need to rekindle the Occupy spirit, educate people about the exploitation of capitalism, and launch a massive propaganda campaign. We should have "isolated revolutions", as I mentioned in my last blog post about Sartre. This should all be done through a sort of revolutionary vanguardist organization that coordinates the parallel institutions and communicates with our parliamentary agents.

Sixthly, At the point when the political climate is strained and a revolutionary mindset has been established, all of our allies in office (the liberals, progressives, socialists, communists, anarchists, etc) should immediately leave. The government will be stunned and paralyzed by the sudden departure of so much of its workforce and be temporarily crippled - at that point, everyone should flock to the vanguardist organization, launch the proletarian revolution, and seize control of the entire State and the means of production. As much as I abhor violence, we're probably going to have to resign ourselves to a militant revolt.

Seventhly, *The vanguardist organization can temporarily use the State structure in conjuncture with its parallel institutions* to repel anti-revolutionary forces, render the bourgeois irrelevant by our controlling all political power, centralize production as much as necessary in the short run, and protect the proletarian State from external and foreign bourgeois powers. We can launch a massive pro-socialist and anti-bourgeois propaganda campaign when we control all State power that will make the one that we had before look like child's play. We'll support revolutions abroad and work to instigate them however we can so as to make sure we don't end up with a Cold War-style "socialism in one country" - whether they be industrialized countries ripe for socialism or backwards ones that we have to temporarily induce state capitalist-like mass industrialization. We'll do whatever we have to (based on those current material conditions) to protect the revolution (so long as it doesn't run against our principals of proletarian liberation and freedom from oppression - there's no point in letting our dictatorship of the proletariat degenerating into a fascist-like police state, because they would profoundly "anti-liberation") and our best to gradually de-centralize as much State power as we can can to the parallel institutions and workers' councils.

Thoughts on Parliamentarianism

"A democratic republic is the best possible shell for capitalism, and, therefore, once Capital has gained possession of this very best shell, it establishes its power so securely, so firmly, that no changes in person, institutions, or parties in the bourgeois-democratic republic can shake it."
- Lenin

The other day I was reading Lenin's *State and Revolution*, and I stumbled across this line of text by him. The moment that I read it, it was as if a lightbulb had gone off in my head. Let me explain.

My first experience with anything from the Left was reading Eduard Bernstein's *Evolutionary Socialism*. The whole idea of using the electoral process to gradually enact policies, one reform at a time, that would bring about a socialist mode of production struck a chord with my fiercely pacifist tendencies. It also seemed to coincide with my then-budding obsession with existentialism à la Jean-Paul Sartre, with the period of gradualist change being a period through which we could gain existential definition through our choices. But, after working on grassroots campaigns for the Democratic Party and finally getting my hands on a copy of the *Manifesto* several years ago, I was able to view a socialist alternative to Bernstein, one that recognized that utilizing the State to abolish the State was doomed to a host of material problems and rested on a revolutionary foundation instead of a gradualist one.

Since then, years have passed - college, additional literature, joining and meeting with the DSA and the SPUSA, and so on. It now makes sense to me, after seeing time pass and hearing self-described "progressive" Democratic candidates promise so much change and reform, that capitalism is not going to be abolished depending upon who we elect into office. It does not matter if that person is a nationalist Republican that identifies with the right-wing of the Tea Party, nor will it make a difference if the person is a partisan, liberal Democrat who jumps at the change to create another social program. While the conservatives openly preach capitalism, the liberals (and I use the term "liberal" in the context of contemporary social liberalism, not Enlightenment-era classical liberalism) claim that their oh-so-tepid reforms will bring about a higher standard of living, a gentler market, and a more equitable distribution of wealth. In reality, though, those reforms do nothing to replace capitalism with an alternative mode of production - all reformism drains the proletariat of its revolutionary zeal by forcing it to accept, piece by piece, a "softer" form of capitalism that is still, unfortunately, capitalism.

Capitalism is capitalism, regardless of who is in charge of the system. Republicans perpetuate capitalism. Democrats perpetuate capitalism. There is no fundamental difference between the two.

Do I still think that we should advocate for reformism? Absolutely. But we should *never* do so under the impression that gradualism itself is going to bring about socialism. It may make the lives of the proletariat ever-so-slightly better by making their healthcare slightly more comprehensive, their tax dollars a little better well spent, or their Social Security a tad more solvent. But, in the end, it does nothing to erase the exploitation of the capitalist mode of production, and it does nothing to fundamentally re-orientate the economy so that it serves the interests of the working class rather than the bourgeois class.

I think that anyone who argues that we should *not* try to influence the political conversation by advocating things such as a national single-payer healthcare, demilitarization, global nuclear disarmament, and comprehensive and solvent social security programs and the like are missing a key part of our vision. We want to raise the proletariat from its level of its current state of exploitative immiseration, and these things are instrumental in helping us socialists do so.

But we have to realize that a reformist tactic is not going to bring about socialism. The only way that there will ever be the establishment of a socialist mode of production will be through an international proletarian revolution. However, the discussion (and implementation) of reforms allow us to approach the subject of what does and does not work in the current economic system, and gives us the political climate necessary to propose alternatives. And, perhaps after having to have pointed out a large enough number of reforms or having pointed out several large, system-wide ones, the majority of the working class will begin to see that the economy is not built so as to serve their economic interests and that it is not sustainable.

Reformism will not create socialism, but it may crate the environment necessary for us to have the discussion about it - we may be able to capitalize on the pro-reform momentum and create a sustainable socialist movement. But, if there is one thing that we have to keep in mind, it is that, *although we may think that our winning of healthcare reform, education reform, etc are progress for our cause because they (ever so slightly) improves the conditions of the working class, they also do us a disservice by leeching the proletariat of its revolutionary zeal by possibly making them complacent with temporary material gains.* It is because of this that we cannot allow ourselves to ever use reformism as the primary tactic through which we get to socialism - it can be *a* tactic that we use, but it should not be *the* tactic that we use.

We can use reformism to a certain extent - by getting into office so that we can encourage de-militarization, disarmament, restricting police powers, cutting "Defense" funding, and so on. They're ways to chip away at the bourgeois establishment: our vote won't bring about socialism, but they can be a way of trying to weaken the military power of the State somewhat so that, when we do have our revolution, they won't have *as much* power as they would have had if we didn't. That being said, their power is still going to be incredible regardless.

I'll admit that I was an idealist and bought into the idea at first that universal suffrage was going to be enough to bring about socialism. My rationale was that a working class with the ability to vote would vote its way out of immiseration and into socialism, but I've since come to see how hopelessly foolish that is. As long as there is a bourgeois class that has control over the media, education, information distribution, communications, and the like, they'll be able to indoctrinate a large enough majority of the population to prevent any democratic transition to an alternative mode of production

Indeed, universal suffrage could possibly be seen as counter-productive to establishing socialism, because - if we are trying to bring it about in a mature, industrialized, democratic republic - the bourgeoisie could influence the proletariat's mindset to such a degree that *the working class could use its majority vote to support, pass, and enact legislation that would legitimize capitalism, reinforce bourgeois dominance, and bring about a democratically-approved corporate police state.*
Although I consider myself a fierce advocate of democracy, we have to realize that the proletariat's vote could be swayed by the bourgeoisie to benefit the bourgeoisie. Voting itself will never bring about socialism.

There needs to be a revolution, that much is certain. There cannot be socialism without the violent overthrow of the State. But there *are* certain small steps that we can take now to prepare for the revolution, and weakening the State from inside seems awfully tempting.

On "Left" and "Libertarian" Marxism

I've continued to do some reading over the past several days - mostly Guérin, Bordiga, and Luxemburg - and I think that I'm beginning to vaguely discover what sort of tendency I identify most with. A large problem that I have with trying to figure this out is that I question each of the readings too much, and I can't fully commit myself to something that I have intellectual reservations about. Yet, I must thank you all, comrades. You're help has been invaluable.

Firstly, it should be known that I reject the libertarian-authoritarian dichotomy. A socialist revolution is going to be very "libertarian" from the perspective of the proletariat, because they are being "liberated" during it; it is also going to be very "authoritarian" from the perspective of the bourgeoisie, because they are being stripped of their power and subjected to proletarian dominance. For this reason, the libertarian-authoritarian dichotomy is inherently false, because it's purely subjective, based on one's economic class.

If we suspend our rejection of the dichotomy for a moment, and take "libertarian" to mean something along the lines of "rejection of the state and all forms of power structures, and a more decentralized approach to socialism", then I can certainly get behind "libertarian" Marxism. I have no desire for a revolution to end up in a sort of state capitalism, or by abolishing a capitalist dictatorship only to replace it with a proletarian dictatorship (vis-à-vis the Soviet Union).

I'm not terribly well-read on the concept of the vanguard party, but I feel as they hold the seed of élitism, and the party leaders could substitute themselves for the capitalist leaders once the revolution takes place. This is partially why I'm skeptical of a party-led revolution; I would rather see a mass strike and mass uprising of the proletariat, but if it needs to have a vanguard party to coordinate the revolution and ensure its success, then that is something that I'll go along with but I'd remain heavily critical of the party during (and even more so, after!) the revolution.

Here's the role of the vanguard party that I would like to see: a sort of revolutionary left-wing socialist-labour party in parliament that acts as a Marxist-DeLeonist "shield" of the proletariat. It would need to be composed of ardent, anti-capitalist revolutionaries, not moderate reformists; it needs to be the parliamentary wing of the revolution that is going to work hand-in-hand with both organized labour unions and socialist revolutionaries. I think that it needs to be one cohesive organization, with three co-equal wings: a political party, labour unions, and revolutionary activists. This way, it can attack capitalism on multiple fronts.

If the socialist-labour party is unable to successfully seize control of the government through democratic elections, then it should form a coalition or front, composed of other labour, socialist, and communist parties. I'm thinking of something along the lines of a radical SYRIZA, or something roughly analogous to it. If the coalition is able to seize power, it would effectively become a one-party state (or, a one-coalition state?), filled with inter-party (or, more accurately, "inter-coalition") debate and democracy. However, I'm not sure that needs to be done to make sure that the coalition stays in power, once it does get there. Perhaps pursuing populist, pro-worker rhetoric would be enough to ensure success in a few elections? I'm not going to pretend to be wise enough to sketch out a perfect scheme of how a party should seize power.

The socialist-labor party isn't going to actually bring about socialism in any way, but it can pass a handful of reforms (socialize the banks, establish socialized medicine, push for nuclear disarmament, end the wars, etc) that could be helpful. It could also act to impede the actions of the state bourgeoisie from taking government action against the revolutionary activists (filibuster, vote against the government, votes of no confidence, etc). I'm sure that there is a few things that it could do to help.

After the revolution, the entire bourgeois political system should be replaced with something akin to a "workers congress" or a "peoples parliament". The way that it could be set up is something along the lines of this: local workers councils are composed of delegates from the community, and help to oversee it and work hand-in-hand with businesses (which are socialized and turned into worker-owned cooperatives). All of the delegates can be subject to immediate recall at any time, an any worker (of legal age) can run for the council, regardless of occupation, gender, religion, what part of the coalition he or she is part of, etc. These local councils democratically elect a single person from the community to serve in another council, which may oversee a state's county or several towns. *That* council would then send a delegate to the next council, which may encompass a particular portion of the state (say, the "Peoples Council of Northern New York State"); that council would then send a delegate to the state council (say, "the Peoples Council of New York State"); that council would then send a delegate to a regional council (say, the "Peoples Council of New England"); that council would then sent a delegate to a national council. This national council would act as the new, proletarian legislature, and could be called the "workers' congress". Perhaps the workers' congress could send a delegate to an international assembly of sorts, where workers from around the world would be able to discuss and debate issues with one another.

  In order to prevent something like what happened in the Soviet Union (where the Supreme Soviet met only several times a year, appointed a Presidium to do most of the work, and acted as a rubber stamp for party-approved policies), I think that the national workers' congress should meet the majority of the year, and whatever sort of executive body that it forms (preferably, of people that are mostly part of the workers congress itself!) would be regulated by the congress that formed it, and could disban the executive body at any time and call for a new one.

  I think a tiered groups of workers councils, all forming one giant federation, could be a way for us to replace the bourgeois system with a proletarian one. The local and regional councils would encourage their local and regional workers cooperatives to communicate with one another, and encourage a sort of decentralized planning. If we were able to incorporate a Salvador Allende-style planning that used computers linked to every council and cooperative, then we would be able to predict and plan production and distribution. I think that the more local and decentralized the post-revolutionary society is, the better.

This is why I like the "left communist" and "libertarian socialist" / "libertarian Marxist" positions so much - they reject the false libertarian-authoritarian dichotomy, hold true to the decentralized (and dare I say, vaguely anarchist?) and communal basis of the left, and are hyper-critical of the Soviet Union. I like that sort of grey-area where class-analysis anarchism meets decentralized socialism.

Thoughts on the Vanguard Party

My thoughts on regards to the existence, role, and function of the vanguard party varied greatly over the past several years. My waning democratic socialist tendencies argue that have a labour party working inside of parliament on behalf of the working class can bring about reforms that will have immediate material improvements for the proletariat - such as enacting universal healthcare, ending corporate welfare, ending the wars, establishing a living wage, etc. While all these things would be well and good to have, I have to be intellectually honest with myself: a labour party cannot bring about socialism, and it will never be able to reform capitalism into socialism because working inside the system involves being incorporated into the system, and the party will merely degenerate into a bourgeois-liberal one. While pro-labour economic reforms are desirable and improve the conditions of the working class, they will be band-aids that temporary ameliorate the contradictions of capitalism, and will not stave off the proletariat's immiseration or capitalism's eventual collapse. Allowing a reformist labor party to actually bring about reforms saps the proletariat's revolutionary zeal, because it will loose its ambition for a radically improved condition for the working class (that is, socialism) and be pacified with the small, immediate material conditions that it obtained.

I think that De Leon put it well in his *Selective Essays On 'Labour Parties'*:

"The woods are full of rumors and of resolutions long as tapeworms favoring a "labor" party. It is timely at such seasons to consider what a "labor" party may or may not mean; what it may or may not accomplish. If a party of "labor" is set up upon the identical economic principals of the pure and simple trade union, it will not differ materially from any middle-class party, and, just the same as all middle-class parties are bound to go down, and for the same reason that the nonpolitical pure and simple trade union could not stand, such a "labor" party, even if it were at all a possibility, would founder as soon as launched."

However, I do think that there should be a vanguard party. Yes, that should make sense to those that adhere to a scientific understanding that the proletariat will most likely not proceed past trade union consciousness, and the already-revolutionary proletarians need to be band together so as to spread the message of socialism. My ambivalence is not whether or not we should have a vanguard party, but what relationship that party should have with the bourgeois parliament. As stated explicitly above, we cannot assume that any involvement that the vanguard party has with the parliament will bring about socialism, but it possible that revolutionaries, anti-capitalists, and radicals could coalesce together into a SYRIZA-like parliamentary wing of the vanguard party and work inside the system, while the other wings of the vanguard party act as revolutionary activists outside the system.

Perhaps this is idealistic; I recognize that. Marxist-DeLeonism's conceptualization of a "socialist labor party" parliamentary wing of the vanguard party to act as the "shield" of the proletariat in order to impede the bourgeois-democratic parliament's enactment of anti-worker legislation is something that I like. It does not advocate a parliamentary group to bring about socialism, but rather one to limit the bourgeoisie.

As De Leon goes on to say -

"The political party fit to serve as the vanguard of the true unionist movement must be one strained through the loins of that movement itself; the true political party of the revolution cannot chose but be a labor party."

Yes, I think that if we, as revolutionaries, consent to the establishment of parliamentary wing of our vanguard party, that that socialist-labor party must be one that is intimately connected to the greater revolutionary movement, composed of dedicated radicals, and makes sure that allows significant inter-party debate so that it can stay true to its democratic and socialist / communist principals.

"Until the true unionist movement has arisen and gathered the strength sufficient to give birth to a labor party, a "labor party" can only be an abortion for the identical reason that anti-"labor partyism" is an abortion today - the latter, as

well as the former, being the spawn of truths so fractional that they are robust untruths, hence inevitably corrupt, neither having anything to twit the other with."

Again, I agree with him. The socialist-labor party that can act as the pan-leftist parliamentary wing of the vanguard party needs to be crafted and founded in an environment wherein a vibrant, energetic, engaged trade union movement can hold it accountable, and provide it with the inspiration and dynamism to actually be a driving force for change. It should not be a socialist-labor party that represents the interests of the working class; it needs to be formed out of the working class itself, a parliamentary extension of the most revolutionary stratus of the proletariat. We want an active parliamentary wing that can bring about some immediate material improvements for the working class and disrupt and stall the bureaucracy of the bourgeoisie from taking anti-worker action, but the goal of the socialist-labor party is *not* to advocate for reform, but to use the national political spotlight as a means through which to spread the socialist message. This parliamentary wing will not bring about socialism - that will only happen through the mass revolutionary action of an enlightened and class-conscious proletariat - but it can provide a springboard through which we can further our cause.

Something that I think that I should say, if merely to reiterate it to myself, is that once the revolution is underway and the proletariat seizes control of both the State and the means of production, the parliamentary wing needs to be dissolved and abolished, because it will have served its purpose. It should exist, I think, merely as a means through which the vanguard party can wrest control of the political apparatus; once the revolution is underway and the proletariat is in power, there will be no need for parliamentary wing to participate in the bourgeois-democratic legislature. The parliamentary wing is a tool, one of several tactics that can be used to attack the capitalist system on all fronts.

This is what I am thinking, at this point in time - a three-winged vanguard party (composed of the revolutionary layer of the proletariat organized together), composed of: the *parliamentary wing* that will work for economic transformations that are pro-labor and in the sole interests of the proletarian class, not the bourgeois class, and will fight for the socialization of the means of production and will use the national political platform to spread the message of socialism so as to recruit more people to the cause; the *labor-union wing* that will push the radicalization of trade unions everywhere, support militant workplace expropriations, lock-outs, and strikes, and aid in the transformation of private businesses into co-operative ones and work create a local (or perhaps regional, or even national) federation of worker-owned co-ops to help set the foundation for a decentralized planning system; and the *activist wing* that will work hand-in-hand with community organizers, civil servants, and activist groups to connect, involve, educate, and recruit working class peoples, as well as spread the socialist message and bring more people into the vanguard party.

    The vanguard party, and its three wings, need to be sure to hold true to its founding principals - democracy, socialism, equality, inclusiveness, and so on - so as to be sure that it does not degenerate into a pseudo-progressive bourgeois party, or be incorporated into the bourgeois-democratic system, or become a party that effectively pushes for a reactionary and anti-proletarian petit-bourgeois interest group.

    Nor can it an organization that is solely exclusive to the socialist intelligentsia, as it must incorporate the entire working class if it is going to have any chance of bringing about socialist transformation.

    I do not mean to relapse into some form of social democratic reformism: when I speak of a vanguard party, I'm referring to something that is *unwaveringly* anti-capitalist and dedicated to the revolutionary transformation of capitalism into socialism. A pan-leftist alliance of communists, socialists, anarchists, etc into a single, cohesive vanguard party that allows inter-party debate and democratic decision-making during it's push for proletarian control of the means of production, the abolition of wages, rent, money, nation borders, the State, etc would be able to a significant amount of difference, I think. The attack against the capitalist mode of production needs to be a multi-front attack wherein we come at the bourgeoisie on a series of different fields.

Nor do I mean to argue that a proletarian party's capturing of the State political apparatus will be the herald of socialism: that will only come about through mass revolution and the forceful seizure of the means of production. The goal is not to have the vanguard party's parliamentary wing win a series of elections; no, this would only result in the embourgeoisement of the socialist-labor party. The goal is to establish a form of decentralized economic planning, to replace the bourgeois-democratic legislature with tiered federations of democratic workers councils and peoples' assemblies, the transfer of the means of production from being privately-owned to being co-operatively-owned through economic socialization, and the abolition of all remnants of the bourgeois past (wages, rent, borders, the State, etc). I would also be supportive of a Marxist-DeLeonist All-Industrial Congress that could possibly replace the bourgeois-democratic legislature.

The end goal, I think, should coincide much more with councilist left communism than any form of Marxist-Leninism.

In short, I mean that a multi-winged vanguard party could be integral in helping us establish a socialist mode of production.

On the Historicism of Bourgeois-Democratic Revolutions

Perhaps I should have titled this "On the History *and Necessity* of Bourgeois-Democratic Revolutions", but I hope to make their necessity explicit enough.

As an existential Marxist, a significant majority of my beliefs are rooted in a sense of intellectual honesty regarding material conditions; specifically, I'm speaking of the presence (or non-presence) of scarcity. As Sartre argues in his *Critique of the Dialectical Reason* ("Search for a Method"), a socialist mode of production cannot be constructed if there is economic scarcity; in order to be able to move into some sort of post-capitalist society, there has to have been a period of intense industrialization (vis-a-vis a capitalist market) that allows the means of production to be come sophisticated enough that they have the productive potential to overcome material scarcity.

This is reminiscent of what Marx said in the *Manifesto*:

"It has been the first to show what man's activity can bring about. It has accomplished wonders far surpassing Egyptian pyramids, Roman aqueducts, and Gothic cathedrals; it has conducted expeditions that put in the shade all former Exoduses of nations and crusades."

Despite the fact that capitalism has many things that we are working to abolish - economic classism, systemic racism, artificial scarcity, exploitation of workers and under-developed countries, and so on - we have to be honest with ourselves by we acknowledging that capitalism has incredible productive prowess. Capitalism has produced more and stimulated more economic growth than any previous mode of production, even though that it has done so at an unspeakable cost. What I am attempting to get at here is that, in order to effective overcome material scarcity, there has to be a period of capitalist industrialization; that is, there has to be capitalism *before* there is socialism, if only to gradually eliminate scarcity. That being said, there will still be market-induced artificial scarcity under capitalism, but the aggregate material abundance in society can be increased to the point where socialism is materially realistic.

This idea that I'm postulating - that we need bourgeois-democratic revolutions to usher in a period of capitalist industrialization that can overcome scarcity before we can move into socialism - has irked some of my other left-wing friends. They argue that we should fight for socialism no matter what, despite the material conditions of the time, out of a sense of leftist purism. But my response is that we have to look at the capitalist-to-socialist transformation in the scope of the historical process. Once cannot jump from agrarian-feudalism into a post-scarcity socialist mode of production if there aren't means of production that are sophisticated enough to sustain the new system; all that may happen will be an "authoritarian" (yes, I use that term loosely and half-heartedly, because I find the authoritarian-libertarian dichotomy to be horribly flawed) state-capitalist system that operates under the guise of socialist rhetoric.

But what does this say about these state-capitalist systems that *do* call themselves socialist? Again, its necessary to look at the conditions of scarcity in a historical context: even though a free-market capitalist system has the potential to overcome scarcity, a centralized government can *induce* rapid industrialization through the use of state capitalism. A bourgeois-democratic revolution can spawn a bourgeois government and "free-market" capitalism (again, I use this term loosely as well, as all of the financial markets and corporations do incorporate elements of internal planning, and no market is completely unfettered and "free"), but a state-capitalist system can forcefully orientate the economy towards industrialization and use command-economy-style decrees to pull a country out of agrarian-feudalism and into a post-scarcity phase.

By this, I suppose that, by extension, I am arguing that certain historical revolutions (such as, say, the Chinese revolution) are essentially bourgeois-democratic in nature, because they are setting the stage for the capitalist industrialization and material production necessary to facilitate the birth of socialism. If I continue this thought, it would lead towards the idea of the "two-stage revolution" - that while industrialized, capitalist nations with a developed proletariat may be ripe for a socialist revolution, the more backwards, under-developed nations need to first go through a bourgeois-democratic economic revolution under the control of Marxist-inspired parties to induce the industrialization needed, followed by a "second", political revolution to transform that democratically-managed state-capitalism into legitimate, post-scarcity, worker-run and council-based socialism.

Does this mean that I support struggles for national liberation? Perhaps. I support the overthrow of imperialist powers, certainly, but we should not fool ourselves into thinking that the under-developed, colonized countries that do so (under the leadership of a vanguard-like revolutionary party) are going to suddenly be "socialist" once their colonizer is gone. National liberation struggles provide us an opportunity to reduce imperialism, yes, but it also gives us the change to set up Marxist-oriented state-capitalist governments that can hopefully overcome scarcity by taking a planned economic approach, rather than a free-market based one.

I think that this presents us with a unique opportunity: to have backwards nations establish Marxist-inspired and centralized governments *an alternative to* the traditional bourgeois, capitalist nations. Both are born out of bourgeois-democratic revolutions, and both help grow the economy so that we can have means of production sophisticated enough to overcome scarcity.

I'm *not* supportive of either free-market capitalism or state-capitalism; they are both things that I think need to be abolished and destroyed, but I'm intellectually honest enough with myself to realize that we cannot have a post-scarcity council-based society if there is not the material conditions to support it. In the scope of the entire historical process, there needs to be a bourgeois-democratic revolution to create some form of capitalism, which in turn can lay the material conditions for socialism.

On Councilism, and Potentially Bourgeois Binaries

Comrades, over the past several months, I have become increasingly interested in Left communism, and the sort of ultra-Left critiques that it has given the Soviet Union, China, Marxist-Leninist and Leninist theory, etc. At the risk of sounding sectarian (indeed, sectarianism really bothers me, and I'd consider myself a pan-Leftist of sorts), I think that the sort of "left" and "libertarian" communism holds truer to the revolutionary and anarchic spirit of Marxism.

I do identify with the left communist tradition, because the ultra-left critiques and proposals that it offers seem more "libertarian" to me. Despite the fact that I've now used the world "libertarian" twice, I think that the libertarian-authoritarian dichotomy is horribly flawed. Absolutist binaries are something that get under my skin very easily and seem crudely reductionist. I also identify with the post-structuralist movement (at least, more so than I do with the post-modernist movement, but I'd consider myself a companion to both), and one of the key concepts of post-structuralism is its unequivocal opposition to binary systems.

The "libertarian-authoritarian" dichotomy is as terrible as the "male-female" binary. They both structurally presuppose the existence of a particular subject as either black and white; the problem with this is that it has a radically *a priori* supposition: that one thing exists only in its relation to the other; that is, black is only capable of actualizing itself when it is compared to the existence (or non-existence) of white. A fundamental problem that presents itself after this realization is that, if black only exists because white does, that white only exists because of the relation that it has to black. Thus we are caught in a cyclical argument over which appeared first in order to give definition to the second, and we cannot answer this because this would negate the entire binary by canceling out its definition by positing that one could come into being *without* the prior existence of the other.

I think a proper understanding of binary structure allows one to understand that a legitimate, pure binary itself is impossible, and that one cannot have a subject and its polar opposite exist simultaneously.

The gender binary (with male standing opposed to female, and with other individuals - intersex, hermaphroditic, transgender, transsexual, agendered, post-gendered, etc - that fall "outside" the bourgeois notion of "gender") is something that I find exceptionally disturbing. As an evolutionary biologist, the idea of "gender" as it is posited in bourgeois society is not something that is found in other biotic subjects. Numerous birds display lesbianism and merge nests after being their male counterpart have died or left; frogs (and other amphibians and reptiles, but frogs serve as the most illustrative example) can rapidly "switch" their biotic sex depending upon the male-to-female ratio in the ambient population in order to facilitate mass reproduction; and a large number of plants (both non-flowering gymnosperms and flowering angiosperms) are capable of being bi-gendered, with their own physiology containing both male and female components, and are able to shift that ratio depending upon environmental conditions.

I think that the gender binary, as it exists under capitalism, serves as effective means through which to facilitate production because it allows a strict, unwavering (at least, somewhat - its rigidity is being challenged by the LGB't movement; and I place the "t" in "LGBT" as lowercase to illustrate how exclusionary and gender-normative the "equality" movement is, and how it poorly treats it transgendered comrades from time to time) categorization of people. By categorizing them and inserting people into socially-constructed demographics, bourgeois society is able to perpetuate its existence by using those categories to facilitate production and reinforce property relations. The gender "binary" is only but a bourgeois facet to the division of labor. Looking at gender, and its relation to production throughout time, confirms this; any anthropologist can explain how gender relations and gender roles differ dramatically across cultures - which, in turn, if we are vulgar materialists, are simply the outgrowth of particular material conditions at specific historical moments.

I will put aside this musing of gender for now; I've gone rather off-topic, considering that the purpose of this blog post was to talk about the relationship between structuralist binaries and councilism. As I mentioned earlier, I do identify with the left communist tradition, although I have admit that I'm much more inclined to identify with the German-Dutch wing than the Italian Bordigist wing. I am a fan of socialist councils - perhaps, for the sake of intellectual honesty, I will admit that I might fetishize them somewhat. What strikes me as interesting is the way that these decentralized, community-based peoples' assemblies are glorified; I expect (global; regional vis-à-vis the "in one country" idea is flawed) socialism to be organized along the lines of council-run communes that are federated and confederated together at regional, national, and international levels.

That is one reason why I like the German-Dutch wing more so than the Italian one; it focuses more so on councilism, while the latter is more "Leninist than Lenin", as Bordiga has been described as. I'm not necessarily anti-partyist or anti-vanguardism, but I don't think that there's a need to have a hyper-partyist fetish, either. But let me skip this side note and explain what the purpose of this whole blog post is - that decentralized socialist councils, despite the fact that they are often portrayed as more "libertarian" than the statist, party-run "authoritarianism", are yet another illustration of a faulty binary.

What I dislike about the "libertarian" councilism is that it does not stand in opposition to the "authoritarian" party-State; it has just as much a chance of being another form of a capitalism, a re-structuring of the commodity-production system if one council-commune is isolated from the rest of the (con)federation. *If a commune is not part of the collective, then it there is the possibility that it will engage in "trade" with the collective; and the moment that material difference exists between the two, an economically classist division has been created that proves that councilism has the potential to be another bourgeois structure.*

The reason that the "libertarian-authoritarian" dichotomy is flawed is not simply because the proletarian revolution is relative; it is "libertarian" to the working class that it frees, and "authoritarian" to the bourgeois class that it asserts its hegemony over. *No, the libertarian-authoritarian dichotomy is inherently flawed because the presupposition that decentralized councilism is more "libertarian" than a vanguard-run State does not take into consideration a particular organization that the council system can take.* One should not say that councilism is "more libertarian" than another system because it the system itself that should be analyzed in accordance with the material and political conditions around it, not simply be granted the label of "libertarian" for the sake of it being council-based.

As someone who supports a council-based system after the revolution, it is important that I be intellectually honest with myself about the economic implications of (con)federated socialist councils. If the entire world is council-ized (for lack of a better word) after the revolution, that is one thing; if there are regions (either small or large) that are not integrated into the system then we will end up with a "councilism in one country" problem. Socialism must be global - it cannot be regional.

On "State-Capital" and Fascist "Justice"

As capitalism develops, and its markets innately trend towards monopolization, the State will begin to centralize its power as capital is increasingly concentrated; this is done (1) to allow for the easier management of the affairs of the bourgeoisie by a streamlined, singular "executive committee" (as in saving capital through effective consolidation, thus pushing profits in the direction of absolute accumulation), and (2) to utilize public funds to subsidize, support, and bail-out oligarchic corporations as they approach near-monopolization, in order to prevent them from rising from the market to a government-insured monopoly.

The anti-trust laws that are enacted by budding bourgeois governments are done as the dialectic antithesis to the market's monopolization thesis, and the too-large-to-fail-but-not-monopolies that arise are the dialectic synthesis. At this point, the State is needed to support them, but they are not large enough to qualify for extraneous anti-trust enforcement.

This suggests that as markets trend towards monopolization, and as the State becomes increasingly centralized, the two will increasingly become one; this indicates that there will eventually be a merger of State and Capital to the point that there is no administrative difference between the two, and it will have transitioned into a compound State-Capital entity. At this point, the State will effectively be constituted of the owners of the means of production itself, and an oligarchic board of directors will effectively be substituted for the State. The State-Capital entity will have used its immense economic and legal authority to have expropriated property from the "private capitalist" to either the State(-Capital) or to (State-)Capital, and have effectively shifted democratic decision-making to unaccountable corporate committees.

The State-Capital hybrid's expropriation of property to either the *State* or to *Capital* will allow the corporate oligarchs to facilitate over a state-capitalist economy. It seems that there is the potential for this sort of government set-up to the embryo of fascism: the imperial conquests that nations go on, and their neocolonial occupations, suggest that a possible antagonism between the citizens of the "nation" and the "colony" based upon a sense of nationalist-supremacy that grew out of the protracted war, transforming them into conflicting serial groups. This nationalism, when coupled with an extensive war, may create the political conditions necessary for a far-right populist political party to be elected to the State (with the help of Capital's rigging of the democratic-electoral system, as is most easily illustrated in the United States), and the State-Capital entity that presides over a centralized economy can transform into an out-right fascist state. Under fascist rule, the centralization of the state-capitalist economy will negate the State's need to use propaganda to establish a totalitarian-normative mindset, and it can openly use police and military forces domestically to ensure that fascism perpetuates.

I am bothered by the current state of the world economy, and seeing neoliberalism preside over the marriage of corporation and government. I see the State-Capital merged hybrid entity as the potential first growth in a world of confederated fascist nations, whose own imperial and expansionistic tendencies will be the first step into an international conflict that has the potential of being a non-violent, economic "cold war" or an out-and-out military "hot war".

I'm very troubled that the inherent trend of monopolization in the market, if coupled with nationalization by right-wing statist-nationalists, could lead to national (or even international) fascism, and that these institutions could enforce bourgeois property law and anti-revolutionary censorship (among other things, of course) to enforce fascism under the guise of "justice" and "enforcement of the law".

The degeneration of the State-Capital hybrids into political fascism holds numerous potential threats, many of which are on a massive, international scale. The State-Capital entity will be the manifestation of the bourgeois class, having turned the bourgeoisie into a class in-itself to a class for-itself. A globalizing system of corporate-mediated state capitalism will prevail over the proletariat, which will remain a heterogenous entity, serialized by identity politics and bourgeois ideology.

When the system becomes completely global (either by confederation of fascist nations, or the merger of all nations into a collective fascist entity) and the tentacles of imperialism are no longer able to feed the cancer that is the center of the bourgeois empire, the internal contradictions of capitalism will manifest at an exponential rate until, at which point, both the objective and subjective conditions for a socialist revolution arise and the proletariat is transformed from a class in-itself to a class for-itself.

At this point, the proletarians, having outnumbered members of the bourgeoisie millions-to-one, will be able to seize control of the State apparatus and, through such, the power of Capital. The authority of the State-Capital entity will be the manifest hegemony of the proletariat as it asserts its dominance as a class, and, when the State-Capital hybrid has effectively destroyed the last vestiges of the bourgeois class, the State-Capital entity will have lost its traditionally Marxian characteristic as a State, rendering it only a centralized administration to manage the common economic affairs of the proletariat. The State(-Capital) of the bourgeoisie under capitalism will become the (State-)Capital of the proletariat under socialism, as the State withers and becomes the simple proletarian-mediated economic administrator of things.

I assume that the construction of parallel structures (militant labour unions, workers councils / factory councils, peoples assemblies and local town-hall style management) will be built at the same time, and that the revolutionary expropriation of the workplace will coincide with the seizure of the State political apparatus.

The assertion of hegemony by the proletariat will include the radical democratization and inter-industry planning of the means of production through the transitioning of private property into collective co-operative property, thus turning the Luxemburgian germs of socialized production into means of socialized exchange. The dictatorship of the proletariat may include the mediation of co-operatives (within the same economic sector, or across industries) into a complex network of inter-connectivity, forming the initial foundation for a democratically-managed economy based on popular worker control. However, this is only postulation, so I cannot say for certain. Given the material, political, and financial situation of the revolution, conditions may end being exceptionally differently than I envision.

If we continue along this line of though, though, capitalist institutions such as marriage will still exist, but it will have lost its civic and financial meaning, and will thus continue only as romantic commitments; in a sense, "marriage" will have "withered away" in accordance with the State's withering. It seems plausible to assume that currency will still exist, but it will have lost its traditionally capitalist character of being "a means of exploitation and commodified worth" and will instead be only "a manner of calculating planned production and exchange" in the proletarian economy.

I suppose that I am looking at socialism as something along the lines of a councilist anarcho-syndicalism, with those local council-assembly groups presiding over the administration of a massive, inter-connected, co-operative economy. In a sense, I'm conceiving it as a form of council-run state-capitalism organized in the interest of the proletariat.

Perhaps I'm completely wrong in my thoughts; I'll have to think more about it. Given both the creative capacity of the human spirit, and the exponential increases in technological innovation, there are infinite ways that we could organize society. There is no reason to assume that what I am saying is historical fact, but merely a personal vision. However, it should be assumed that the future, post-capitalist society will include democratic management and worker-ownership of the means of production, at the very least. As for what comes with (or after) that, we shall have to wait and see as the historical conditions unfold.

As socialism progresses, all institutions will continue to loose their capitalist characteristics; as one institution begins to "wither away" and loose its capitalist function, so do all the others that gain their meaning based upon their relation to that primary institution. As a result, all social and financial institutions, and all power structures that were either born from or dependent upon capitalism, will "wither away" after the final, extinguishing moment of the State's withering abolition.

I believe that the "withering away" of the State will be joined with (or, shortly proceed) the "withering away" of social and economic power structures that are dependent upon the State; this will cause a cascading domino effect wherein one capitalist institution after another begins to loose its bourgeois meaning.

At this point, I think, a "higher" communism will be prepared to be ushered in. I am not prepared to try and envision how a communist society would be organized exactly, but I picture this post-revolutionary socialism in being something along the lines of the means of production will be sophisticated enough to overcome material scarcity, the State will have had withered away, and democratic management of the workplace has been initiated. Of course, this minimum-program prediction is not a picture of what socialism will perfectly look like; when the proletarian dictatorship spreads democracy from the political sphere into the economic, social, and cultural, a cascade of society changes are to occur that will make any prediction difficult to see.

Capitalism will transition to socialism when the State, and the classes whose conflict it mediates, is abolished. At the point wherein the residual power structures left behind wither away in the wake of the State's abolition, socialism will transition into communism.

On "Socialist" Co-Operatives, and the State's "Withering Away"

I have had some interesting conversations with some of my fellow comrades regarding the nature of co-operative businesses, and the potential for their utilization as a method of transforming the capitalist mode of production into a socialist one. There have been several interesting conversations. Let me summarize what has been said and the general thoughts that I have at this point in time.

Of course, no vanguardist State is going to be able to use federal authority to create socialism, and no government administration is able to dictate the exact structure of the economy; the revolutionary transformation of the economy will come about through the expropriation of the workplace by a class-conscious proletariat, not State decrees.

However, this does not change the fact that the State - armed with incredible legal, economic, and political authority - can use its powers to support the endeavors of the proletariat. Under the dictatorship of the proletariat (wherein the working class seizes control of the State political apparatus and uses it to assert its classist hegemony over the bourgeoisie), the proletarian-controlled State can enact fundamental, systemic change by altering the legal code so that the workplace can be easily and effectively transitioned into collectively-owned, worker-managed co-operatives.

No one is arguing that the State can establish socialism by decree, but certain reforms would certainly improve the immediate material conditions of the working class. Universal, non-profit, single-payer healthcare, for example, is not socialism in and of itself, but it is something that we, as socialists, should support because it serves as a means of expropriating control over healthcare (that is, literally human life) from the clutches of profit-driven corporations to those of a proletarian State. If nothing else, the usage of the State's right of eminent domain - something that, dialectically, is decried as the most unholy of bourgeois property relations - is exceptionally useful when that right can be seized and utilized by the proletariat correctly.

Would that not mean that the economy would then be organized along the lines of state capitalism, where a single entity takes up the role of being the "national" and "collective" capitalist, rather than the "private" and "individual" one? That is, would not rampant nationalization under a proletarian State simple be the substitution of the bourgeois by the collective? Would the economic authority of the individual "private" bourgeois capitalist be replaced by the "national" proletarian State, and property (that is, the means of production specifically, at least in the commanding heights of the economy) would now be the "collective" property of the proletariat proper when under the control of a proletarian State?

Would such economic collectivism be socialism, or would it be state capitalism?

Then again, is there necessarily a difference between the two?

A State is an organ through which one class asserts its hegemony over another, a product of the irreconcilable antagonisms between the classes competing for domination over scarce material resources. The dictatorship of the bourgeoisie is the usage of the State political apparatus against the proletariat; the dictatorship of the proletariat, inversely, is the usage of the State against the bourgeoisie.

Is that the destiny of the socialist movement? To end up with an economic system of intense centralization under the control of a proletarian State, which, after the relations of production have been fundamentally altered, will be nothing more than an "organ" to facilitate the continued operation of state capitalism? Is "socialism" simply analogous to worker-managed state capitalism?

Engels put it aptly in his work *Socialism: Utopian and Scientific*: *"The proletariat seizes political power and turns the means of production into State property. But, in doing this, it abolishes itself as the proletariat, abolishes all class distinctions and class antagonisms, abolishes also the State as the State."* He also goes on to say that *"State interference in social relations becomes, in one domain after another, superfluous, and then dies out of itself; the government of persons is replaced by the administration of things, and by the conduct of processes of production. The State is not 'abolished'. It dies out."*

By using the State to fundamentally re-define property relations, the proletariat is able to set the stage for a new mode of production.

Engels does seem to suggest that a proletarian State, complete with the full nationalization of the economy, represents the ushering in of socialism. Lenin continues this train of thought when he argues the that implementation of socialism in Russia required the establishment of state capitalism. Indeed, he argued that a period of state capitalism is necessary to lay the economic foundations of socialism, at least for the overcoming of material scarcity by inducing rapid industrialization. If we extrapolate, we can assume that "socialism" is related to nationalization by a proletarian State.

No, that cannot be the case, because to assume that socialism is only "proletarianized" state capitalism would also be to assume that the revolution that established such would have been a nationalist one; that is, a revolution that ends with a political organ wielding central power (the State under the proletariat) assumes that the organ to do so would still be, in effect, a bourgeois government, as multitudes of which across the world would still exist, and thus would "nations", in the traditionally Marxist sense of the word. It assumes and presupposes that revolutions would work within the structural framework of capitalism, and that the revolution would occur within the boundaries of a particular country and relate to the seizure of particular government apparatuses.

By having the workers of a particular country rise up and seize control of their government, they seize it in the context of a national government; the transfer of power from the bourgeoisie to the proletariat does not abolish the State, borders, nationality, etc. They all continue to exist, but the capture of the State by the proletariat foreshadows its gradual withering away, which in turn will cause the withering of related power structures.

During the revolution, parallel structures will work to take up much of the local and regional (and, perhaps, even "national" or "international"?) responsibilities of their mirroring bourgeois one. These can include local peoples assemblies, town-hall style meetings, democratic community councils, and the like. As the revolution progresses and bourgeois power wanes, organic parallel institutions will spontaneously arise to take over the responsibilities lost by the bourgeois State. The grouping of citizens into local assemblies is the natural political order, as people are be definition structural animals: the tendency of animals to group themselves into packs, engrained into them by the evolutionary understanding of power-in-numbers, is a political extension of a natural, biotic tendency.

By doing this, they will be revolutionarily expropriated authority from the bourgeois domain to the proletarian one; that is, the "State", the hegemonic organ, will be fundamentally transformed so that it no longer be the manner of bourgeois elections; a profoundly apolitical and spontaneous town-hall assembly councils will replace the majority of what the State once dictated over.

The bourgeois State is manifest in the forms of oppressive government institutions and political structures; the proletarian State will be manifest in decentralized and democratic organs that are run exclusively by the proletariat itself. These proletarian organs will eventually replace the State in numerous economic spheres.

These town-hall, community assembly, and workers' council institutions that will arise during the revolution will be the new political organ that will replace bourgeois political structures and "elections"; they will serves as the decentralized means through which the state capitalist economy, built out of State centralization, can be locally and democratically managed. This will allow a form of decentralized, councilist organs to manage the common affairs of the proletariat and preside over a form of councilist anarcho-syndicalism.

Thus, the transformation of businesses into co-operatives is something that we, as socialists, should fully support because it provides the Luxemburgian "germs of socialized production" to also become "germs of socialized exchange" if they are networked together into an ever-expanding matrix of worker-run enterprises. One of the great problems with co-operatives is that, while they act as the first seeds of socialist economics, they are seeds that have been planted amongst a capitalist economy. They do not exist in an environment that is conducive for their growth and development - power structures, particularly the reining financial multinationals, have a vested interest in crushing co-operatives before they can arise as a genuine economic alternative to their own hierarchical, top-down management.

Often, they are bought out and purchased by corporations so as to minimize the danger that emanates from them; corporations can also use their vast economic power to out-compete and out-spend co-operatives, thus driving them into financial ruin and out of the market completely. Co-operatives are destroyed by capitalist powers before they have a chance to fully thrive and develop. However, if they are able to opt-out of the market and remove themselves from competitive capitalism, then there is a great deal of potential in them. Co-operatives that form stable, long-term business contracts with each other and with public agencies, and which continuously grow to incorporate more and more co-operatives, can form a powerful economic network that will be able to use inter-network planning avoid the damaging market mechanisms that corporations use to crush them.

Large networks of co-operative enterprises, other worker-owned and worker-managed businesses, and local, decentralized community councils can help set the foundations for a new economy, and a proletarian State can use its immense authority to help do so.

As private institutions are democratized and genuine community decision-making is actualized, then councilist anarcho-syndicalism (that is, "socialism") can be actualized. The political ramifications of this new economy, and the host of socio-economic and cultural power structures that it will topple, will potentially set the basis for real-world communism.

This appears to suggest that there will be a succession of events that will occur in a cascading fashion: firstly, that the bourgeois State will be captured by a proletarian party, who will use its immense economic and legal authority to orientate the economy in the direct interest of the working class by facilitating the transition of private-hierarchical businesses into worker-managed co-operatives and by nationalizing key sectors of the economy (banking, healthcare, education, transport, energy, etc); and secondly, the revolutionary expropriation of the workplace by the workers themselves, either in concurrence with the first event, or shortly thereafter, after which the new proletarian State has laid the legal framework for private-to-cooperative business transition. Both of these will be accompanied by the networking of co-operative businesses with one another - in the same industrial sector, in the same geographic region, with other co-operatives in associated and secondary sectors, etc - in order to maximize production, minimize waste, democratically manage the workplace, and provide long-term business contracts between co-operative enterprises in order to set the foundation for decentralized economic planning.

But this still presents numerous problems. Primarily, the transition from a bourgeois State to a proletarian State, and from privately-owned workplaces to worker-owned workplaces, does not abolish wage-slavery, capital, classes, nations and borders, etc. It presents a fundamentally altered economy: the contemporary neoliberal situation is gone and a co-operative and syndicated economy has been established, but it does not eliminate many of the structural problems that are present under capitalism. It does improves the situation for the working class, but it does not establish socialism or communism.

To this, we can say several things.

Firstly, that the proletarianization of the State (that is, the dictatorship of the proletariat) means that the hegemonic class is no longer the bourgeoisie, and that the bourgeoisie has lost its traditionally dominant political power. This has fundamental and far-reaching consequences, because the "withering away of the State" throughout this dictatorship will cause the class character of numerous power structures (economic, social, cultural, etc) to wither along with them. This will cause a cascading change in social relations in society that will gradually transform the entire social superstructure - as the landscape changes economically, so will the social phenomena that they create. Numerous things will be subject to change.

And, as one power structure after another begins to loose its class character, so will others. The primary power structures that are defined by their relationship to the State will wither along with it, and the secondary power structures that are defined by their relationship to the primary ones will slowly begin to transform. The withering of the State, primary power, and secondary power will all occur as the proletarian State facilitates the creation of a co-operative economy. All of the individual socio-economic narratives that, collectively, constitute the superstructure will gradually loose their class character.

Secondly, the capture (and subsequent usage) of the State political apparatus by the proletarian party will not be the only action engaged in by the proletariat. Concurrent with democratic and electoral procedures, parallel institutions will spring up organically in communities and will assume control over many spheres that once belonged to the bourgeois State but were removed from the jurisdiction of the proletarian State. That is, local town-hall assemblies and community councils will assume authority over things that the State no longer controls: management of communities and local social relations, for example, will fall under their control while the proletarian State concerns itself with the establishment of the networked co-operative economy. We cannot assume that the transformation from capitalism into socialism will be dictated by the decrees of a "socialist" government, but rather through the revolutionary action of the proletariat itself. A surge in democratic involvement (which will culminate in the seizure of the State by the proletarian party) will go hand-in-hand with a surge in civic involvement, causing organic peoples assemblies to grow in concordance with the State's proletarianization. Political proletarianization will happen at the same time as the hatching of organic socialist councils.

Thirdly, the withering away of power structures and the establishment of parallel institutions presupposes, logically, that the two will be connected. As bourgeois power increasingly withers away, proletarian power will increase proportionally; the eventual "abolition" of the State (that is, the historical moment where its withering has been completed and the last vestiges of class character in the State have been fundamentally removed) will be the specific point wherein socialism has been established. As power structures and the State continually wither away, the authority of parallel institutions will grow and assume control over the spheres of authority that originally fell under the jurisdiction of the bourgeois State.

The conclusion that can be drawn from these three events (the withering away of power structures, the birth of parallel institutions, and the assumption of authority by them) will represent a potent transformation of society. In essence, democracy will be moved from just the purely political sphere to include economic, cultural, and social matters.

Then again, was democracy ever really present in the political sphere? Or has public power been transferred to unaccountable, bureaucratic power structures - corporations, committees, oligarchic cabals, élite circles, etc? Has enough decision-making authority been handed over to institutions that are not accountable - either through direct democratic action, or through the action of republican representatives - that the peoples' political involvement is effectively rendered meaningless? Do we have a democratic republic that is neither democratic or a republic - has the democratic rule of the people been replaced by the decision-making of a handful of corporate aristocrats?

Unfortunately, the answer is yes. The voice of the people in the democratic process has been effectively silenced since the 1970s, when the American Republic was essentially replaced by the Corporate Empire through the vicious campaign of financial deregulation under the Reagan Administration and the transformation of the Treasury Department into the political arm of Wall St.

What I am currently thinking is that the abolition of the State will mean the newfound hegemony of the democratic peoples assemblies; this historical moment represents the terminal death of capitalism and the ushering in of socialism. The economy will be orientated along councilist anarcho-syndicalism and democracy will saturate every aspect of society.

On the Transitional Period, and the Initiation of Planning

Harris, Kiernan, and Miliband's *Dictionary of Marxist Thought, Second Edition* has an extensive passage on both the "dictatorship of the proletariat" and the "transition to socialism". At one point, they describe the latter as following:

"The Marxist concept of socialist revolution implies that there must be a period of transition from capitalism to socialism. In contrast to bourgeois revolution which is an overthrow of the political power of the aristocracy at the end of a long process of growth of the capitalist economy and bourgeois culture within the framework of feudal society, the seizure of political power from the bourgeoisie is, according to Marx, only 'the first episode' of the revolutionary transformation of capitalism into socialism. Marx (Critique of the Gotha Program, sect. 3) distinguishes between the lower phase of communism (a mixed society which still lacks its own foundations) and its higher phase (after the disappearance of the 'enslaving subordination of the individual to the division of labour' and of 'the antithesis between mental and physical labour', when such abundance would be attained that goods could be distributed to each 'according to his needs'). Most Marxists identify the lower phase as 'socialism' and the higher phase as 'communism'."

Harris *et al* make several good points, and they subtly reiterate something that I think needs to be more properly understood by the Left: a bourgeois-democratic revolution is going to be the catalyst to show the transition of feudalism into capitalism, and a proletarian revolution is going to be the catalyst that brings about socialism. Only countries that have been sufficiently industrialized enough to generate means of production that are sophisticated enough to overcome material scarcity are going to be able to lay the economic foundation of socialism. Not only does scarcity have be overcome, but it has to be done in a way wherein the aggregate material output is effectively past the point of net-zero scarcity, not equal to or less than it. A given society that does not have material abundance is not going to be lay the ground for any effective and sustainable communitarian economy.

I do have to say that I agree with them when they differentiate the "lower" and "higher" phases after the proletarian revolution - perhaps I'm simply being nostalgic for early-generation Marxist terminology, but I prefer to use the terms "socialism" and "communism" rather interchangeably. I would rather have them be synonymous because I think that having their definitions overlap shows how connected the two are, and to effectively illustrate how the two "phases" are different periods in the same post-capitalist era. I understand that the two terms are different, of course; I just think that the difference between them has been too conflagrated and over-exaggerated. The post-capitalist period that we find ourselves in after the revolution need not be ruined by rampant sectarian definitions over a handful of theoretical terms; we need not concern ourselves with the philological impact of the different "-ism"s that we name something, or waste our time continuing century-old sectarian feuds. Our attention should be focused on working together in solidarity in order to build a sustainable socialist economy.

For public reasons, I am more apt to describe myself as a "socialist" because I think that it has been tainted less by the Western propaganda machine than "communism" has, but I would not deny either if I was called one. What I do dislike, though, is when someone assumes that because I'm a socialist / communist I'm just "a very liberal liberal", or something along those lines. The absolute lack of understanding that most lay people have for political theory is outstanding. Then again, they should not be burdened with an "irresponsibility" for their ignorance - the fault lays at the hands of educational power systems, which have a vested interest in a thought-controlled populace that is trapped within a certain State-defined boundary of discourse.

They go on to say:

"The original programme of Marx and Engels, formulated in the Communist Manifesto, was quite flexible and construed the transition to communism as a series of steps which eventually revolutionize the entire mode of production, classes generally, and its own supremacy as a class. In order to specify

the character of the workers' state Marx used the term 'dictatorship of the proletariat', which was controversial in his own time and is challenged by many democratic socialists today. Anarchists (especially Bakunin) objected that the idea would help perpetuate the existence of an authoritarian state and of a tyrannical bureaucratic ruling elite. On the other hand, reformists (e.g. Bernstein) rejected the idea of political revolution since they thought the very economic process of capitalism lead spontaneously towards socialism."

    I think that the dislike that many anarchists have for a proletarian dictatorship is rooted in their misunderstanding of Marxist syntax rather any genuine theoretical qualm. A "dictatorship of the proletariat" does not necessarily mean that there is a legitimate political dictatorship in the liberal democratic sense of the word; it does not mean a horribly totalitarian oppressor is going to use all manner of government power to squash individual freedom. The dictatorship of the proletariat is simply going to be the proletariat organized as a class for-itself, rather than a class in-itself, that will seize control of the State political apparatus and use its tremendous economic and legal authority to assert its hegemony over the bourgeoisie. What a proletarian dictatorship refers to is the working class assuming control of the State and using it in their own direct economic interest. Also, I would argue that many (not all; there are a fair number of class-analysis anarchists) of the anarchists that do not subscribe to Marxian class-analysis have a profoundly unscientific paradigm. In order to properly understand power structures, one needs to be able to deconstruct its class character, not simply point a figure at it and decry it as "authoritarian".

    One can also make the argument that there would be several similarities between the proletarian class dictatorship and the liberal-democratic political dictatorship. Chief among these would most likely be the political disenfranchisement of certain demographics. Under proletarian control, the State would bar the bourgeoisie from taking part in managing any economic affairs; the transfer of economic decision-making from corporate boardrooms to co-operative workers' councils and union assemblies would effectively remove large numbers of bourgeois individuals from political power. Élitist bourgeois democracy, the hegemonic rule of small aristocracy, will be replaced by proletarian democracy, the political supremacy of the working class as it marches towards socialism.

After all, what is political power if not economic decision-making? And if that power has been delegated to the proletariat, than has the working class not been elevated to the position of political supremacy? We, as Marxists, know that the relations of production, and the economic-interest conflict between the two classes, is the motor of history. If the economy is serving the economic interests of the proletariat rather than bourgeoisie, than we can safely assume that the guiding economic interest (and thus, the very motor of history itself) will move in a diametrically opposed direction than if it was still under bourgeois thrall.

"The economic program of transition expounded in the Communist Manifesto comprised measures meant 'to wrest, by degrees all capital from the bourgeoisie', 'to centralized all instruments of production in the hands of the state' and 'to increase the total productive forces as rapidly as possible'."

This sounds like a quote that evolutionary socialists, social democrats, and other gradual reformists. I'm not downplaying the victories won by progressive in parliaments: the enactment of single-payer healthcare, social security systems, welfare nets, quality education, etc are certainly good. But the reforms that are enacted via the bourgeois State political apparatus generally serve as a de-radicalizing mechanism for the proletariat; by winning several small politico-economic victories, the working class becomes increasingly apathetic as its immediate material conditions (e.g., standard of living) rises. The slow and small improvements of economic conditions in a given nation cause that country's electorate to gradually loose sight of the final socialist goal and grow complacent with immediate reforms. Reformism can improve certain economic conditions, but it cannot build a new mode of production. We have to be honest with ourselves and realize that any fundamental reconstitution of social and economic relations is going to require a (potentially violent) revolutionary transformation in society.

Only a class-conscious proletarian revolution holds the possibility of creating socialism.

". . . This kind of society [the USSR] does not nearly approach the goal of the entire process of transition which Marx described (in the Communist Manifesto) as 'an association in which the free development of each is the condition for the free development of all'. Such a goal requires different means and different stages of the transition process. Under the pressure of powerful social movements, and the need to resolve various inner contradictions, some important reforms have been accomplished even within the framework of the old capitalist society (progressive taxation, nationalization of some key branches of the economy, workers' participation, planning, social welfare, socialized medicine, universal free education, free culture, humanization of work etc). The political supremacy of radical socialist forces may take place near the end of this process rather than being its precondition. Once they prevail these forces will be able to turn the state into self-governing rather than authoritarian structure ... Means of production would be socialized and put under the control of self-managing bodies."

The goal of the dictatorship should not be simply to facilitate the transition of for-profit capitalist enterprises into worker-owned and democratically-managed co-operatives, nor is just to link the co-operatives into an ever-expanding conglomerate. Yes, co-operatives should be unwaveringly supported, but they should not be supported because they are co-operatives; they should be supported because they hold inside them the seeds for an industrial democracy, with working individuals holding the power of economic decision-making.

A co-operative economy is a means, not an ends. It is the first step in a transformation of productive relations by replacing hierarchical, top-down bourgeois management with democratic, collective decision-making by the workers; it is a threat to the bourgeois structuralism of the workplace.

Co-operatives that are franchises (for lack of a better word; that is, co-ops that have numerous facilities that stretch across a large region) may feel the need to form an inter-industry republic to manage its executive affairs. By this, I mean that each individual co-operative may, from within its own ranks, democratically elect one of its own workers to represent that particular facility in a conference of all the facilities in a certain industry. In essence, the workers of a particular co-operative franchise would form an industry-specific syndicate council, composed of its own workers, to form a central committee that would act the place of a corporate board of directors.

In a sense, these syndicates will form the basis of industry-specific republics, whose highest ranks will be the guidance force of that particular industry. This would allow the bourgeois "board of directors" to be substituted with the proletarian "democratic delegates".

The various industrial syndicates - the democratic-republic structure of a large economic enterprises - may have the possibility of democratically selecting, from within their own ranks, a number of delegates to a "supreme syndicate". This supreme syndicate could manage the common affairs of the economy, and form the basis of a "workers congress" at the national level, or work hand-in-hand with a proletarian party-controlled legislative institution, or even be subordinate to the "national" legislature (as "nations", the traditionally Marxist sense of the word, would have withered away with the various bourgeois States) and enforce its directorates. There are infinite possibilities how a post-capitalist and post-scarcity society could be organized.

However, the supreme syndicate should not be able to dictate all of the decisions that a complex economy and a dynamic culture would need decided. There would need to the input of non-labor; that is, those who are not necessarily taking part in directly contributive material production should have a say in the democratic decision-making process. This may include those physically unfit for labor, retired or handicapped individuals, non-working students, stay-at-home family members, etc. This is why the supreme syndicate should, I would argue, remain subordinate to the "national" legislature. This can possibly be done by having the multi-head presidium executive appoint a number of individuals to take part in the syndicates - say, one-third, so that the remaining two-thirds workers delegates would still be able to out-vote the appointees.

What does this say about economic planning? If we have found that a series of steps (democratic seizure of the State by a proletarian party, usage of State power to cooperativize private business enterprises, and the linking of these new co-ops into ever-growing conglomerates with worker-appointed directive syndicates) to create a progressive economy, what can we do after this to ensure that it grow towards socialism? What can we do to make sure that this "worker-managed capitalism" that will exist under the revolutionary dictatorship of the proletariat blossoms into a fully socialist mode of production, wherein the all of the means of production are held totally in common and production-for-use, rather than production-for-profit, will be the guiding economic principal?

This is where I have heard several conflicting theories, for some assume that a co-operative economy would be socialism in itself, and that we would have reached the end goal already. No, we are looking not at how the proletarian dictatorship can go about creating a co-operative economy for its own sake, but rather that it can start to place in the means of production under workers' control so that we can lay the foundations of socialism. Our co-operatives are the tools with which we will plant the seeds of the new economy. As State power withers away and various power structures gradually loose their class character, those seeds will bloom and socialism will begin to actualize itself.

To cite Harris *et al*'s *Dictionary of Marxist Thought* again, there is an interesting entry on economic planning. It discusses, in significant detail, the planning-or-market debate between Oskar Lange and the capitalist theorists Hayek and Mises. In it, Hayek based his argument against planning on:

"the impossibility of gathering and processing information that would be needed to work out centrally an efficient allocation of resources could result only from the

operation of market forces, with market-determining prices having the central role of conveying information to decentralized decision-makers ... Hayek was not concerned with the conditions needed for a strategic Pareto-efficient allocation of resources. They insist that his concern was the process of resource re-allocation resulting from the continuous responses of decentralized decision-makers to the ever-changing information available to them, with market-determined prices having the role of co-ordinating their independent decisions."

It seems that the cliché line of market fundamentalists - that when purchasing something, we cast an "economic vote" to show what material goods we do and do not want produced and exchanged - has yet another gaping hole in it. Not only to corporate producers opt-out of market forces by operating on the basis of inter-industry planning (tiered sharing of information, intimate communication with similar vertical and horizontal corporations, insider trading, activity based on stock-holder interest rather than share-holder impact, etc) that invalidate may "economic votes", but the numerous "votes" create such a chaotic, ever-changing situation in the market where the aggregate supply and demand both fluctuate from moment to moment, creating a situation wherein no "decentralized decision-maker" can objectively look at macroscopic economic conditions and see how his or her "vote" will impact anyone (or anything) else than him or herself.

Purchasing goods on the principal of informed and rational self-interest, say many neoliberals and Objectivists, should be the basis of economic decision-making. To this, I say that they are wrong; the numerous conflicting "economic votes" that are continuously being cast create an anarchy in the market wherein some goods are over-produced, others are under-produced, prices are skewed wildly, and the volatile economy leads to massive material waste.

"Economic planning enables the [anarchic] inter-dependence to be taken into account. Investment decisions, to be rational, should be made on the basis of the expected future pattern of relative costs and prices, not the existing pattern. Uncertainty about the actions of others prevents atomized

decision-makers from making estimates of the future that are as good as is possible in a planned economy. In a planned economy, major investments bringing about non-marginal changes can be planned together and co-ordinated in advance before resources are committed ... The historical antithesis between plan and market has been largely abandoned and some form of 'market socialism' has emerged as the principal economic model advocated by socialist economists. However, the experience of Eastern Europe, particularly of the New Economic Mechanism in Hungary in 1968 ["the shift to decentralization in an attempt to overcome the inefficiencies of central planning", The Economic Reforms in Hungary, Balassa], has led to increasing skepticism about the possibility of anything resembling earlier Marxist concept of economic planning. The basic argument is that for enterprises to have an incentive to make efficient use of the resources and local knowledge at their disposal, they must be fully autonomous. They can only be fully autonomous if they make their own decisions, including investment decisions, and benefit or suffer according to whether or not they are successful. This requires a capital and labour market, with investment decisions being co-ordinated and resources reallocated through the operation of market forces."

    I think I should start by saying that I think that markets and socialism are incompatible. Of course, some sort of distributive system will exist under socialism, but it's not going to be a "market" in the Marxian sense of the world, because markets are intrinsically classist because of the unequal distribution of capital between those participating in it. The market is exploitative and bourgeois; the with the withering away of the State, the market will wither as well, and a "market" mechanism devoid of its class characteristics will manifest that will act as a sort of proletarian distribution medium.

    That being said, we can confidently say that markets, as we know them, will not be preset under socialism - and, if economic planning requires a rapid and transparent information-system, then the solution to creating an effective, minimally wasteful, reflexive planning system may be in the arrival of cybernetic technology.

I'm thinking of something that is akin to Project Cybersyn (portmanteau of "cybernetics" and "synergy"), the 1971-73 project under Chilean President Salvador Allende attempted to construct a decentralized decision-support system to manage the national economy that was based on the principal of viable system modality. By this, I mean the usage of a complex network of computers to form a neural network throughout the economy; public services and enterprises, co-operatives, and government branches would be equipped with computer software that would continuously monitor the input and output of each enterprise and transmit it to a central planning organization. This information could be fed into statistical modeling systems and simulators (such as Allende's Cyberstride, or the Chilean Economic Simulator [CHECO]) that would issue alerts, directives, warnings, and indicators in real-time (such as raw material supplies, worker absenteeism, etc) to alter the workers of a particular industry. A sophisticated operations branch at the central planning organization would provide a space wherein planners could view relevant data, formulate responses, and act as the hub of economic communication.

Electronically-linked co-operative conglomerates could use both inter-conglomerate planning and conglomerate-to-conglomerate telecommunication to set the foundations for a planned socialist economy. A well-structured computer system can provide the in-depth, high-quality rapid responses needed, and can incorporate second-by-second information from various economic sectors and run it all through numerous simulators.

Perhaps this is the way that we start building the foundations of a socialist economy: seizing control of the State, converting private enterprises into worker-managed co-operatives, the linking of these co-operatives together into ever-growing conglomerates that employ internal planning mechanisms and moment-by-moment telecommunication, the formation of long-term business contracts between co-ops with public and private institutions, and profound re-orientation of the economy in the direct interests of the working class.

It may not be much, but it can be a first step. It can be a start. It can be one of the first things that the revolutionary dictatorship of the proletariat can do to start planting the seeds of a new, progressive, socialist economy amongst the roots of the old.

In section three of Engel's *Socialism: Utopian and Scientific*, he says:

"The proletariat seizes the public power, and by means of this transforms the socialized means of production, slipping from the hands of the bourgeoisie, into public property. By this act, the proletariat frees the means of production from the character of capital they have thus far borne, and gives their socialized character complete freedom to work itself out. Socialized production upon a predetermined plan becomes henceforth possible. The development of production makes the existence of different classes of society thenceforth an anachronism. In proportion as the anarchy of social production vanishes, the political authority of the State dies out. Man, at last the master of his own form of social organization, becomes at the same time the lord over Nature, his own master - free."

Engels reiterates something here that I think is not properly understood by some Marxists who assume that a change in political relations (seizure of the State by a proletarian party, legislative support for labor, nationalization, etc) will bring about a fundamental change in productive relations. The goal is not to win political battles (e.g., elections) against bourgeois parties in order to then go about using State authority to re-define economic relationship, but rather to socialize and democratize economic decision-making, so that new economic relations will yield new political relations. A newfound economic hegemony of the proletariat will, in itself, be its political supremacy. Revolutionaries can change politics by changing economic conditions, not change economics by changing politics.

By socializing the means of production, the proletariat creates the political conditions necessary for the fostering of socialism.

To return to *Harris et al*'s *Dictionary of Marxist Thought* one last time, there is a good entry on "self-management":

"In the most general sense self-management is the basic structure of socialist society, in economy, politics and culture. In

all domains of public life - education, culture, scientific research, health services, etc - basic decision-making is in the hands of self-management councils and assemblies organized on both productive and territorial principals. In this sense it transcends the limits of the State. Members of the self-management bodies are freely elected, responsible to their electorate, recallable, rotatable, without any material privileges. This puts an end to the traditional State, to political bureaucracy as a ruling elite and to professional politics as a sphere of alienated power. The remaining professional experts and administrators are simply employees of self-management bodies, full subordinated to them. Self-management involves a new socialist type of democracy. In contrast to parliamentary democracy it is not restricted to politics, but extends to the economy and culture; it emphasizes decentralization, direct participation and delegation of power for the purpose of a minimum of necessary coordination. Political parties loose their ruling function and oligarchical structure; their new role is to educate, express a variety of interests, formulate long-range programmes and seek mass support for them."

I agree with them. Any fundamental transformation from one mode of production to another is going to require a class-conscious proletariat to engage in a (possibly violent) revolution to take over the workplace, thus asserting their political hegemony. A proletarian dictatorship can help set the foundations for economic planning by linking their newly-seized co-operative enterprises together into powerful, worker-run conglomerates.

On Purist Decentralization and "Market" Socialism

I think that it's important to note that market and socialism are incompatible. Markets may be an effective mechanism for commodity distribution, but that strength is also their greatest flaw: they allocate *wants*, not *needs*. They do not serve as an effective means through which the materials and resources conducive for human survival are able to reach those whose survival is most precarious. In this, the market creates an economic precariat out of the proletariat, whose economic security is continuously in question and always based upon the momentary fluctuations of the market. The participation of individuals in a market is contingent upon an unequal distribution of capital, who each engage with one another in the hopes of "winning" - that is, making a higher profit, accumulating more capital, obtaining a greater quantity of commodities, etc. Or, for the proletariat, it is a coercive mechanism through which capitalist participation and conformity is enforced, as participation in the market is necessary for survival. It's very existence is dependent upon inequality and an anti-humanist compulsion. Doing so is a vivid illustration of the estrangement that the "early" Marx discusses in his humanist writings, although I think it's somewhat inappropriate to consider the "early" and "late" Marx to be epistemologically different; he may have been passing through a period of philosophic growth during his university studies, but one should take all of his writings and pronouncements into account in order to see his philosophy in a complete, larger context. I do not agree with the assertion that Marx was subject to epistemologic break during his life.

    I think that there will be some sort of "market" that will exist under the revolutionary dictatorship of the proletariat, to use the term loosely. The capture of the State political apparatus by the proletarian vanguard is not going to mean that markets will suddenly vanish overnight - there will be period of radical transformation as the economy is oriented in the direct material interests of the working class. During this period, the State will gradually loose its class characteristics and it will be de-politicized from a "hegemonic organ of class rule" to a democratic "administration of things". This seems to suggest that politico-economic organs will continue to exist, but will be perceived by, and function in the interest of, the working class in a different manner than they do currently. The State withers away and changes form; is it so wild to think that markets may do the same, or that they may serve some auxiliary function to support mainstream economic planning?

The market that exists under capitalism may, like other power structures, wither so that it gains a different political connotation. Instead of being a means of capital re-allocation and commodity exchange, the withering away of the State may result in a contingently de-politicized "market" that continues to distribute goods in a manner that is conducive to socialist construction. By this, I mean that the withering away of the market may be parallel with the withering away of the State - as the State is a classist organ, its dissolution will cause other related classist institutions to predictably dissolve as well. Thus, the eradication of the State as a class organ will cause the market to be eradicated, and, just as the State changes form, so too will the market. I have discussed the withering away of the State, and the contingent withering of primary and secondary power structures, in other works, and it is thus not necessary to do into extraneous detail here.

The structure of the market after the withering away of the State can be predicted to be dissimilar to the market that exists currently. That is, the bourgeois market and the proletarian "market" will have several profound differences. Amongst them will be that it will no longer exist as a means of capital accumulation; instead, it will be proletarian mechanism through which participating individuals will be able to cast economic votes to decide what, how, and where they want material goods (that is, material *wants* rather than *needs*, or goods that are not needed for survival, growth, and creative development) to be allocated, given that those goods are not already being distributed through the embryonic planning initiated by the proletarian State and the co-op conglomerates.

I think that "market socialism" is an improper term, because I believe that socialism will only truly exist when the State has withered away, and the "market" that exists at that point in time will be de-politicized to such an extent that it will have lost (or, be in withering process of) its own class characteristics. I cannot postulate the exact structure of a post-State "market", nor can I think of another term to call this new-found proletarian distributive mechanism, but I can say with relative certainty that it will no longer exist as the class organ that it is under the dictatorship of the bourgeoisie. In accordance with base-and-superstructure theory, any economic change in a particular mode of production is going to contingently result in some sociologic change as well. Thus, because the global economy will be altered by the dictatorship of the proletariat, the market will have undergone a fundamental change that radically transforms its social role. It will no longer be a bourgeois market; it will be a proletarian one, a capitalist residue that will be fundamentally altered as it withers away in the wake of the State's vanishing.

    The market may exist as a "market" while (or shortly after?) the State withers away, but the historical dialectic shows that it, like other economic relics of the past, will eventually undergo a revolutionary re-constitution and take new form. The capitalist market gains definition based on the existence of the State; when the State is gone, the market will take on a fundamentally new structure. It is logical to think that, like all bourgeois institutions, the "market" that will replace the market proper will eventually be eclipsed and overshadowed by an economy based primarily (or completely?) on economic planning.

    As I have said before, it makes more sense to me to have economic planning be decentralized. Federations of democratic workers' councils, town-hall style assemblies, co-ops, etc that are built based on voluntary association appear to be the most effective way to replace local, regional, and even national bourgeois-political structures. However, pursuing decentralization *for the sake of it being decentralization* is a purist argument; one should not advocate either centralized or de-centralized planning on an ideologic ground, but rather use a hybrid amalgam of the two, with each being applied to different sectors of the economy in accordance with whichever is the most effective, productive, and democratic. Certain things, such as energy production, need to have a "national" solution (I place it in quotations because nations, in the liberal democratic sense, would no longer exist) so as to ensure equitable access to electricity for the entire populace. If energy production was decentralized, it may result in an unequal distribution of electrical power due to poorly connected communes, in the same way that confederated workers' councils may lead to capital inequality. Yet even though certain sectors of the economy may require a "national" and centralized solution, this solution must be profoundly democratic and directly accountable to all of those that are connected through it.

Dialectically, purist decentralization has the possibility of resulting in communes, businesses, and communities being inadvertently isolated from one another in such a manner that detrimental, self-destructive inequalities may grow amongst them. Again, it is not necessary to go into extraneous detail here, as the bourgeois, reductionist, and explicitly totalitarian nature of binary systems has been discussed by Derrida in great detail in ways that I cannot. However, let me add that I believe that decentralization is essential to any successful socialist project, given that the decentralized units are federated together in a manner that is conducive for collaborate work, because it will institutionalize a system that is not conducive for the centralization of politico-economic power in either a single individual or a single organization.

A decentralized economy also intuitively appears to be the system wherein there can be the most direct local accountability, and if this system is going to function based upon federations of workers' councils and co-ops, then it could logically be assumed to be the most democratic structure, if contemporarily ideologic notions of "democracy" are operant. The more "local" the system is, the more direct the connection between it and the populace; and the more direct the connection, the more accountable and "democratic".

Both centralization and de-centralization have their merits and faults, but it appears that any effective post-capitalist system is going to require them to both be used in varying degrees for different economic sectors, and the ratio of the two in a specific sector may fluctuate in accordance with material production, consumption, and needs. This is because any centralization or de-centralization needs to be the organic product of an economy that is fundamentally structured in working-class interests. Yet, in order to be intellectually honest, I must be willing to point out the flaws of the decentralized system that I propose. A system that is radically decentralized based on purist notions of anti-centralization has the potential to be inefficient, poorly networked, and unnecessarily bureaucratic; however, one that actually de-centralizes economic decision-making for the sake of legitimately improving efficiency is grounded in logic and reason.

I think that is important for me to connect this idea to others that I have postulated in the past. As I have argued before, the final abolition of the State will herald the beginning of socialism, and the final abolition of power structures that gain their socio-political authority by their definitive relation to the State will herald the beginning communism. Generally speaking, I would rather use the terms "socialism" and "communism" interchangeably, so distinguishing them them in such a manner is rather uncharacteristic of me; however, I think it is necessary in this particular instance to show the difference between the socio-political climate in the "lower" and "higher" phases of the post-capitalist epoch.

Of course, the initiation of planning by the proletarian State and the co-op conglomerates (via democratic inter-business planning, long-term public contracts, vertical and horizontal networking, a Project Cybersyn-like national software, etc) will gradually cause the proletarian "market" to become increasingly obsolete. Markets will no longer be the means for material allocation; as economic planning is ushered in via the proletarian State and its contracted co-op conglomerates, the material needs of the working class will be met directly, rather than through the market's fickle fluctuations. The capture of the State political apparatus by the proletarian vanguard, and its eventual withering away, will contingently result in existent economics gaining new political connotations.

Section Two:
University Newspaper Articles

Democracy Endangered

The Supreme Court's infamous *Citizens United* decision represents the beginning of a dangerous phase in American history. It represents the transition from a people-driven democracy to a corporate oligarchy, wherein the say that you and I have becomes increasingly unheard while the voices of the ultra-rich are amplified.

Of course, there are those who will support the Supreme Court's decision out of a genuine belief that spending money equates to free speech. But this view run in direct opposition to the well-being of America and its people. *Citizens United* has nothing to do with "free speech" or the liberty to take part in the electoral process. How does the legalization of super-PACs and groups with the ability to spend *unlimited* money in elections reinforce liberty or democracy? How does it do anything to better America and improve the lives of the working class? The simple answer is that it does not; allowing money to flood Washington does not make our voice there any louder. It only silences them.

The amount of money that one has should not equate to how much say they have in government; democracy should go hand-in-hand with political equality, not economic classism.

What does that say about our Republic? What sort of message are we projecting to both our citizens and those abroad when we let super-PACs trample over us? What sort of Republic are we, when things such as *Citizens United* and voting identification laws begin to undermine the system that made this country the envy of the world? It is not a good one: we are setting the stage for both potential disenfranchisement and the very end of representative government as we know it.

Elizabeth Warren put it spectacularly when she said that "corporations are not people. People have hearts, they have kids, they get jobs, they get sick, they cry, they dance. They live, they love, and they die. And that matters. That matters because we don't run this country for corporations, we run it for people."

Bernie Sanders, the longest-serving Independent in the history of Congress, has offered a proposal that seems logical to us but will be extraordinarily difficult to pass through the capital-riddled system: the *Saving American Democracy Amendment*. It states that corporations are *not* people, and only living, breathing human beings are entitled to the freedoms enshrined in the Bill of Rights. Amending the Constitution is not something that should be taken lightly or be done often. Such discussion should only come up when the existence of our Republic is in peril and, unfortunately, we are at that dreaded point. Which path will we take? Will we go down the road wherein the ultra-rich wrest total control of Congress from the people, or will we rise up and demand a preservation of democracy?

Is this what we have come to? A time wherein our supposedly-democratic Republic and its representatives can be bought and sold by the corporate élite like so many commodities? What would our Founding Fathers say, if they knew that our most hallowed institutions have been infected with the cancerous influence of capital? President Lincoln's famous declaration of our nation being "of the people, by the people, for the people" is increasingly slipping away, piece by piece.

This is not an issue like abortion, same-sex marriage, universal healthcare, or the host of other mundane things that Democrats and Republicans bicker about every day on the news. The condition of our democratic system transcends this - *Citizens United* has been the subject of sharp criticism from both the Left and the Right. We may argue over talking points throughout the course of the presidential campaign and be divided amongst which candidate to choose, but we are all united in our desire for fair, pure, and transparent democracy.

This is not an issue that divides America, splitting it into liberals against conservatives - it literally represents a turning point in America, a presentation of two very distinct paths that our country can take. Will we follow the one that leads towards corporate ownership of government and the death knell of representation? Or will we do overturn *Citizens United* and do as Senator Sanders says, and "wage a moral and political war against the billionaires and corporate leaders, on Wall Street and elsewhere, whose policies and greed are destroying the middle class of America"?

The solution is clear: we need to purge corporate money from Washington, and get the lobbyists out of the people's Congress.

The choices that we make in the coming months are going to have effects that resonate for generations - we have the momentum on our side to overturn *Citizens United*. Numerous states have passed resolutions condemning the Supreme Court's decision and its potentially fatal blow to American democracy, and we have the opportunity to send a strong and powerful message to the government this election: we can say that it can no longer be in bed with the corporations, that people come before profit, and that people - and only people - are entitled to the liberties that our Founding Fathers fought and died for. All this rhetoric that we spin when fighting abroad - that we're doing it for humanitarian reasons and that we're working to bring democracy to tyrannical nations - will only remain rhetoric and speech if we do not work to undo this devastating ruling.

Romney Is Not A Working-Class Hero

Has President Obama made progress? Absolutely - there is no disputing that. We cannot be intellectually honest with ourselves when we say that he has done nothing or that he is destroying America. These ideas that he is a closeted socialist intent on bankrupting the United States has no grounding - if 31 consecutive months of private-sector job growth and a net addition of 5.5 million jobs, coupled with 18 tax cuts and a revitalized auto industry, is not indicative of him being an effective capitalist, then I do not know what is.

His progress is not limited strictly to economic matters, however: the first bill that he passed, the Lilly Ledbetter Fair Pay Act, cuts down on pay discrimination based on gender. He repealed the "Don't Ask, Don't Tell" policy, and refusal to defend the constitutionality of the overtly bigoted Defense of Marriage Act has put the issue of same-sex marriage on the track to being reviewed by the Supreme Court - potentially as early as its next term.

No one could have walked into the Oval Office and turned the economy around overnight - no Democrat or Republican could have pulled us out of Great Recession and brought us directly into a flourishing market. The ravaging of the working class lasted for decades, and it's going to take time to get us back to the point wherein we can have total economic security again. President Obama has taken bold steps to fight the Recession. He has done much, but there is still plenty of work left to do.

We do not want a corporate aristocrat leading our nation - we want someone of integrity and spirit, someone that is able to identify with the working class and understand the struggles that it goes through, day in and day out. Can Romney identify with workers? Absolutely not. Obama can - being raised in a profoundly middle-class family and struggling to get from a fatherless household and into Harvard University. If President Obama is not a shining example of what a contemporary rags-to-riches story would be, then I do not know what would be. His history encompasses the rhetoric that so often use in America -

that working hard, persevering, and putting in diligent effort can lift one out of poverty and will be appropriately rewarded.

A man who inherited enormous wealth cannot understand what it is like to scrape together money to buy used textbooks; one with multi-million dollar off-shore bank accounts does not understand the struggle of putting food on one's table and feeding one's children, or having to choose to pay for either one's rent or one's medications. Mitt Romney is not someone who exemplifies the American Dream or common man - he is an alien, someone that is separated form the working class by such a wide margin that he cannot understand the mere *concept* of the working class. He cannot empathize with the poor, the middle-class, the marginalized, and the impoverished when he was born with a silver spoon in his mouth. No matter how many photo-ops he may take part in or how many times he wears flannel and bluejeans, he will never fool working families into thinking that he is one of us.

Today, too many people are working too many hours at dead-end jobs, barely able to earn the subsistence wages necessary to keep their homes and families afloat. *These* are the people that we should be rewarding and focusing on. Why do we continue to glorify the ultra-rich and their shady business deals as being the "hard workers"? No, I dissent from this: the working families, the struggling poor, the middle class and everyone fighting to get into the middle class - these people are the backbone of our economy. *They* are the ones that get up every day and do the manual work that keeps our infrastructure running smoothly, to stay up late and grade their students' papers, to staff our hospitals and keep us healthy, to go to work and keep the economic gears turning. The working class is the backbone of the United States, not the ultra-rich, and our value systems should be those that recognize and exalt the common, struggling Americans, not greed-driven bankers.

There are so many things that we need to do over the coming years. Not only do we need to resist cuts to Social Security, but we need to demand that the ultra-rich pay their fair share and contribute to this nation. We need to not also oppose cuts in Medicare and Medicaid, but we must join the rest of the industrialized world in guaranteeing healthcare as a fundamental human right through a single-payer Medicare-for-All system. We must end unfettered free trade agreements that ship our jobs oversees, end *all* of our wars abroad, and end discrimination against *all* peoples across different sexual and gender spectrums by instituting national gender-neutral marriage. We must develop a new perspective that glorifies the working class, not the exploitative class.

We do not want a soulless opportunist sitting in the Oval Office - we want someone who understands the middle class by actually having experienced it.

We must stand together against this attack on the working class. Do not vote in accordance with your parents or the never-ending television ads: vote with your conscience. Which candidate will work to end bigotry and promote tolerance? Reduce dirty energy production and encourage sustainable green power? Strive for a responsible end to the war in Afghanistan, just like in Iraq? Push for greater access to healthcare? Tell Wall Street to play by the same rules as Main Street?

We are not going to finally step into modernity and heal our nation until we do these things, and we are not going to be able to do any of them if we have Romney sitting in the Oval Office.

Obama Re-Elected

What sort of things can we expect over the next four years, now that Obama has been re-elected? At the very least, we can see the determined expansion of his Affordable Care Act, ensuring that millions more will have access to equitable healthcare; at the most, we could see a forceful push on the Supreme Court to strike down the overtly-bigoted Defense of Marriage Act.

Now that he no longer has the pressure of impressing the electorate, Obama can push forward and work to enact a truly progressive agenda. I expect to see another vote Congress to pass the DREAM Act, the legislation that would have granted undocumented immigrants who were brought here as very young children a potential path to citizenship. I'm also expecting another attempt by Obama and Republican Speaker John Boehner to have a "grand bargain" that cuts federal spending while increasing taxation on the ultra-rich.

Despite what the cynics say about the President and his re-election - that the world is going to end, that we're rushing towards Grecian debt, or that we're tumbling down into socialism - I remain cautiously optimistic. There are so many challenges that lay ahead of us - domestic energy, national security, our sovereign debt, inequality, and bloated military budget. The list goes on. As daunting as I realize that these obstacles are, I'm fully certain that they will be met. President Obama has not shirked the issues, and anyone who says otherwise is simply a cynic or nay-sayer. The man inherited a broken nation, and he was worked day-in and day-out to make sure that our country's best days are not *behind us*, but rather *in front of us*. We need to build on the momentum that we have and continue to heal our economy; we need to push forward and guarantee marriage, education, and healthcare as fundamental human rights.

But the progress that we've made isn't simply reflected in the man that New Hampshire chose to send back to the White House - very fundamental changes have taken place here, within our state's own borders. Maggie Hassan is our next governor, and I breathe a sign of relief knowing that there is finally someone in the governor's office who is not afraid to freeze tuition, restore university funding, and invest in our education system. Carol Shea-Porter and Annie Kuster will be able to fight to women's rights, equal pay, and an equitable economy when they head to Congress in January.

We have done so much, America, but there is still so much more to do. We all took part in making history yesterday, whether we voted for Romney or Obama. Our political landscape has fundamentally changed. We mustn't think that the fight ends here, however. There are so many more things that we need to accomplish, so many obstacles that need to be overcome. I have no doubt that they will be overcome, now that we have chosen to send a voice of compassion and reason back to the White House.

In 2008, we started a campaign. In 2012, it became a movement. In the coming years, we are going to be able to ride this momentous wave of hope into cultural modernity and economic stability. We did what the cynics said we could not, and we persevered. If our president works as hard the next four years as he did the last, we are going to see tremendous, positive change in our country.

American Foreign Policy Gone Wrong

The first years of the United States were remarkably free from governmental involvement; federalism was still in its infancy, and the nation had not grown to the point in which the state-country relationship had evolved so that the former was not consumed by the expanding power of the latter. Individual liberty was at its zenith: judicial precedents, legislation, and executive orders had not yet been set down that restricted self-government. The dawn of America could be considered the advent of a libertarian utopia and the 'proven' success of classical liberalism.

Yet the existence of world wars, political conflicts, and ideological schisms have all proven to contribute to the perversion of America. We were an embryo for liberty that could have very well have evolved into a glorious, people-driven republic, but we have not followed that path: we've entered the era of the corporate police-state, with boundaries set upon our civil rights. Time has not proven the American experiment to be true, but rather has warped it into something that our Founding Father would decry.

Modern America prides itself on being that, though - we pride ourselves on being the paragon of Western democracy, acting as the singular and last night in the darkness of emerging statism and collectivism. We desperately try to ignore the fact that our nation has changed; we hold fast to the concept that we are still the freest country on earth and the only place where freedom and patriotism truly exist. We do not willingly acknowledge the fact that the government's control is rapidly expanding or that our civil rights are being constricted at an accelerating rate, but rather remind ourselves that we are still the home of the free and land of the brave.

We allow everyone - both ourselves and our self-righteous politicians - to flippantly throw around the words 'freedom' and 'liberty' without thinking critical of what they mean. We tell ourselves that we are a free and democratic country and that we advocate for democracy abroad, but we shut our eyes to our own government's foreign policy. We ignore the

American-sponsored dictators of Latin America, the generous donations and double-dealings with Middle Eastern radicals, and the intervention into the affairs of governments of other countries. We pray that our "democratic" country will live forever as the bastion of liberty while cringing away from the thought that our nation is involved in some of the most undemocratic actions conceivable.

Newly-founded America gave birth to free markets and constitutionalism. The free market gave rise to capitalism and personal profit, and even this mutated into corporatism and outright imperialism. Economic and social intervention is now the lifeblood of our government, and imperialism is the new patriotism that our country espouses.

What of the propaganda that we savagely throw against Hugo Chávez, calling the man a tyrannical leader that has dictatorially nationalized Venezuela's petroleum industry and erected a statist bureaucracy? Is this propaganda truthful, or is merely a slander campaign against someone who no longer agrees to run his country based on America's economic interests in the South? In reality, Chávez has done wonders for the people of Venezuela - he does not flippantly talk about "democracy" as we do, but has rather supported it by helping his citizens create over 100,000 new worker-owned cooperative businesses. Yet because he does not the share the same economic interests as the U.S., we have launched a full-scale media war against him, the same as we did in the early 1970s with the wildly popular and democratically-elected self-avowed Marxist president of Chile, Salvador Allende.

What is most troubling nowadays, though, is an over-zealous support for Israel. Now, it needs to be said that there is nothing wrong with Israel itself, and the nation has the right to exist and defend itself from any and all threats. We should support and protect our allies, but we should not do so blindly. What's most disturbing is the way that some support Israel despite the human rights violations that it continuously commits - such support for Israel stems from a need to reaffirm oneself as patriotic, as if an unwavering, absolutist commitment somehow makes one better and more valiant than those that do not. They support Israel simply because it *is* Israel, not because of any specific or noteworthy thing that the nation has done.

Israel's attempt to preserve its purity by disenfranchising Palestinians does not promote democracy or liberty in any way - it exacerbates ethnic tensions and political conflicts. The way that the Israeli state - and the Israeli Defense Forces, in particular - treat Palestinians, Muslims, and other non-Israelis does nothing to bring about a peaceful solution to the never-ending conflicts in the Middle East. Yes, there are Palestinians who have engaged in radical policies (indeed, some that may even warrant the over-used title of "terrorist", but both sides are guilty for past crimes), but that is not justification for the complete marginalization of an entire racial group. If there is anything that history has taught us, is it that the things that Israel is doing will not end the Israeli-Palestinian conflict: bombing, slandering, and subjugating a race of people in the hopes that they give up and acknowledge defeat is not wise. It only angers them more, and fuels both of them. Both the Israelis and Palestinians are willing to fight to the death, and one perpetually assaulting the other is not conducive for a productive outcome.

Both sides need to come to the table and have an honest discussion about their past actions, future goals, and where they can meet in the middle so as to establish a two-state solution. If we are going to have a peace accord between Israel and Palestine, we need to end the incessant American intervention and warmongering and actually promote diplomacy and pacifism.

Obamacare, and Other Evil "Socialist" Ideas

I'm astounded to hear some continue to call President Obama a socialist. In the U.S., it seems, it is used it as a political cudgel to associate one with the totalitarianism of the Soviet Empire, as ex-presidential candidate Newt Gingrich so fondly calls it. As I have said before, we cannot be intellectually honest with ourselves when we say that Obama is a socialist. His capitalist résumé is incredible: 32 months of consecutive private sector job growth, 18 middle-class tax cuts, the creation of 5.5 million jobs, every job lost throughout President Bush's years have been restored, the auto industry is revitalized, and the United States is on track to produce more oil than Saudi Arabia starting in 2020.

Obamacare is not socialism, and the overwhelming majority of the law is a conservative cop-out. It was originally conceptualized by the Heritage Foundation, a right-wing think tank, in 1993. The bill's "mandate" that every citizen purchase insurance only serves to provide insurance corporations with additional customers, revenue, and profit. It stabilizes the private sector by dramatically expanding the number of people that take part in it. Even Stewart Alexander, the Socialist Party USA's 2012 presidential candidate, calls it a "corporate restructuring of the healthcare system in America".

The Heritage Foundation's proposal was supported by Congressional Republicans in 1993, who supported it as the market-friendly alternative to the proposal of First Lady Hillary Clinton's. Hillary's legacy has lived on, however. The progressives in Congress rallied in 2008 and 2009 for a government-sponsored public insurance option to compete in the market with private insurance. Congressman Alan Greyson's simple Public Option Act would have done just this: allowed those who want private insurance to keep it, and allow those who want public healthcare to receive it by purchasing Medicare participation. The drafts of Obamacare (such as proposals H.R. 3200 or H.R. 3966, America's Health Choices Act of 2009 and Speaker Nancy Pelosi's proposal, respectively) each had such a public option, but it was eventually dropped due to conservative opposition that it would eventually evolve into a fully government-run Medicare-for-All system.

Medicare-for-All is single-payer healthcare: a single, non-profit financial pool that we all contribute to through our taxes, and which from all healthcare expenses are drawn from. This is the way it is financed in Taiwan and the United Kingdom, and to a lesser extent in Canada. Single-payer was scored by the Congressional Budget Office as saving as much as $400 billion per year but cutting bloated CEO salaries, bureaucracy, and eliminating the 10-30% administrative cost of corporations and replacing it the 2-3% cost for Medicare. The growth of our healthcare costs would decrease by nearly 40%, putting us closer to Canada's levels. They spend 10% of their GDP on healthcare; we currently spend 16-17%.

The rhetoric about socialism is blown completely out of proportion. The idea that Social Security - a publicly-funded safety net designed to combat a senior poverty rate of 50% at the time - is the cause of our nation's bankruptcy is an absolute farce. Nowadays it's 10%, proving that it's has done what it was designed to do. The Congressional Budget Office has announced, again and again, that Social Security has not contributed a single nickel to the federal deficit, has a current $2.6 *trillion* dollar surplus, and is able to pay out every cent in benefits to every eligible American for almost the next three decades. A simple lifting of the payment cap - instructing those who make more than $500,000 a year contribute more to it than someone who makes $20,000 - would keep it solvent *indefinitely*.

We should not balance our nation's budget on the backs of the working class. We need to expand Medicare to cover everyone, and we need to re-write the ridiculous tax code that allows Exxon-Mobile to pay an tax rate of 0%. Closing those loopholes would bring in $500 billion a year. A simple 30% tax on multi-millionaires was proposed by corporate financier Warren Buffet, generating nearly $47 billion in new revenue.

Letting the Bush-era tax cuts (which the CBO estimates is the result of 48% of our debt) expire would bring in $950 billion. Ending *all* of the wars in the Middle East would save us nearly $7 billion a week - adding up to $364 billion *per year*, and seeing as the CBO scores laws over a ten-year period, the end of the so-called "war on terror" would save an astounding $3.6 *trillion* over a decade.

The libertarian Cato Institute makes a logical argument when it says that drug legalization would save sums of money. If the U.S. was to legalize marijuana (as is now the reality in Washington state), an estimated $41.3 billion would be saved from cutting the wasteful spending in arrests, prosecution, and incarceration. Portugal enacted universal decriminalization - on everything from marijuana to heroin. If we did, we would save an additional $38 billion a year, and national same-sex marriage - something that the Supreme Court is finally considering - would pump nearly $750 million into the economy in consumer spending on marriage-related expenses in the first year alone. Other estimates show this figure being as high as $1 billion.

There are realistic steps that we can take to reduce the deficit without doing so at the working class' expense. If we want to avoid the fiscal cliff and national bankruptcy, we need to readdress our priorities.

The End of Reaganism

Ronald Reagan single-handedly presided over the attempted pulverization of the working class. Under his watch, economic productivity increased by a noteworthy 45%, but it came at a terrible cost. Wages for working families remained frozen, while the tax rate for the richest 1% of earners was cut in half; household credit debt exploded, spiking to be over 110% of the nation's GDP as workers lost their economic purchasing power; middle-class bankruptcies escalated 610%; the prison-industrial complex privatized countless prisons, and incarcerations jumped 355%; and the usage of high-dosage anti-depressants skyrocketed 305% as working people succumbed to the economic stress, straining the healthcare system and increasing its cost by nearly 80%. Despite the damage to working households that he caused, the DOW Jones exploded nearly 1,400% and the ratio of employee-to-CEO pay grew to 1:649 as wealth was redistributed upwards.

Reagan did not preside over a period of economic growth - he set the stage for a corporate re-structuring of our financial system and padded the pockets of the ultra-rich at the expense of the working class.

This is not all that categorized the Reagan Era. The social conservatism that reigned that the time was little more than cultural backwardness; the "traditional values" that were held on so dearly were merely philosophically-justified bigotry. At the time, same-sex couples were considered abnormal. Marijuana usage was considered to be on the same level as hard drugs like cocaine and heroin. Us libertarian socialists were equated with the authoritarianism of Marxist-Leninism, and any critique of domestic policy was indicative of Sino-Soviet sympathy. It was an era that was fiercely anti-progressive and anti-equality, and riddled with elements of overt nationalism.

History progresses dialectically. As time goes on, policies become increasingly progressive; American culture moves slowly and surely to the left, and acceptance of ethnic and sexual minorities is all but certain. But just because the arc of history bends inexorably towards justice, as Martin Luther King famously said, does not mean that it will occur with a full consensus. Even though Reagan's presidency is (thankfully) in the past, elements of the zealous devotion to unfettered capitalism that his oligarchy spawned still exist today.

The Tea Party views Ronald Reagan as if he was a god, as if he was the patron deity of prosperity and freedom. Any legitimate analysis of his tenure proves only the opposite, but he hid the immiseration he caused by speaking endlessly of liberty, evoking patriotic sentiments that caught the populace up in a wave of mindless America-obsession and made them refuse to question anything that it did.

Despite the overwhelmingly moderate reform that President Obama tried to pass in the first two years of his presidency, the ultra-rich - angered that his legislation would run counter to their economic interests - funded a political movement in the hopes that it would restore the rampant nationalism of Reagan so that they could get Obama out of office and replace him with yet another corporate puppet. It's very name - the "Tea Party" - drips with overt hyper-patriotism.

Rupert Murdoch and David and Charles Koch have poured billions of dollars into a faux "grassroots" movement that reeks of the toxic filth of nationalism and free-market fetishism, all hidden behind the thin veil of "patriotism" and "liberty". There is nothing organic or spontaneous about the Tea Party - from its conception to its electoral victory in the 2010 midterm elections, it was flooded with money by the same people who financed the pro-Romney super-PACs.

Yet despite its unrealistic and backwards agenda - from the abolition of corporate regulation to the full regulation of all civil liberties - the country presses inexorably onwards. When the United States elected an African-American as its president, the far-right recoiled and hardened its views; when Obama's healthcare reform passed and was declared constitutional by the Supreme Court, it radicalized even further; and when the next presidential election came, it tried to oust the so-called communist by reaffirming its conservatism by rejecting immigration reform and obsessively adhering to the cultural norm of the Industrial Revolution.

Despite all of this, the United States has pressed on. The nation voted for Al Gore to be president in 2000 and gave him the popular vote, and even though the State preserved its tyranny by unconstitutionally declaring George Bush president, it declare its desire to push forward and enter cultural modernity by electing Obama twice. Healthcare reform (despite the final bill being only a shadow of a compromise) passed, cannabis legalization has begun, same-sex marriage will be nationally recognized after the Supreme Court hears cases for its constitutionality in late March.

Barack Obama's re-election, despite what conservative political commentators and pundits say, will not herald the collapse of our Republic, nor will he usher in an era of Soviet-style authoritarianism. In reality, it is the pronouncement that the United States will finally join the rest of the industrialized world in actually promoting tolerance and social equality, and finally recognizing economic logic by leaving fanatical neoliberalism behind. Obama does not represent the death of America - he represents the end of bigotry, the end of economic backwardness, and the end of cultural intolerance - he represents the fortunate end to Reaganism.

Capitalism is Killing Our Humanity

If people judged capitalism by the same standards that they judged socialism with, they would have declared it a failure generations ago. The rampant intellectual dishonesty amongst the anti-Left crowd is astounding - the mere idea that anyone would vocally support a system that is able to sustain itself by the plundering of under-developing countries reeks of soullessness and an utter disregard for human welfare. The parasitic relationship between First World nations and their Third World subjugates serves only to treat those in developing countries as tools, as completely commodified machines whose only purpose is to continue their forced labor for the mass-production of super-cheap imports.

It is even more unbelievable that people continue to equate socialism - real, genuine, unfettered socialism - with the atrocities committed by Stalin and his Marxist-Leninist allies. Anyone who has taken the time to sit down and read legitimate socialist literature will most likely find a deeper hatred for centralized State bureaucracies like the former Soviet Union than for capitalist nations. It's also incredibly amusing that the right-wing radicals that rail against President Obama's alleged European-style "socialist" tendencies or the Soviets' Marxist-Leninism are, in reality, woefully uneducated on the subject, and choose to regurgitate the racist nationalism of Fox News instead of deciding to pick up a book on proper socialist theory.

When the ruling class apologizes to the working class for: pre-emptive war, colonialism, the 14-hour work day, child labor, the Massacre of the Paris Commune, apartheid, international war, deforestation, Exxon Valdez, and the military suppression of democratic movements in Latin America and the replacement of their elected leaders with CIA-backed fascist dictators for the sake of economic interests, then - and only then - will I even consider apologizing for the errors committed in the name of "socialist" countries.

The capitalist mode of production does nothing to expand "liberty" or raise the standard of living for the people that live under it. In reality, a capitalist nation commodifies the workers, turning them into cogs in the profit-making machine without their awareness or consent of it. The "high standard of living" that the far-right often evokes is only sustained by the outrageously parasitic behavior that we continue to exhibit.

A system that disproportionately redistributes all wealth upwards while reducing aid for the working class is not sustainable. Capitalism is not something that can last indefinitely; it is a cancer that needs to stretch its malignant tendrils abroad in neocolonial, imperialist war in order to seize natural resources and exploit cheap labor. One day, when this cancer has no more resources to draw upon, it is going to collapse in upon itself, and the working class will be left to pick up the pieces of the world that the corporate aristocracy's greed had destroyed, and will have to built a new one from the ashes of the old.

Although, to even talk about the possibility of having an economic system other than capitalism is heresy in the United States. Capitalism has been intricately tied to "liberty" and "freedom" by the right-wing nationalists, who throw the words around at every possible chance that they have, draining them of any real meaning and using "liberty" to justify unfettered corporatism.

The burden for the recession should not be placed on the backs of the workers, of the citizens who spent their entire life playing by the rules only to have the programs that they paid into their entire lives be slashed in order to continue the budget-busting tax cuts that we shower the ultra-wealthy with. Some rebuke this by saying that we have the highest corporate tax rate in the world; however, that 35% tax is so riddled with loopholes that the *effective* tax rate for hovers just below 9%. In reality, we have one of the most lax tax systems on the entire planet. The Bush-era tax cuts (which, thankfully, have been repealed for individuals making $400,000 or more, and for households making $450,000 or more a year) cost this nation a staggering $100.2 billion a year. In the past decade, that amounts to over a trillion dollars in hand-outs to the top 1%.

    The idea that slashing the federal budget in the hopes that reduced aid for special education, the handicapped, and our seniors will somehow create limitless prosperity for all is not simply foolish - it is downright cruel. The proposed changes to Social Security would save approximately $10 billion a year (which is barely a drop in the bucket, in comparison to our over-16-trillion dollar deficit), and it would do so by tweaking the Consumer Price Index for Urban Wage Earners and Clerical Workers, what is generally referred to as the CPI, so that the benefits that are based on inflation would be calculated differently. If put into practice, it would mean that Social Security benefits would become much less comprehensive - a senior citizen who lives on Social Security collects just under $15,000 a year in total pay, and the affect of the CPI "tweak" would cost them $650 a year. As inflation continues and the market fluctuates, the cumulative effects of the CPI change will result in American senior citizens being stripped of $1,000 or more.
    The fact that we are allow such a system to exist is mind-boggling. The complete disregard that some people have for our fellow brothers and sisters in this world is heartbreaking; the absence of human solidarity is disheartening. I look forward to the day when our country enters cultural modernity and we decide to work together for a system that puts human well-being over short-term profit.

Legalizing Marijuana is Only Step One

      The recent public hearings on the New Hampshire General Court's possible passage of legislation that would legalize, decriminalize, or make marijuana medically available shows that we New Englanders continue to be leaders in issues of civil liberties. If our nation's glorious Constitution (and dare I say, the spirit of liberty that it embodies?) speaks of anything, it speaks of inalienable autonomy, of the right of each citizen to do with his life and to his body as he sees fit. There is no reason for our current drug policies. If we want to stay true to our cultural ethos, we need to change our laws: we need to legalize drugs - from marijuana to crack-cocaine and heroin, and everything in between - in order to rein in our out-of-control police spending and reaffirm our devotion to liberty.
      What evidence is there that prohibition of any kind works? One needs only to look at our own drug policies and compare them to those in other countries that have been taken. In Britain, where the the single-payer National Health Service allows drug-users to give hospitals their used needles in exchange for sanitized ones. As a result, HIV transmission and infections associated with needle usage plummeted, as addicts were no longer using, re-using, and sharing needles amongst each other and for multiple drugs. The number of addicts to drugs that require (or can be taken with) a needle decreased by a striking 54 percent. The cost of supplying these hospitals with clean needles is only a fraction of the outrageous strain that emergency medicine requires when treating overdose and withdrawal. In the end, England was able to *save* money by focusing on preventative care and public health, rather than emergency care and a budget-busting police state.
      Portugal is a unique case: the drug reform that went into effect in summer of 2001 decriminalized *all* drugs. While drug trafficking and distribution is still considered a criminal offense, their usage and ownership was changed to an "administrative" one, roughly equivalent to small misdemeanor here in the United States, and is treated as a medical condition rather than a federal

crime. This, coupled with a needle exchange program in their local pharmacies, modeled after the hospital program that British neighbors have, that also comes in a kit fully equipped with rubbing alcohol, condoms, and information on HIV transmission and treatment. They also took the money that their police forces were saving by not arresting small-time drug offenders and invested in their healthcare system, building additional rehabilitation and treatment facilities across the nation.

    The results? An astounding drop in drug usage by 49%. By treating drug addiction as a medical issue and enacting bold, progressive policies, the number of drug users has nearly been cut in half. With our Nixon-era war on drugs having cost us over $1.5 trillion in police enforcement and judicial bureaucracy, it is time for a different approach. The fact that we have increased spending on the war on drugs nearly ten times over, despite a stubborn rate of illicit drug addiction at 1.3 to 2 percent that has refused to go down, shows that throwing more money at the issue is not a solution. We shouldn't just shower our police in taxpayer money and intensify the legal penalty; we should be smart about how and where we spend our tax dollar, and spending them on preventative healthcare and rehabilitation is both logical and fiscally responsible.

    Drug profits are extraordinarily high because they exist in the black market; because drug dealers are not able to use the property law and legal contracts to enforce their deals, they are compelled to enforce their deals through non-legal means - primarily, through violence. Those that finance drug traffickers by providing transportation, guns, crude chemicals, and safe houses are able to take part in an international industry that constitutes 8% of the global economy. Cannabis provides only an estimated 25% of cartels' revenue at most; by legalizing it and taxing it as we do with alcohol, it would inject approximately $10 billion in consumer spending into the economy in the first year alone. A legalization-and-taxation policy for cannabis, coupled with a legalization-and-rehabilitation program for hard drugs, would render our national and international black markets obsolete. Numerous economists estimate that it would bring in up to an astounding $100 billion in federal revenue is taxed and sold like alcohol, and the additional state employees necessary to grow, cultivate, distribute, and sell it would support up to 75 jobs per state county, on average. This would yield a quarter-million new jobs overnight.

Of course, many will argue that we should not legalize drugs; this will encourage usage and normalize addictions to hard drugs, they say, and will cause more problems than solutions. But which system is better: the one that compassionately rehabilitates addicts and teaches them to be productive and contributing members of society, or the one wherein the State yanks children away from their parents by throwing the former into a corruption-riddled foster-home system and the later into an inhumane prison-industrial complex?

Which one encourages accountability, responsibility, and liberty? The answer is clear.

A market for illicit drugs will always exist; whether or not we make it a criminal black market or a legal, regulated one is something that we, as a country, have to answer. If we continue the budget-busting policies that spawn gang violence and allow our civil liberties to be eroded by ever-expanded police powers, we can go with the former. If we want to retain our freedom and keep our fiscal house in order, then we need to legalize all drugs.

Let's Not Forget the 'T' in LGBT

The "Transilience" film that Dr. Joelle Ruby Ryan of the Women's Studies department presented to the public in the MUB last week is something that all UNH students should see. For those that missed it, it can be found online on Youtube. It is not a Transgender 101 film; it is not something that is meant to be an introduction towards the transgender community. It the third installment her film series that gives one the chance to see how she, as a gender outlaw and proud activist, has dealt with the challenges presented to her by a cis-supremacist society that does not value gender diversity. It is not meant to represent the trans community as a whole; no one person can speak for an entire movement, but Dr. Ryan does a fantastic job of highlighting how we, decades after the civil rights movement, still marginalize entire sections of the American populace.

There are numerous people here at the University that would do well to take a Women's Studies class, and I encourage everyone to do so. It is a learning experience that some people are in desperate need of, as there continue to be to many people who are needlessly vicious to the department and take part in the oppression of trans minorities, while at the same time garbing themselves in the rhetoric of "liberty" and "freedom". How can one proselytize about our enduring "liberty" when entire social groups are shunned by society and treated as deviant outcasts? One cannot.

The fight for gender equality - and even the fight against the compartmentalizing concept of "gender" itself - is the next great civil rights struggle of our time. Yes, the LGBT community is going to score a major victory this coming spring when the Supreme Court declares the constitutionality of same-sex marriage, but we should not focus the argument entirely on those of the same sex; we should not forget our transgender comrades who have had to deal with oppression in a way that the mainstream LGBT community cannot even think of. To have a non-heterosexual sexual orientation is certainly against the grain of America's viciously patriarchal society, but to actually be transgender puts one on a whole different level. Name changes, gender-reassignment surgery, systemic legal oppression, economic classism - the transgender community has had to face persecution and brutality in a way that no other minority has ever had to. I cannot imagine the struggle that my trans friends have to go through, but the fact that they do - and that they persevere and come out stronger - makes me indescribably proud of them. They deserve the utmost respect and support.

If there is one thing that the trans community can remind us of, it is that is how desperately important it is for us to live our own truths. There is a particular kind of joyful pride at being able to inhabit one's own skin and readily accept one's identity. Of course, being "different" will always be difficult, but those that do - and those of us that stand side-by-side with them in unwavering solidarity - are helping to pave the way for generations that will come after, and are changing the world by resolutely stating the truth,that all people are created equal, and that everyone should have the right to live their life in a way that brings them the most joy.

UNH has made excellent progress on trans issues, and I applaud them, but there are still issues that need to be faced. The Transgender Policy and Climate Committee (T-PACC) is a sub-committee of the President's Commission on the Status of GLBT Issues, and is dedicated to monitoring the campus climate for trans students, faculty, and staff. It works to recommend and implement policy changes to promote an environment that reaffirms gender diversity. Thus far, it has worked with Health Services to explore resources available for trans students, and has approached the Registrar's office in the hopes of initiating a system change to better serve the trans community on campus by potentially changing the "sex" categories on university applications and paperwork.

Unfortunately, there continues to be a faction of radical "radfem" feminists that are extraordinarily hostile to transgender and transsexual people, especially trans women. Radfems in Western society are viciously obsessed with the concept of "woman" and involve themselves with calling out, and working to abolish, male patriarchy in the name of female empowerment. In the process, though, they unfortunately alienate those that do not adhere to a strict male-or-female gender binary. The radfem faction of feminists, and their overtly black-and-white pro-women views, unfortunately caused them to be estranged from their fellow social revolutionaries. Why is it that this rampant sectarianism has to continue to plague the feminist community? Why do the radfems continue to marginalize their trans comrades in the name of women's liberation, when, if united together in a feminist popular front, they could be a force to be reckoned with against the patriarchy?

    Everything that people do counts, and no action is "too small". Whether someone is heterosexual or homosexual, cis-gendered or transgendered, makes no difference; if there is systemic oppression and rampant inequality in our world, we should work to resolve the problem together. Us cis-gendered allies can be effective catalysts for change if we stand together and not just accept but actually fight for our transgendered brothers and sisters. Activism can be as simple and everyday as interrupting an offensive joke, or calling out rude comments in public. Start where you are, and remember that your actions will have a ripple effect. Trans rights are human rights, and we all benefit when we are all liberated by the ability to be able to live our lives without fear, shame, or judgement.

The Sequester: Another Attempt by the Corporate Élite to Crush Labor

The news has been up in arms recently about the economic sequester that is, as the Republican Party says, an attempt to offset the "reckless spending" of our leaderless and partisan President. Even though the sequester cuts only a mere 3% of federal spending - which, in the scope of the nation's $15.1 trillion GDP and $16.72 trillion federal deficit - is only a drop in the bucket, it represents a particularly dangerous road for us to take if our goal is to balance the federal budget. Despite the fact that the working class' discretionary income has stayed fairly consistent (and, in some regions and demographics, even dipped), inflation has reduced its economic purchasing power, leaving the middle class with increasingly little influence over the economy. As capitalist-style "tax reform" continues to redistribute wealth upwards, workers have less power to influence the state of the economy; the only other entities with enough purchasing power to impact the state of the economy are: first and foremost, the federal government, with its incredible collective bargaining power accounting for trillions of dollars and millions of participatory taxpayers; and secondly, to a lesser extent, private corporations, who currently sit on over $2.2 trillion unused and untapped assets and armies of lobbyists (nearly 5 per every 1 member of Congress).

If individual consumers no longer have the power to impact the economy through their elective expenses, then we need to have the second and third most powerful economic entities take responsibility and do something to defibrillate the American economy. Private corporations have no desire to do so - not only does the *Dodge v. Ford* Supreme Court case requires them to operate in the interests of profiteering shareholders rather than in the economic interests of the community, but they exist to generate profit regardless of their legal obligations. We cannot trust in the corporate aristocracy to work in the interests of the working class. I am not arguing that we should place our faith in federal institutions rather than corporate ones (indeed,

I'm much more a fan of the abolition of the State), but we need to be intellectually honest with ourselves by acknowledging that the federal government has enormous power, and it has the potential to use that power to jump-start the economy.

At the risk of sounding like an angsty, deficit-spending-obsessed Keynesian, we need to use the government's extraordinary budget to invest in the working class. Gutting the federal budget in such a delicate time is not something that will serve the direct interests of the American middle class.

The sequestration is not a good idea; we should not be pulling billions of dollars out of the economy when our recovery is still so fragile; we should be pumping money into it, be investing in the working class and small business, and enacting massive public works programs that hire millions of thousands of American citizens to repair, expand, and modernize our roads, bridges, ports, and infrastructure.

There is nothing about this "sequestration" that involves fiscal responsibility; the entire concept reeks of a overt attempt by the bourgeois class to initiate privatization at all levels under a fabricated illusion of financial collapse. Without these budget cuts, they cry, our debt with skyrocket to a point wherein our interest payments to China will consume our entire budget, and it, and other foreign powers, will effectively own the rights to our economy. Without this sequestration, the evil "socialist" president that we re-elected (by voter fraud, some right-wing maniacs argue) our debt will grow to consume our entire budget and a second Great Depression will be ushered in by our outrageously left-wing president.

The entire sequestration is the result of an illusion by the corporate aristocracy, who are so outrageously financially irresponsible that they are unwilling to claim responsibility for the Wall Street collapse of 2008 that they are willing to create an elaborate illusion of pending economic collapse in order to have the working class shoulder their burden, rather than accept responsibility. The sequestration is an attempt to shift the responsibility for our economic woes from the 1% to the 99%; it is a way for the élite to shift responsibility to the Average Joe through a series of intricate lies about the state of the economy.

No matter what Wall Street says - about the "bankruptcy" of Medicare in the coming years, the shrinking Social Security surplus, the atrocious tax-and-spend policy of our "far-left" President, or the budget-busting cost of our progressive Congress - we are not broke. The United States is not poor; we are not out of money. We have the funds to do anything that we want - the problem is merely that we have chosen to spend our tax-payer dollars in horribly irresponsible ways. Of course, why on Earth should we invest in modern, eco-friendly green energy when we can fund the construction of ten thousand more wartime missiles instead? Why should we spend our money on universal healthcare, comprehensive education, or the mass-repair of our national infrastructure when we can spend it on a bloated Pentagon bureaucracy and imperialist war?

If we want to be intellectually honest with ourselves, we need to realize that the host of economic reforms that President Obama has passed - from the Affordable Care Act to the Economic Recovery Act - have already begun to pay off and have started to defibrillate our economy. The reckless spending of the previous administrations has hit a critical point wherein its begun to compound at an exponential rate: Nixon's two-trillion-and-counting "War on Drugs" and Bush's $2.2 trillion "War on Terror" - when combined with the post-2001 tax cuts for the rich that constitute 48% of our entire federal debt - put Obama's entire "socialist" agenda to shame. I am not defending the Democratic Party in any sense; the Party is riddled with internal corruption and financial waste, but, if we want to have an honest conversation about our federal deficit, we cannot blame the current administration. Our debt is the result of generations of tax-and-spend obsessed bureaucrats, not a single President.

It is time that the American people stop blaming President Obama for every economic woe that comes their way and start being honest with themselves about the government's electoral history and start taking responsibility for themselves for electing those those petty bureaucrats into office. Now is not the time to play the blame-game in D.C.; now is the time to take responsibility and set aside partisanship to actually work towards an economy geared in the economic interests of the working class.

The American Republic has Become the American Empire

At what point did we allow our country to turn into a corporate police state? When was it that our great American Republic mutated into a nationalist Empire? Did it start when President Obama expanded the use of drone strikes in the Middle East, bombing women and children in the hopes of potentially eliminating a single al Qaeda agent, or when his Affordable Care Act restructured our healthcare system to reinforce, and even mandate, participation in a for-profit and anti-trust law exempt market? Was it then, when his healthcare and financial "reform" padded the pockets of the ultra-rich at the expense of the working class?

No - the situation that we have now is the result of more than a generation's worth of political apathy, of allowing capitalist bureaucrats and Wall Street financiers to make our decisions for us. Being an angsty, anti-establishment government-basher has become fashionable; sitting around and pointing out the flaws of the nation, without making an effort to take a part and offer a practical solution, makes one "cool" and "edgy".

The USA PATRIOT Act codified many of the wishes of statists into law. Whether we're talking about the Act's regulation of bank accounts, the broadening of the government's authority to deport citizens, or the authorization of roving wiretaps and non-consenting business record searches, the Act is only the first brick in the construction of the modern police state. We have also had the unfortunately passage of the National Defense Authorization Act of 2012, which appropriates and divides up Defense and war spending, but contained a blatantly unconstitutional clause that gives the government the authority to indefinitely detain American citizens. And now - even after the intense political backlash against the NDAA 2012, our Congress has the gall to discretely slip another clause into the NDAA 2013 that repeals the World War II-era legislation that prevents the government from using State-approved propaganda, and would make Washington immune to any court cases challenging them.

The entire NDAA 2013 sets the stage for an Orwellian thought police program, complete with the blessing of our elected representatives. The impacts of these laws - both constitutionally and as a matter of personal liberty - become even more frightening when we realize that they do not stand alone; hosts of other bills - from the surveillance-expanding USA Act of 2001 or the Antiterrorism and Effective Death Penalty Act's drastic expansion of state-approved execution, or even the protest-restricting Federal Restricted Buildings and Grounds Improvement Act that was passed during the populist Occupy Wall Street uprising - are also on the books. One could fill an entire library with books full of these heinously unconstitutional laws that the élite class uses to secure its hegemony. When coupled with the push for prison "reform" vis-à-vis privatization, expanding TSA and Homeland Security powers, and the government's recent mass purchasing of guns and ammunition, it seems that we are getting dangerously close to fascism.

All of the dozens of harsh, inhumane bills that were passed from the FDR era and on are nothing compared to the outrageous human rights violations that have been committed in the name of "liberty" and "democracy" since 9/11. We have allowed the bourgeois élite to take advantage of us by uniting us against the "terrorists" by appealing to a demagogic and emotionalist sense of nationalism and fear - by uniting us against a common "enemy", they have expanded and centralized police power. Since that tragic day, the profiteering élite have created a false threat, a faux-strawman of pending immediate danger of the foreign terrorists who want nothing more than to end our entire way of life and kill all of us, for no other reason than our being "free" and "rich", not in retaliation for the toppling of their democratically-elected leaders and incessant bombings.

The Middle Eastern neo-colonialism of the Bush-Cheney regime reeks of overt imperialism. Who are we to colonize and occupy foreign lands, topple governments that we do not like, and establish radical ones that serve our economic interests? How can we go about proselytizing incessantly about "freedom" and "liberty" while presiding over the systematic eradication and political disenfranchisement of millions of our fellow human beings?

It does not matter who the president or the current administration is, or what political party controls Congress or the governorships; every single politician that takes part in the government is guilty of the construction of the American Empire.

We should not be encouraging an expansion of State power; we should not crushing ever single liberty that our Founding Fathers fought for, especially amidst cheering and applause. We should be championing the abolition State authority in all spheres, not supporting it. If we continue to rely on the State to solve all of our problems, than we have no one else to blame for our country's descent into fascism than ourselves.

Proposed Immigration Reform Doesn't Go Far Enough

The immigration reform that is being drafted in the U.S. Senate does not go far enough. Like President Obama's Affordable Care Act, almost all progressive elements have been stripped from it in order to get the votes necessary for it to pass. Now is not the time to allow yet another watered-down centrist band-aid; our broken immigration system is in dire need of immediate repair and needs a complete overhaul. The entire system needs to be redesigned, and the proposals from the so-called Gang of Eight senators - four Democrats, four Republicans - does not come close enough to addressing the problem.

Immigration reform should be something that allows us to unite our immigrant brothers and sisters with their families back home, and create an atmosphere that invites hard workers to come and take part in the American Dream. The senators' draft bill has several components that do not do this. Rather than try to create a peaceful bridge between the Untied States and other countries, the draft bill creates harsh barriers between us. It builds over 350 miles of new fencing along the U.S. - Mexican border, implements biometric scanners at airports and seaports near them, radically increases the number of border security agents, and installs a massive, border-wide camera-and-radar system to track movement across it. This is not a "progressive" reform in any way: it is a nationalist's dream of radical isolationism mediated by a police state.

There are dozens of clauses in it that would create a harsh, anti-immigration environment that would dissuade many of the immigrants already here from coming out into the open, from a dramatic increase in fines for knowingly employers for hiring non-citizens to cutting their access to public and social services, even if they are below the poverty line and need drastic medical care. Of course, there are several mildly good pieces to the bill - mostly, by streamlining and accelerating the naturalization process, and creating a 10-year program to allow undocumented individuals to become citizens - but the negative far outweighs the positive.

What disturbs me the most is the rhetoric that's being thrown around during the immigration debate. The labeling of people as "illegal aliens" strikes me as exceptionally dehumanizing and derogatory. No human being is "illegal" for the sake of their birth; simply because one is born on a different side of a bureaucratically drawn line does not mean that that person has less value, or that they are not entitled to the same liberties as every other human being. If we truly believe that all peoples are created equal, and that we have inalienable rights given to us by our Creator, then we have to realize that no human being should be treated differently than another, and we should embrace everyone - both legal and "illegal" - with open arms. Our "reform" should allow anyone and everyone that wants to take part in the American Dream to be able to; it should welcome every single person that's willing to come and work hard.

What we need is an immediate, universal amnesty program to allow every undocumented individual in the country to immediately recognized as an American citizen. The people who have spent years here, working strenuous hours, taking part in the community, raising a family, and saluting our flag are already Americans in everything but name. It's time that we recognize that these people are just as valuable as we are, and that we need to treat them as equals in every respect. The idea that we, just because we were born inside of those bureaucratic lines, are better than others drips with the toxic filth of nationalism, of an intolerant classism hidden behind the romanticized rhetoric of "exceptionalism".

We need to drop this hyper-patriotic language and realize that every human being on this planet is equal in every way - no nationality, creed, language, culture, or religion makes anyone any better or worse than anyone else. Comprehensive immigration reform is not just something that is economically beneficial for our nation; it's not just something that will enrich our culture and introduce millions of consumers and potential job creators. It's more than just a social justice movement; it's a matter of basic human rights and individual dignity.

Our immigration "reform" is an absolutely joke, yet another shadow of a compromise, another failed attempt at a potentially transformative piece of legislation. If we seriously fix some of the problems that are plaguing our nation, then we have a long list of things to do: a universal and non-profit single-payer healthcare system; a massive banking regulation and monopoly-busting program; national gender-neutral marriage; an unprecedentedly large public works program; and a national program to convert private enterprises into worker-owned co-operatives and the advocacy of economic democracy. Each and every one of these things needs to be enacted immediately side-by-side with a universal amnesty program, and every moment that we do not is a disservice to the millions of undocumented peoples here that are American in every single way other than on paper.

Recent UNH Transgender Conference a Wild Succe

By hosting the second annual Transecting Society transgender conference this past Friday and Saturday in the UNH MUB, Dr. Joelle Ruby Ryan of the women's studies department continues to advocate for one of the most important social justice issues of in world history: the universal equality and value of all people. There can be no higher praise that can be given to her, and the other speakers, for their unwavering dedicated to equality, love, and human liberation.

To those UNH students who were unable to attend the conference, I would recommend logging into Youtube to watch Dr. Ryan's "Transilience" film that she premiered several weeks ago. It provides a glimpse into her life as a transgendered individual and exposes people to an entire social demographic that is repeatedly marginalized and forgotten.

One of the things that I took from the Transecting Society conference is that it highlights an issue that continues to plague the LGBT community - the rampant sectarianism of the gay-lesbian faction that all-too-often alienates its fellow transgendered comrades. It is unfortunate that the LGBT community repeatedly marginalizes transgendered individuals and acts as an LGB clique, not a trans-friendly and all-inclusive human rights movement. Too often, the "LGBT" community only comes across as "LGB" instead.

And speaking of a "human rights" movement - let us not forget that the Human Rights Campaign has continuously sidelined transgendered people. It is not an organization devoted to the universal acceptance of all people; it is a political money-making machine that refuses to champion trans issues simply because there is not a financial incentive to do so. If there is one thing that my transgendered comrades have taught me, it is that we need to think outside of the simple man-woman gender binary. Gender is not so black and white; across all organisms in nature, we see an enormous gradient of sexuality and gender. Why are we so afraid to acknowledge that our conceptions of "gender" and "sex" and "orientation" are social constructs created by the patriarchy in order to perpetuate its chauvinistic hegemony? Why are we afraid to openly say that every human being, regardless of what each person chooses to identify (or not identify) as, is infinitely precious and is holy and perfect just as they are?

The HRC gay-equality agenda does not take into account those individuals who lie outside the gender binary. The capitalist patriarchy has created an anti-trans social environment which, as a result, does not produce a market mechanism thorough which HRC can raise millions in profit by supporting trans issues. The "Human Rights" Campaign is not an advocacy group for universal equality, nor is it all-encompassing; it is the ultra-rich lobbying group for privileged, élitist, white gay population whose support for same-sex couples reeks of a reinforcement of the gender binary.

We need to abolish these antiquated an chauvinistic concepts of "gender". A human being is a beautiful human being, regardless of whether bureaucratic government paperwork inscribes a simple "M" or "F" next to their name. Transgendered individuals are no less valuable than anyone else in society - in fact, in many ways, I would argue that they are *more* valuable, because they are wiling to open their hearts to love and expression in all forms, not simply the ones sanctioned by bourgeois society.

We all need to stand in unwavering, unconditional solidarity with every human being. Equality is not negotiable; human rights are not something that should be subject to debate.

The Transecting Society conference is something that every single student at UNH Durham should have gone too. Far too often, the issues of our transgendered brothers and sisters - shunned into the shadows, forgotten, marginalized, and denied equal and equitable rights - are forgotten and ignored. Despite this, these are the people that I look to for inspiration - their hope, their love, and their unwavering hope in mankind serves as a mode of creativity through which I push myself and hope for the best.

We should not forget our trans brothers and sisters. We need to stop viewing the gay liberation as an élitist "movement" yearning for financial compensation and instead recognize that it is intimately connected to a greater collective liberation. We need to realize that all people, independent of sexuality and gender, are completely equal and that the systemic disenfranchisement of an entire demographic of society - while at the same time incessantly proselytizing about how we are the nation of "liberty" and "democracy" - is outrageously hypocritical, and that we need to enact immediate legal protections and pro-trans legislation to protect them from the patriarchal, binary-fixated society that has dealt them so much injustice.

    The Transecting Society conference discussed a variety of important issues in an extremely progressive and visionary manner. Dr. Ryan and the UNH administration are taking positive steps forward to educate the general public about the immediate steps that need to be taken to bring justice to the trans community. In the coming years, as the conference continues to grow and attract more trans academics and gender theorists, it is sure to be a driving force for change in the political climate throughout New England.

US-UN Sanctions Created the North Korea Disaster

If North Korea really does have nuclear capabilities, and if it uses them in any capacity, there are two possible outcomes. Firstly, the reactionaries who are in bed with the military-industrial complex could retaliate by carpet bombing and drone striking their entire country in order to secure the United States' global hegemony. Alternatively, it could violently destabilize the North Korean government and collapse its economy through crippling sanctions, removing them as an international threat completely.

It doesn't matter which path is taken. Innocent lives will be lost and the average working-class citizen will be the victims of an international power-play.

The countless economic sanctions that the world powers have thrown at North Korea at are not dissuading it; the endless cease-and-desists orders are ineffective. No matter what we do, its ruling élite and the military junta are going to have all their material needs met - they will have all of their luxury and food desires met satisfactorily. What we are doing to them only hurts their working class; the normal citizen is the one that is taking the brunt of our sanctions.

How can we continue to call ourselves the pinnacle of "freedom" and "democracy" when our entire foreign policy is to cause the direct immiseration of working-class people overseas? How can we say that we defend "human rights" abroad when our tactics strip them of food and water, subject them to drone strikes and pillaging, and occupy their nations with endless waves of troops? If we turn the entire international community against another country simply for ideological differences, how can we not expect them to say and to things back to us in direct retaliation?

The slew of threats coming from North Korea are because we have worked consistently, for more than a generation, to undermine their economy and government. They have every right to hate us. Rather than say that we will respond for their threats with military force and crippling economic sanctions, we should be removing barriers to trade, establishing mutual embassies, engaging in diplomatic talks, and removing each and every sanction that we have put on them that hurts their citizens.

The number of bombs that we had - and still maintain - is mind-blowing. Physicist Julius Oppenheimer, the director of the Los Alamos nuclear research facility that developed the first atomic bomb, admitted in 1953 that the U.S. had already stockpiled over twenty thousand varying bombs in case of an open hot war with the Soviet Union, and that it had every intention of continuing to make more. In 1963, after another decade of U.S. bomb-building, the Soviet Union only had 42 inter-continental ballistic missiles. Of course, 42 ICBMs is still a large number, especially when one takes into account that six of them could carry 3-megaton warhead and the other thirty-six could carry up to 6-megatons.

To help understand this concept, take note of the fact that the Hiroshima bomb was approximately 15-megatons, and the Nagasaki bomb was nearly 21-megatons. The bombs that we used in Japan were much larger than those owned by the Soviets, but this still gave the USSR the power to level a city.

The exact number of nuclear weapons owned by the United States and the Soviet Union at the height of the Cold War is highly classified, but partial declassification vis-a-vis the Freedom of Information Act has put the estimation around eleven thousand active nuclear warheads. The USSR was estimated to have just over two thousand, scattered sporadically across Soviet-allied states.

The discrepancy between US and USSR military power could not have been wider. If the Cold War would have turned into a hot war, the Soviets would have been obliterated. Their budding economies, barely starting to enter a quasi-industrial revolution, were completely unable to match us, even though they were pumping a majority of their gross GDP into the creation of national war machines.

Despite the nuclear threats from the Soviets, the Middle East, and now North Korea, the U.S. has prevailed. If we could survive decades of Soviet-American tension, open animosity, and borderline nuclear war, then we can surely survive threats from

North Korea; a single small, angsty, economically-backwards, isolationist nation does not present a threat anywhere near the level that the mainstream media portrays it as.

    I am not afraid of North Korea, and you should not be either. Even if they decide to launch their barely-functional missiles at us, the international community is so allied against them that they would be swatted out of the air like so many flies. Their Korean-nationalist version of Marxist-Leninism (or, what we in the West refer to as "Stalinism"), Juche, is simply a push for radical autarky. If we would just stop this vitriolic rhetoric and instead work productively with them like we do with so many other countries, then many of the problems that we face would evaporate.

Americans Should Support New Venezuelan Leader
Originally, "Ongoing Coup d'État Against Venezuelan President Maduro Doomed to Fail"

Hugo Chávez presided over a period of rapid economic expansion for Venezuela. By nationalizing the oil-rich country's massive natural resources, he was able to provide low-cost energy to Venezuelans and pump billions into the economy by selling oil internationally. With nearly 296 billion barrels of oil now under Venezuelan control, it is freeing itself from the chronic imperial dominance of ultra-rich Western nations.

What did Chávez did with this sudden surplus of state funds? He didn't waste it on undeserved corporate tax breaks, and certainly didn't start budget-busting wars. Instead, he invested it directly in the working class - greatly expanding public healthcare and education, doubling the number of students in college, tripling the number of retirement pensions to combat poverty, and giving labor unions greater say in the workplace.

The result? Thousands of worker-owned and worker-operated co-operatives have spring up across the country; both poverty and unemployment have been slashed in half; extreme poverty was cut by just over 70%; and townhall-style *consejos comunales* ("community councils"), wherein local citizens form neighborhood-based assemblies and decide democratically what to do with increasingly-large block grants. More than 30,000 of these have have sprung into being, and Chávez worked to put direct, participatory democratic structures into the country to allow the Venezuelan citizens themselves to take ownership and control of their own immediate community.

The *consejos comunales* are using their ever-expanding authority to build and expand schools, improve hospitals, repair roads, clean up water supplies, and improve their community's infrastructure. This faint element of decentralized, populist, people-driven socialism is one of the cornerstones of Venezuela's budding *chavismo* ideology. Of course, Venezuela is still very much a developing capitalist nation, but at least there is a modicum of desire to orientate the economy in the direct interest of the working class.

Unfortunately, Chávez passed away on March 5th from a long and painful battle with cancer, which was cured, returned, and eventually took his life. Before he died, he gave his blessing to his vice-president, Nicolás Moduro, and hoped that his United Socialist Party would nominate and vote for him in the election that would be constitutionally required after his death.

With the post-Chávez election results coming in, Maduro prevailed against right-wing candidate Henrique Capriles Radonski of the unapologetically neoliberal and anti-progressive Justice First Movement. What response did Capriles give Maduro - congratulations, support, an extending of a constructive, bipartisan relationship? No, Capriles invoked his right as a presidential candidate to request a recount, clogging the government up in a morass of bureaucracy and inaction in the hopes that it will slow the implementation of the dynamic reforms Chávez started and Maduro is continuing.

Of course, Capriles (as well as his capitalist Western allies, who have a vested financial interest in the continued imperial exploitation of Venezuela's budding industrialization) is going to continue to call Maduro an illegitimate dictator. It makes sense for him to do so - the far-right, with its fetish towards de-regulation and insatiable money-making, regardless of the social consequences - is able to legitimize its own economic philosophy only through a barrage of *ad hominem* attacks.

Capriles' supporters, duped by false anti-Chávez propaganda, have staged violent protests and riots in the streets. Doctors have been kidnapped, hospitals have been set on fire, members of Maduro-sympathetic peoples militias have been murdered, and dozens of innocent people have been grossly wounded. If that wasn't enough, the death toll stands at eight while I write this, and the corporate-financed and self-righteous Juventud Activa Venezuela Unida (JAVU), the radically pro-capitalist student protest group, has led numerous protests that have resulted in excessive property damage. JAVU has pined down over a dozen innocents with active mortars.

Is this what democracy has come to? When the people vote, democratically in open and free elections to orientate the economy so that it serves the common man more so than the corporation, is it appropriate for the quasi-fascist far-right to stage a military coup d'état in the hopes of ousting someone who (despite the pro-labor rhetoric he used to win his election) has no desire to abolish classism or money?

President-elect Maduro of Venezuela is not the heartless dictator that Capriles has made described him as; that being said, he isn't the savior of the Left, and he isn't going to usher in a sort of *chavismo* socialism any time soon. Historically, Maduro is a moderate, but the things that he and Chávez have done have resulted in real, immediate improvements in the standard-of-living for the working class. We should all stand in unwavering solidarity with the Venezuelan people denounce the violent intolerance of the country's right-wing militants. The imperialist West will not recognize Maduro as Venezuelan president until Capriles' election-recount demand is met, but the democratic will of the people does not need government permission to be legitimate.

No matter what the bourgeois West or the Capriles-sympathizing insurrectionists think, the people of Venezuela have spoken - Maduro is president, *chavismo* will endure for the time being, and their working class will continue to have the economy molded to its fit its interests better.

America Needs Political Change to Restore Liberty
Originally, "Solidarity Can Overcome Any Problem"

Noam Chomsky, a linguistic professor at the Massachusetts Institute of Technology and a fellow libertarian socialist, put it well when he said that "propaganda is to a democracy what the bludgeon is to a totalitarian state". What is it that we learn in our schools - history (taught from an imperial and nationalist perspective), literature (that reinforces a hegemonic ideology), social studies (that impose patriarchal heteronormativity), and science (geared toward capitalist production)? The school systems that we take part in have been so radically politicized that they have been turned into State tools of indoctrination, where we are told *what* to think and not *how* to think. Everything that we are taught is done to reinforce and perpetuate bourgeois philosophy.

Us students that are able to put ourselves through school by acquiring large debt are unlikely to think about radically changing the world. The debt that we accrue acts as a disciplinary technique that forces us to work for capitalist employers in order to make the ridiculous sums of money needed to pay our schools back. We come out of school freshly programmed by the State, and have also internalized the disciplinarian culture of a capitalist society. We are manufactured to be State-supporting automatons that are efficient components of a consumer economy.

It reminds me of the famous (and unfortunately anonymous) quote: "Go to work, send your kids to school, follow fashion, act normal, walk on the pavement, watch TV, save for your old age, obey the law .... and repeat after me: I am free".

We have problems other than just education. The entire system does not work, and 18 million die each year from poverty-related causes. Current global agriculture production can feed 118% the world's population, despite the fact that the bureaucratic morass of the market allows a UN-estimated 868 million to starve each year. There are more than 5 vacant homes for every homeless person, and 77.5% of the occupied ones are in debt; of them, 1 in 7 is being pursued by a debt collector. Nearly 50 million American citizens are without healthcare, and the unemployment rate stands at 14.3%, if one takes into consideration the unemployed who have given up looking for work, as well as those who work but do not make enough to regularly stay above the poverty line.

How do we go about fixing this problem? Is it through electing populist candidates that promise "reform" and "change"? No. It doesn't matter whether we elect some pseudo-nationalist conservative or a partisan progressive. After all, the two are distressingly similar - two people that went to similar universities, have massive fortunes, are both financed by the same corporate institutions. At the Democratic Convention, President Obama said that "only in this country, only in America, could someone like me appear here". Really? The fact that he had the gall to explicitly state this perturbs me. In other countries, people much poorer and much more disadvantaged have not only be keynote speakers at massive political conventions, but have even been elected president.

Take Luiz Inácio Lula de Silva, the former President of Brazil. He had a peasant background, was a union organizer and advocate for the poor, and never went to school. Despite this, he ended up becoming president of the second-largest country in that hemisphere. Or Salvador Allende, the first democratically-elected self-proclaimed Marxist, whose pro-poor economic reforms earned him a CIA-sponsored military coup d'état that put fascist dictator Augusto Pinochet in power, amidst the cheers of Thatcher and western conservatives?

"Only in America"? Yes, only in America can a genuine candidate of the people be suppressed by military and corporate interests, and only in America are they shunned so utterly from the political process. Only in America can someone who was elected president twice and committed heinous war crimes vis-à-vis the drone-strike bombing of Middle Eastern women and children (am I speaking of Bush or Obama - but then again, is there a difference?), and only in America can someone who exposes war crimes be locked in solitary confinement for two years and be called a terrorist (I mean Bradley Manning, of course).

    We have numerous problems here in the Untied States - exploding poverty, indoctrinatory education, a patriarchal culture. The list goes on, as does the to-do list of policies that need to be immediately enacted to bring back both liberty and a growing economy. We need a massive public works program, single-payer healthcare, gender-neutral marriage, an unprecedentedly large investment in alternative energy, economic democracy and unionization in the workplace, transitioning private property into cooperatives, and an end to corporate personhood and the rule of the financial élite.

    There is nothing that we, as Americans, cannot accomplish when we stand together in unwavering solidarity and confront our problems side-by-side. We have already been through so much, from economic depressions to imperialist wars, and we have survived; we will continue to thrive, no despite how much the corporate oligarchy wishes to push us down, so long as we remember that the working class outnumbers them millions-to-one.

Is Our Education an Indoctrination System?

Noam Chomsky, the linguistics professor at the Massachusetts Institute of Technology who was famously declared by the New York Times as the "most important intellectual alive", put it wonderfully when he said: *"Students who acquire large debts putting themselves through school are unlikely to think about changing society. When you trap people in a system of debt, they can't afford the time to think. Tuition fee increases are a disciplinary technique, and by the time students graduate, they are not only loaded with debt, but they have also internalized the disciplinarian culture. This makes them efficient components of the consumer economy."*

Professor Chomsky is absolutely right. After all, what is the education system? As one local professor said, the modern classroom is nothing more than an authoritarian, thought-controlling institution complete with a truth-inscription board, all designed to induce a psychological obedience to the State. Overwhelmingly, people do not go to universities for a sheer interest in learning. Rather, people spend tens of thousands of dollars for a piece of paper that creates a sense of productive legitimacy, a piece of paper whose sole purpose is to prove to corporations that they have spent a number of years in a brainwashing "school" that has molded them into efficient cogs in the capitalist system. In the end, is that not what an "education" is nowadays? Is it not merely an investment in economic conformity?

Is this what education has come to? Has it degenerated into an indoctrinatory tool of the bourgeois State into forcing the working class into a never-ending cycle of debt enslavement and brainwashed social conservatism? Has it lost the sacred position of being a means of pedagogic, intellectual maturity and collapsed into a propagandistic profit-making machine?

Education is no longer about self-improvement. It is a tool of the ruling class to induce a particular social mindset. It no longer produces revolutionary scholars; it produces endless cogs in the machine - cogs who, as if suffering from Stockholm Syndrome, worship their oppressor with nationalist fervor.

What can we do to fix this? What can we do to turn the State brainwashing camps back into institutions of academic self-betterment? Primarily, we would need a new, democratic economy based on collective production-for-use rather than individualistic production-for-profit. But short of that, the first thing that anyone should do is step back and look objectively at the situation - look at the social and economic roles that schools occupy in a regional economy, and understand the deeply political character that they have. Schools have the power to employ thousands and move markets, but they also have the power to be tools of mass sociologic propaganda.

Understand the political space that the education system occupies, and question it. Question the role, existence, and authority of every aspect of our academic bureaucracy. Question why some things (such as the Predator drone strike program, which PolicyMic reports accidentally kills 50 innocent civilians for every 1 terrorist - and then question whether the State-designated "terrorist" is justified for his actions based upon objective conditions) are funded by tax-payer money, while others such as the school system are the victims of deep, brutal budget cuts.

To the new students, here is my message to you: do not be afraid to engage in revolutionary acts of sedition. To to challenge social and economic power structures that you have taken for granted your entire life. To be brave enough to question every professor, every moral, every social norm, everything that you have ever learned. To be and express yourself in a way that you choose, no matter what the system does to try and condition you to be otherwise. Question everything. Accept nothing.

Do not be afraid to fight for liberty, in the most radical and literal sense of the word, or to demand the unconditional emancipation of all of humanity from the terminal disease that we call capitalism. Do not be afraid to demand that education, healthcare, housing, and green energy production be of a higher economic priority than weapons development or war spending. But do question why the latter is of greater economic importance - is it for the righteous cause of spreading democracy and freedom to an oppressed, war-torn country? Or is it to secure imperial military hegemony in one of the most oil-rich regions on the planet, all in order to facilitate world domination from a police-state Empire?

Don't be just a "liberal" or a "conservative", but a warrior for social and economic justice - do not be afraid to fight the class war on the side of the working class. Do not be afraid to get engaged civically, discuss revolutionary politics, and debate anti-establishment philosophy. Do not be afraid to stand together in united solidarity and openly challenge power structures, and do not be afraid to question every aspect of the education you obtain here. In the end at graduation, you may learn what there is to know in your given degree field, but it may be more important to know *about* what you know and place it in a larger anthropologic context.

Good luck, new students. We were all in your position once, and we stand in solidarity with you. I wish you the best in the coming weeks and look forward to seeing you all around the campus.

No War but Class War

On September 13, America and Russia came to an agreement to place Syria's chemical weapons under international control. President Obama has beaten the war drums again and proved that the government will not tolerate any undermining of its imperial hegemony in the Middle East - but due to overwhelming popular opinion, he were forced to back down. The U.S. has historically flexed its muscles in one CIA-funded coup d'état after another, under the politically-correct veil of "regime change" that is, in reality, nothing more than the political re-structuring of puppet client states so as to make them work in the economic interests of the American corporate aristocracy. History proves that the U.S. is the imperial power par excellence.

We should not go to war with Syria, even though the media continues to repeat the need for immediate action for the sake of "humanitarian intervention". But we know what the media really is: the public relations arm of the totalitarian police-state. It's the tool used by our super-PAC-appointed politicians to manufacture consent among the masses for whatever initiative they want enacted at a given time. It's not world news; it's sensationalist propaganda force-fed to the working class in order to induce a particular mindset that serves the interests of the ruling class. It breeds racism, hetero-normativity, cis-gender supremacism, trans-misogyny, a viscously patriarchal culture, and (possibly worst of all) the toxic filth of nationalism.

Despite what the "media" says, there is no reason to go to war with Syria other than to re-enforce our current military presence in the area. The cascade of riots and revolutions during the so-called "Arab Spring" have weakened our military dominance, and President Obama and his fellow aristocrats want to spend American resources to re-establish imperial hegemony in the area, a hegemony so absolute that it will secure America's neocolonial control of one of the largest oil-rich regions in the world for another decade. War is an excuse for the U.S. to strengthen its military control over finite energy resources. Humanitarianism is the public-relations justification for war - it's a façade trying to hide the fact that the government desperately needs a reason to legitimize its extensive military presence in the Middle East.

Think of the new 800km-long oil pipeline project from the Kirkuk oil fields in Iraq to Baniyas, Syria that pumps 300,000 gallons of crude oil daily. Private oil contractors would love to get their hands on it, like Dick Cheney's Halliburton corporation that got oil contracts and openly stated that "oil remains, fundamentally, a government business" after 9/11. Or Donald Rumsfeld, the ex-Secretary of Defense, who lied to Congress in 2002 when he stated that Iraq has "stockpiles of chemical weapons - including VX, sarin, cyclosarin, and mustard gas" and "anthrax and botulism toxin, and possibly smallpox". A decade later, we've found no Iraqi stockpile, but spend nearly $11.26 million per day on the "war on terror" since 2001.

We should not give in the "media" and jump into war. It costs trillions of dollars (currently over $1.4 trillion, according to the Defense budget passed this March!), developing machines designed specifically to slaughter other human beings, and spills innocent blood (be it of men, women, or children) in the name of economic conquest. No human should advocate war under any circumstance - to do so speaks volumes about their own soulless lack of humanity and support for the big-brother Empire. To go to war isn't just a moral perversion but also a direct violation of the principals laid down in the Nuremberg trials that convicted Nazi officials of war crimes in World War II.

If we want to be the model of "freedom" and "liberty", we need a drastic re-assessment of our foreign and domestic policy. If Obama wages war against Syria, he'll continue the trend that Reagan started: the conservative dream of transforming our democratic Republic into a corporate Empire by transferring decision-making power from democratically-accountable public institutions to unaccountable corporate boardrooms. There is only one war that needs to be fought: the class war. The working class should not be on the defensive. It needs to be on the offensive, and the offense it launches against the chronic parasite called Wall Street needs to be powerful enough to completely eradicate it, to abolish every aspect of its cancerous politics and dirty money. Economic decisions need to be made in a decentralized, democratic manner by the individuals who are impacted by them, not by centralized, oligarchic powers.

The working class needs to seize control of the State and use its immense legal and economic authority to re-direct the economy in *their* direct material interests. It's interesting how it's "class warfare" when the working class tries to fight back, but "the status quo" and "the way things should be" when its being absolutely pulverized by capitalist economics.

It's wrong to go to war against Syria - we need to leave the Middle East alone and focus on our own internal problems. Rather than wage another "war on terror", we should be waging a class war. There is nothing more important than the emancipation of the working class from all forms of oppression, be they misogynistic conservatism or corporate-dominated politics. Do not be afraid to stand in open opposition to authoritarian power structures and demand their unconditional destruction; to do so makes you a champion of liberty and a warrior for justice. We don't have to live under capitalism - with the exponential growth of technology and the infinite creativity of the human spirit, there are endless ways for us to organize society. There is no reason to assume that society today is the *only* way to live. Another world is possible - don't be afraid to fight for it. Don't be afraid to fight for liberty, socialism, and democracy; don't be afraid to shake up the system and propose radical alternatives.

Do Not Accept the Police State

"When fascism comes to America, it will be wrapped in the flag and carrying a cross." Sinclair Lewis spoke this words in 1935, but they seem to have a disturbing validity today, especially in the post-9/11 era where we seem so ready to give up all of our freedoms to the ever-growing police-state. It does not matter if the politicians use sensationalist rhetoric and emotion into scaring you to give up your freedoms in the name of "national security" - there is nothing as sacred as freedom, in the most radical and literal sense of the word. Do not let it be taken from you, whether the politician in question is a big-government, war-loving Republican or a politically-correct Democrat.

The police state has been growing, little by little, since World War II. By its close in 1945, many of the major world powers were in shambles. Europe was decimated and Japan was reeling from two atomic bombs. This meant that the United States had little international competition; it could safely assert its political and economic supremacy over countries that were shattered by Nazi atrocities. Since that historical moment - that period of absolute, undisputed world dominance - our government has systematically turned their unconstitutional war-time practices into every-day law.

Examples are abound. The US PATRIOT Act expanded phone wire-tapping and made it easier for the State to seize and search your bank records. The Federal Restricted Buildings and Grounds Improvements Act, known by some as the "Anti-Occupy Act", allows federal authorities to declare certain areas as protest-free zones, erasing the right of assembly from the books. The National Defense Authorization Act of 2012, which allocated Defense department spending last year, happened to contain a clause that would legally allow the indefinite detention of an American citizen in the name of the "counter-terrorism".

We don't have to accept the police-state. We don't have to accept having police everywhere that we go, having them zooming back and forth on their segways around our campuses, airports, and cities. We don't have to live in a world where the

NSA reads our emails and the FBI wire-taps our phones. Imagine what this country would look like if "war on terror" legislation was repealed, the NSA was abolished, and the FBI prosecuted the corporate aristocrats (oh, excuse me - "job creators") that crashed the world economy. And then imagine what America would look like if we spent all of our imperial war spending on education, healthcare, and anti-poverty programs.

Question the role of police - what is the sociologic, political, and economic space that they occupy? Do they serve a universal, cosmic Justice? Or do they, more often than not, serve as the foot-soldiers of the State, breaking up workers' strikes and constitutional protests (Occupy Wall Street, anyone?) in the name of totalitarian property laws? Is their political function to protect 'human rights', or to enforce social conformity and perpetuate the economic supremacy of the bourgeois class?

The police serve the political function of being an organized instrument of State repression, an enforcer for the capitalist class. They are the facilitators of an economic dictatorship and the perpetuators of the State. We Marxists identify the State as being the hegemonic organ to facilitate class rule, which arises out of irreconcilable class conflict. The economic conflict between the "have" élites and the "have-not" workers creates political and sociologic friction; if left to build, that friction might grow enough to burst into violent revolution. But the State - the courts, police, army, culture, and everything else that the bourgeoisie uses to keep us wage-slaves in line - can be seized democratically, through the ballot box, by a true working-class labor party and turned around to serve the economic interest of workers.

The police are the last resort of the State to enforce political conformity - any dictator would prefer to rule through non-violent means, but they are not above using force if the situation demands it. Normally, the revolutionary friction gradually dissipates - piecemeal, compromise "reforms" sate the workers' desire for change; the "media" manufactures a particular political atmosphere; and a patriarchal, nationalist culture ostracizes dissenters more effectively than any Orwellian thought-police. But if capitalism fails to peacefully purge any potential revolutionary zeal, then it calls in its "justice" system to violently legitimize its dominion and restore order.

Do not ask for "change" or "reforms". Instead, demand revolution. Demand a radical, fundamental change in all social and economic relationships. Demand a whole new economy that is geared in the direct material interests of the working class: single-payer healthcare, public higher education, co-operative business enterprises, gender-sexual liberation, and a political system that truly is run *by* and *for* the people through federations of decentralized, democratic workers' councils. Do not fall for the bourgeois nonsense of social-contract theory, liberal democracy, and conservative morality - after all, when did we sign the social contract? When did we agree to be born, live, and grow inside this system? When did we explicitly consent, and when did we agree that we wanted to sacrifice unnumbered natural freedoms in order to build a collectivist State? When did we agree that hetero-normativity, cis-gender supremacism, racism, and nationalism were the cultural ethos that we wanted to live by?

At what point did we all agree to live under this government? The answer is that we did not. We were born here, born in chains that we can no longer see or recognize because they have, over time, because habitual and normalized. We do not understand that we are not free because we have not had the opportunity to be exposed to something else. We are living George Orwell's *1984* without realizing it. When you step back and look objectively at our government, you'll realize it's neither a democracy nor a republic, but rather a corporate-sponsored police-state.

Partisan House GOP vs The Working Class

Earlier this week, the U.S. federal government shut down because the Republicans in the House of Representatives were unwilling to continue to fund the government unless that resolution included clauses to repeal a key funding mechanism for President Obama's Affordable Care Act.

The longer the government shutdown goes on, the more profound its effects will be. Many of the programs and services being shut down are basic social services - literally, the economic security of the working class has been thrown out the window, and it will only get worse as time goes on. Before the shutdown, working families were struggling to survive; now, instead of barely keeping their head above water, they're going to slowly sink as social program after social program is going to have their department budgets dry up. The effects are wide-spread. The National Institute of Health is stopping accepting patients, the Centers for Disease Control is ending the seasonal flu vaccination program, and the Department of Housing and Urban Development is no longer providing vouchers and subsidies to low-income families to help them pay their rent. Homeland Security's E-Verify program, which checks people's immigration status when applying for the job, is no longer operational; national parks (includingYosemite, Alcatraz, and even the Statue of Liberty!) are closed. The Environmental Protection Agency looses almost all of its regulatory power during a government shutdown, and the Commodity Futures Trading Commission looses most of its ability to regulate market transactions and financial derivatives on Wall Street. Veteran's hospitals will be unable to hold hearings and process paperworks, causing a massive disruption and delay of care for our country's finest. Even the websites for federal departments are shut down - preventing students and professors alike at UNH from accessing information, resources, and materials needed from the Energy, Agriculture, and Education departments that we rely on Monday to Friday.

And, if the shutdown lasts for more than two or three weeks, the Department of Veteran's Affairs will run out of its emergency funds and may have to completely stop disability claims and pension payments, leaving an estimated 3.6 million veterans without an income.

Vincent Gray, the Mayor of Washington, D.C., said that his office has enough money to fund "police, firefights, and EMS units" and "services like trash collection and street sweeping" for two weeks. After that, basic municipal programs are going to be completely stopped until Congress intervenes and passes a federal budget. And Mark Zandi, the chief economist of Moody's Analytics (yes, the same Moody's that got rid of the country's triple-A credit rating) estimated that 800,000 federal workers would be without jobs and the economy would bleed $200 million for ever day the government's closed. Economic growth, he said, would be cut by 0.3% - and seeing as last year's was by only about 2.2%, the difference between 2.2% and the possible 1.9% could mean tens of billions of dollars being pulled out from underneath the still-struggling economy.

The government should be shut down, but not like this. What needs to be shut down aren't social programs and day-to-day public services, but rather the military-industry complex, the revolving door between Congress and Wall Street, and the hundreds of billions handed out in corporate welfare. If we're going to cut spending and reduce the size of the federal government, let's do it in a way that doesn't have the potential to violently throw tens of millions of working-class families into abject poverty.

Now, imagine what will happen if the debt ceiling is not raised by October 17th. If we don't have an operating government, we cannot vote on matters pertaining to our national credit; and, without that vote, the U.S. will default on its international monetary obligations for the first time in American history.

Should the government be shut down? Yes, but not like this! We need to shut down the bloated, bureaucratic spending at the Defense Department that sucks up more money than the Health and Human Services, Education, Transportation, and Energy departments combined, *not* Meals on Wheels for seniors and Head Start for struggling students. The blatant disregard of the House GOP for the status of working families is only further evidence that they - and their antiquated, colonial-era notions of patriarchal "freedom" - deserve to be thrown into the dustbin of history. They have again proven that they are inadequate of managing a government and have virtually handed the next election to the Democrats. They've created a dream scenario for a fully Democratic Congress to be ready and waiting when Hillary Clinton sweeps her way into the White House in 2016.

Neither of the two capitalist political parties in the U.S. have the vested interest of the working class at heart, but it should now be apparent to all that they will not let anything - seniors' food, children's education, public healthcare, or even day-to-day social services - stand in the way of their campaign to minimize (and eventually privatize!) all aspects of the U.S. government. If you're not angry, then you're not paying attention. Wake up, and don't be afraid to rekindle the Occupy Wall Street spirit and take the fight directly to the Republicans. Don't be afraid to throw them out of office and replace every single one of these nationalist bigots with progressive champions of the working class.

Don't just sit there and be angry about the situation in Washington. Don't be afraid to stand up and demand that the entire system be replaced with one that works in our direct economic interests, rather than those of the Defense weapons contractors and Wall Street aristocrats. It's your government - don't hesitate to rise up and seize it back from them.

A Co-Op Economy Can Effectively Replace Wall Street

What my "From the Right" comrade Philip Boynton continues to miss, week after week, is that an endless regurgitation of antiquated, colonial-era moralism and FOX News romanticism does nothing to improve the material conditions of the working class. The élitist notion that a cabal of financial aristocrats know what is best for the economy is one of the most cancerous, anti-democratic parts of corporate ideology. The transnational companies that control the flow of the economy, and who warp elections with million-dollar super-PACs, need to have their hegemony brought to an end. Corporations need to be fundamentally changed, to be radically deconstructed and re-built in a manner that is conducive for economic security, working-class prosperity, and a dedication to legitimate democracy.

"Democracy" is not just a sensational talking point, comrade. It is not rhetoric, it is a legitimate way of organizing society. Democracy and capitalism are mutually exclusive and completely irreconcilable.

The banks can no longer privatize successes and socialize losses. How long are we going to allow the redistribution of wealth upwards? How long are we going to let these parasites use their super-PACs to appoint our Congress or dictate how the economy run? Capitalism is not just unstable, but also profoundly undemocratic; it is characterized by the monopolization of economic decision-making by people who are not proletarian. Capitalism is antithetical to liberty and the embryo of totalitarianism.

The banks must be nationalized because State power is the only force strong enough to legally wrest ownership of major industries from the ruling class. If the workers can politically capture the State, and have the State capture major industries, then steps can be taken to make the now-public businesses into full co-ops. Nationalization is a means, not an ends; the ends is always local, decentralized control of the economy by the working class so that it functions in their direct interest. By nationalizing industry, it can be expropriated from the hands of profit-driven aristocrats and turned to serve the interest of the working class by changing it into worker-owned and worker-managed co-operatives.

An economy based on competing co-op conglomerates that enter into large, long-term business contracts with public agencies has the potential to phase out the market and introduce economic planning. It has the potential to be the seeds of a new economy - an economy where resources are allocated through the decentralized, democratic decision-making of workers councils, not the heartless up-and-down of the market. People would actually have a say in how the economy is structured, and the input of the common worker would have more weight than that of the corporate accountant hundreds of miles away.

All power needs to be given to the workers. They need to collectively own and democratically manage the workplace as equals - as a genuine co-op. These co-ops need to join together into large industry-specific or cross-industry conglomerates and be left to compete against one another, mixing both a competitive market mechanism and direct worker control. The best conglomerates would win stable, long-term business contracts with government institutions. This new system would be simple, democratic, and worker-based, and holds the seeds of a truly democratic economy.

Think of the wild threats that this would pose to the top-down, hierarchical sociology that we have now. Imagine an co-op economy, where the workers actually own and manage the workplace and run it in a way that's conducive for their own economic security. Imagine the profound impacts that this would have on all social and economic relationship if we had both political *and* economic democracy?

In practice, a very real possibility would be to do something akin to what President Salvador Allende did in Chile from 1971-1973, before Nixon ordered the CIA to violently topple him and appoint fascist dictator Augusto Pinochet and a military-junta government - but never mind that British Prime Minister Margret Thatcher said Pinochet "brought democracy to Chile", even though he was indicted for human rights violations, suppressing and assassinating political dissenters, and embezzling taxpayer funds for personal profit. Under Allende, the Chilean government began a famous program called Project Cybersyn. With it, various business enterprises installed computer programs so that information - employee hours, material input and output, quotas, shipping manifestos, manufacturing statistics, etc - could be readily and instantaneously shared, turning a single workplace into constituent pieces of an enormous, multi-business network. The "Cybernet" networks could be plugged into the government's "Cyberstride" software program to provide detailed, minute-by-minute statistical models of how the national economy was doing. If the economy was not doing well, it would automatically alert all those in the affected Cybernets and offer incentives (tax breaks, funding, regulation changes, etc) to improve them as positive reinforcers to encourage economic growth.

Rather than punishing poorly-functioning businesses by cutting their funding and tax benefits as in done under capitalism (think of Bush's No Child Left Behind, or Obama's Race To The Top, which cut funding to failing schools), Project Cybersyn encouraged innovation by providing a series of instantaneous incentives to motive the workers. It was a united, digital economy. It opened the door to economic models other than that of corporate bureaucracy and promised that workers would have both democratic control of the workplace and the national economy.

Wall Street is afraid of this. The corporate and political aristocracy in Washington, D.C. are afraid of economic alternatives - they enjoy sitting in a position of power, able to tell others what to think and what to do. An economy wherein businesses become democratic co-ops, and wherein they join together into ever-growing networks with collective bargaining power, has the potential to shake the foundations of contemporary capitalism.

The ruling élite are afraid of a democratic economy. They are afraid of the working class being in control. They are afraid of a co-op economy. They are afraid of socialism.

Democrat, GOP "Reforms" Don't Go Far Enough

We should not pass short-term band-aid "reforms" that throw taxpayer money at a problem in the hopes that it will go away - i.e., Obamacare, the stimulus and bail-outs, Dodd-Frank, and others. There needs to be a radical deconstruction of the system's entire structural framework. There needs to be a revolutionary reconstitution of all social and economic relationships. Democracy needs to exist in the economic sphere, not just the political one. As Jefferson himself put it in his letter to William Smith in 1787, "the tree of liberty must be refreshed from time to time with the blood of patriots and tyrants". There is nothing more conducive to freedom than the revolutionary overthrow of a totalitarian system, and I will stand for nothing less.

If we want to improve the direct material conditions of the working class, then there are several things that can be done in the short-term. The end goal is, and should always be, a fundamentally different economic system, one based on decentralization and democracy - but that does not change the fact that there are things that should immediately be done to help the working class.

If we wanted, the FDA could be the means through which the government enacts mass-distribution of food and medicine. It could be the tool used by a progressive administration to enact a real "war on poverty" by ensuring that every American citizen has access to fresh, chemical-free organic produce. The FDA could be used to eradicate mass hunger and starvation in every corner of the country, and could make sure that everyone – young and old, rich and poor, black and white – never has to miss a healthy meal by enacting regulation, subsidy, and funding changes that would induce a market response to universally reduce food prices. An eco-friendly, healthy "food-for-all" social program in our schools and neighborhoods would cost only a fraction of a percent of our imperial war-spending, and it would be a significant first step towards the eradication of hunger and malnutrition in the country.

The right to high-quality healthcare is one of the most fundamental things to which public taxpayer funds should be directed. It's an industry that you can't chose to be part of (or not be part of), because your very existence, by contingency, means that you will require medical care at some point in your life. Whether it's your birth, death, sickness, etc does not matter – you are intimately part of the system. You cannot interact with it out of your own volition - the fact that you exist means that you have an intimate relationship with public healthcare, and this makes it radically different than sensational, consumerist industries. A universal Medicare-for-all national insurance that covers every American citizen from birth till death would cost less than the current bureaucratic private market.

If everyone paid a 3.3% tax rate on their income – less than the 6.5% or more that some insurance corporations charge in premiums! – every citizen could charge all of their medical, dental, and optic bills to the Medicare program and it would remain indefinitely solvent and fully funded. Every child could get the vaccines, braces, glasses, contraception, and prescriptions they need. H.R. 676, the bill in Congress that would enact single-payer healthcare, has been re-introduced several times in the past year and Congressional budget analysts say that it would save the country $300 billion each year by consolidating savings from getting rid of wasteful corporate bureaucracy.

A public works program – in the spirit of FDR-era New Deal projects – would hire millions of citizens and have them repair our nation's infrastructure. If we brought back FDR's Workers Progress Administration, the government could hire citizens to re-pave our roads, re-build our bridges, modernize the energy grid, repair our crumbling schools and neighborhoods, and revitalize our cities. A public works program has the power to cut the unemployment rate to a near-zero level overnight; it has the potential to drag our infrastructure into economic modernity and make it stable for another dozen generations.

A Workers Progress Administration must go hand-in-hand with a national project to completely re-design the country's energy industry. It should immediately nationalize all energy production to expropriate natural resources. The earth is not something that one can "own" - it is something that we all share, and as such should all be held by the public and run in the direct interests of the public. The project can build massive fields of solar panels in the Midwest fields, hydroelectric facilities along the coasts, and wind turbines along the jet stream. Not only would this allow universal access to non-profit, clean energy to everyone in the country, but it would make oil wars in the Middle East obsolete. If we truly wanted to, we could re-structure the energy industry through subsidizing massive green energy development *instead* of dirty oil and gas manufacturing. We could incentivize alternative production with specific market mechanisms if we wanted to, but the political will for this does not exist in Washington.

If we can find money to wage war, we can find money to help our own citizens. If there's money for drones and corporate welfare, then there's money for hospitals and textbooks.

I would rather have my taxes go towards cutting-edge universal healthcare, high-quality education, and massive infrastructural repairs for me and my fellow Americans than fund the imperial colonization of the Middle East. Why can't we do some nation-building here at home? It's not a matter of impossibility or lack of funding, but rather a lack of political will. If we wanted, we could orient our government - and all of its immense legal, economic, and political authority - to fundamentally re-structure the economy in our interests.

Two-Party System is Anti-Worker to the Core

Poverty is not "natural". It is a social construct unique to the human race. The sociology of poverty is a construct generated by an unequal distribution of fiat capital in the market, and radical poverty among our fellow American citizens has been normalized by the generations-long propaganda campaign that the ruling class launched to condition the public that there is no plausible, effective alternative. We created the market, decided to give it value, and chose to perpetuate it; we have the power to abolish and replace it with something else.

The truth of the matter is that there are infinite ways to organize society. The market is only one; there are countless others that have been proposed that are profoundly more democratic than market fundamentalism, such as Pannekoek's councilism, Rocker's anarcho-syndicalism, and Albert and Hahnel's participatory economics ("parecon"). I encourage each and every one of you to look into these, and into others. The more you analyze the system, the more that you realize that it is not geared in your interests. To think otherwise only proves that the post-New Deal propaganda campaign (that is, mass media) to normalize fetishized, unregulated corporate hegemony has proven to be effective.

The GOP is collapsing from an internal civil war. Moderate Republicans are being purged from the party while science-hating, reactionary nationalism is on the rise, cloaked in the sensationalist rhetoric of "liberty" and "freedom" while at the same time destroying both. The Republicans' reckless behavior is ripping our economy apart at the seams - if the 2011 downgrading of U.S. credit under their economic management (or the budget sequestration, or the government shutdown, etc) isn't blatant enough to show their incompetence, than nothing will.

The Republican Party fought for (and won) hundreds of billions of dollars in tax breaks for the top 2% of income earners. They put two imperial wars on the nation's credit card and handed the Medicare prescription program over to for-profit pharmaceutical corporations that have repeatedly been charged with Medicare fraud and artificially raising prices on patients.

This corrupt party - one that privatizes gains amongst a handful of aristocrats, but socializes losses amongst the entire tax-paying public - needs to be relegated to the dustbin of history. It is an organization whose leaders are nothing more than the generals in the class war - Paul Ryan, Mitt Romney, John Boehner, Mitch McConnell, and other jingoist neoliberals are the ones leading the campaign to obliterate working class in order to continue their generations-long plot: the centralization of all political and economic decision-making power in non-democratic, unaccountable corporate board rooms, all for the sake of profit. They do not understand what it is like to live from paycheck to paycheck, carefully managing every cent in their bank accounts in the hope that they'll have just enough money to buy food, gas, rent, and medicine. They do not understand what it means to be "working class" and fight desperately for economic security.

The modern-day GOP establishment drips with the toxic filth of nationalism, imperial conquest, and anti-intellectualism. It is not the party of Lincoln or of "liberty". It has been completely taken over by violent, reactionary elements that have dragged it from being a centre-right party to a profoundly far-right one, and it is terrifying to think of what a Tea Party president could do with a fully Republican Congress.

Yet, I do not mean to come across as partisan. The overwhelming majority of the Democratic Party is as deep in the corporate aristocracy's pocket as the Republicans are - they're just the 'good cop' to balance out the GOP 'bad cop', a gentle face to violent oppression. It disgusts me when white-privileged, cis-gendered liberal élites occasionally call upon populist and progressive rhetoric. They are not "progressive", bur rather "oppressive". They may pretend to speak the language of the working class, but they're just posers - they know nothing of the struggles of the chronically poor and violently discriminated. These "progressives" are no comrades of mine.

The two capitalist parties continue to prove that they are incapable of properly managing an advanced, industrial economy and running in it the direct interests of working people. What is needed isn't a liberal Democratic administration, and certainly not a Republican one of any kind, nor do we need to have romanticized "bipartisanship"; after all, how can there be any when Congress is occupied by one party, and one party only - the Business Party? It has its internal factions that pretend to be political enemies but who always, in the end, cave in to the demands of their corporate masters and their lobbyist armies. The Democrat-Republican binary is a false one. At the end of the day, they are both the puppets of Wall Street aristocrats and rely on their unlimited-spending corporate super-PACs. They do not care about the people; we need a real working-class political party.

What are we to say about Republican *laissez-faire* economics - are we to equate them with "freedom", even though the philosophic founders of capitalist theory themselves refute the idea that there is an intrinsic connection between liberty and the market? Whether it is Adam Smith's ambivalence towards the moral debauchery of that caste systems that markets create, or Friedrich Hayek arguing that a freely-competitive market can be socially destabilizing and destructively cyclical, there have always been philosophic undertones of the ethical disapproval of capitalism by market theorists.

Even though capitalist fundamentalists - like Ayn Rand and her Objectivist cult that preach the virtue of selfishness - believe in the romanticized notion of feedback-controlled supply-and-demand and in self-regulating competition, it does not change the fact that markets trend towards monopolization. Market fetishization denies economic logic and assumes that the "perfect competition" is more than an idealist pipe-dream. The internal contradictions in this idea are too numerous to count, if for nothing else other than the fact that competition naturally erases others and consolidates power.

Those who worship at the alter of market fundamentalism put self-righteous ideology before working-class reality. They are radically disconnected from the day-to-day struggle of working people and blindly place colonial-era notions of "liberty" before real-world, practical reforms that would improve working-class conditions. The intellectual dishonesty and fanatical anti-workerism of market advocates is appalling.

"Liberty" is More than Just a Word

Freedom, liberty, patriotism, equality - these are all words that are thrown around far too carelessly. Too often, they are thrown around and used in a context wherein they are drained of all substance; and even worse, there are times that they're invoked and used, in a perverted and convoluted way, to justify heinous human-rights violations. A prime example of this double-think is the current terror campaign being waged in "Afghanistan".

I place Afghanistan in quotations to show the ridiculous hypocrisy of it all - we are not in Afghanistan alone, but rather 74 sovereign nations across the globe, and many of them without the explicit consent of their governments. Why are we doing this? The answer is simple. It is not to spread "democracy" and "freedom" to some war-torn country; we are not being valiant champions and saving oppressed Afghani citizens from their tyrant-presidents.

We are there to secure out position as the world hegemon, nothing more, nothing less.

Despite the fact that domestic oil, coal, and natural gas production is experiencing explosive growth in the United States (set to outpace even Saudi Arabia by 2020), the Middle East is still a source of an enormous amount of oil. We may not need their oil ourselves - our own energy production, when coupled with trade deals with Canada, give us enough energy to completely ignore the Middle East. But just because we don't need access to additional energy resources doesn't mean that the imperial State wouldn't enjoy having undisputed, complete control over them; having that kind of power gives the State incredible clout in international affairs and geopolitics.

World population is growing exponentially - it's not unfeasible to agree with leading international economists when they say that the aggregate human population may as much as double in the next generation or two. Some people say that food production is not high enough to feed everyone on the planet, but this is false; there is enough agriculture at this exact moment (either in existence being used, or free and usable if governments actually had the political will to invest in an anti-poverty healthy-foods campaign) to feed almost twice the world's population. What we lack isn't agriculture, but a decentralized, worker-managed system of distribution that would allow local input to be the the mechanism that dictates where foodstuffs are allocated. The people should vote how and where their foods are produced and shipped, not bureaucratic power structures whose only vested interest in profit instead of filling the stomachs of working-class families. Hundreds of billions of dollars of food goes to waste each year in the European Union because of the different food production/distribution regulations that are so different from country to country. Because of all the red tape, regulations, and bureaucracy, entire warehouses of fresh food go to waste while working families go hungry - not because of incompetent farming, but because of incompetent governments that do not operate in the direct material interests of the working class.

    A growing world population means that there will need to be additional technology built to help take care of them - computers, manufacturing facilities, coal plants, infrastructure expansion, etc. Each and every one of these pieces of technology are not going to be able to run themselves - they are powered by energy, and the energy production that we have (thanks to the large agriculture corporations, who have successfully fought a generations-long fight to have taxpayer funds subsidize their costs and contribute directly to their profits) is limited. We do not have the means necessary to produce "unlimited" energy at this point in time. If we truly wanted to, we could enact massive legislative change (affecting energy, commerce, manufacturing, etc) that would induce market mechanisms designed to lower the cost of alternative-energy production and have a market-based solution to encourage transitioning to green energy.

    Or, we could join the rest of the industrialized world and nationalize our energy sector so that it can be run as a non-profit, worker-owned and worker-managed co-op conglomerates. But no, that is not a possibility - because, in the United States, anyone who proposes any non-market (or dare I say non-capitalist?) solution is instantly slandered by violent power systems that have a vested interest in perpetuating their hegemony and crushing any viable alternative.

The growing world population means that additional technology is required, and additional technology is going to require additional energy to power it. These means that the people who control our planet's finite energy resources are going to be in a unique position, a position of supremacy wherein they have the power to dictate how economies, populations, and political policy are formed. It will give the Corporate Empire (that is, the U.S. since Reagan) the power to control the rise, fall, and structure of fossil-fuel dependent economies across the planet.

We are in "Afghanistan" not because of "freedom" or "liberty", but because it gives us a justification for indefinite military seizure of natural resources in order to secure international economic hegemony. Anyone who thinks that our actions in the Middle East are anything other than blatant neocolonial conquest (violating too many human-rights conventions, international treaties, etc to count!) is only mindlessly reciting the rhetoric of Fox News and the Republican establishment. Our actions there are not conducive to foster freedom; they crush freedom, in every one of its domestic manifestations, with imperial drone strikes and never-ending troop surges.

It is time to stop being intellectually dishonest and look at the situation objectively. "Afghanistan", and the other 73 countries that we are militarily active in, do not want us there. It is time for us to end the wars, bring the troops home, and re-direct that war funding towards cutting-edge education, single-payer healthcare, and non-profit green energy production. To argue otherwise is illustrative of an internalized disregard for human life and overt nationalism.

Amnesty for "Illegal" Immigrants is Step One

There is no such thing as an "illegal" human being. Things are only "illegal" if a bourgeois State decides to declare it so - there is nothing inherent or intrinsic about a person that makes them "legal" or "illegal". There is nothing about the Mexicans down south or the Canadians up north that makes any human in their borders any more or less valuable than anyone else in any other country. To argue that people who are American are more valuable than any other human shows not only a callous disregard for our fellow human beings, but is also evidence for the internalization of State-worshiping nationalism, hidden under the guise of "liberty" and "exceptionalism". It distresses me to think that there are people who think that "American exceptionalism" exists - this is not true. The idea that Americans are more valuable than other human beings is a dangerous one - it's the embryo of violent discrimination and imperial conquest. It sets the foundation for a world-view wherein there are two, and only two, categories of people: the "exceptional" Americans and the "less-valuable" non-Americans.

Blind nationalism de-humanizes non-citizens, and far too often it enters mainstream discourse under the label of "patriotism". There is nothing "patriotic" about viewing foreign individuals - particularly those in the Third World and developing countries, or the imperial puppet-states whose own citizens we're taught to hate (Islamophobia, anyone?) - as less valuable than yourself. That's not patriotism. That's arrogant close-mindedness.

A human being is not "illegal" because some government decides that he or she is. Borders are a political lie. They are bureaucratically-drawn lines that exist for the sake of asserting a particular geographic hegemony and for managing mass populations. There is nothing real or legitimate to them; they are completely existential and only have as much value and meaning as we decide to give them. To declare that there *are* borders is a radical political statement, because it imposes absolutist human-designed concepts on the natural earth. It replaces the "natural" with the "man-made". But to declare that borders should be defended, strengthened, and fortified means that the people who declare such are brainwashed to such a degree that they no longer question the most basic foundations of government.

It bothers me when have establishment liberals try legitimize themselves as "multi-cultural" when they consciously populate their photo-ops with minority individuals. Doing so doesn't make them progressive or supportive of minorities; it does the exact opposite. It reeks of hypocrisy. They create a sort of fake, synthetic image and only exploit the reformist demands of minorities in order to create the illusion of "multi-culturalism". Far too often, Democrats try to look as if they're minority-friendly but inadvertently champion policies that are, at their core, profoundly anti-immigrant. They may use minority rhetoric and occasionally discuss equality and immigration, but never actually enact any fundamental change to reduce the systemic xenophobia that runs rampant throughout the current system.

Yet no matter how two-faced establishment liberals can be, at least their behavior does not sink into the only racist undertones of Tea Party rhetoric. The constant chanting of "American exceptionalism" and "illegal immigration" by the far-right preaching choir (that is, Fox "News") has been going on for years, and it's grown to a breaking point: people no longer question the meaning of "government", "nationality", and "borders". They take each and every one of them without question, accept them readily, and refuse to deconstruct them and analyze them philosophically.

This is dangerous. Not only do we no longer questions the chains that governments put on us, but we don't even see them or realize that they're there - and this sort of enslavement is much worse than an open dictatorship. It's not just physical or economic slavery; it's complete, total indoctrination to the point wherein you literally can't think outside the box.

The DREAM Act is one of the more recent comprehensive immigration reform proposals. Senators Dick Durbin and Orrin Hatch first introduced it on August 1, 2001 under the name of "the Development, Relief, and Education for Alien Minors Act", but it was later edited and re-introduced in 2009 after President Obama won his landslide Democratic election in 2008. Under the 2009 DREAM Act, certain individuals (those who arrived here "illegally" before the age of 16, have lived here for *at least* 5 consecutive years, have finished or are in public education, etc) gain the right to be a "legal" alien for six years. After six years, if the "legal" alien can prove that he or she (it's interesting to note the gender-binary language of the Act and how it generally targets only high-skilled cis-gendered individuals, not the poor, handicapped, or economically non-productive) has been furthering their education or being engaged with some branch of the Armed Forces, then that person is allowed to apply for citizenship and begin the formal process required to be an American.

I have many issues with the DREAM Act, which are all far to numerous for me to go into any detail here. Even though the Act is a step in the right direction, it's similar to the Affordable Care Act ("Obamacare") in that it's a temporary, short-term band-aid that does nothing to address the underlying structural causes of immigration. A better approach would be across-the-board amnesty for all "illegal" immigrants *as a first step*, followed with the gradual abolition (dare I say "withering away"?) of governments and their borders. No human being is "illegal" - to think that they are is dehumanizing and nationalist.

Fascism is Becoming Mainstream

In a previous article, I opened with Sinclair Lewis' quote that "when fascism comes to America, it will be wrapped in a flag and carrying a cross.". It is something that I think should be reiterated here, because it is disturbingly true. We are sitting passively aside and allowing racist, nationalist, sexist, and openly fascist rhetoric to be used in mainstream American discourse; our apathy has allowed truly dangerous rhetoric to become normative and conventional. We have allowed these sentiments to enter mainstream debates under the guise of "liberty" and "freedom" - terms which serve, in actuality, only as overly-romanticized illusions that try to legitimate the truly imperial beliefs that many people are conditioned into thinking.

Of course, no one can blame people for having a degree of internalized hetero-normative nationalism, especially when the corporate media is constantly bombarding us with waves of capitalist and patriarchal propaganda designed to induce manufactured consent amongst the masses.

Fundamentalist conservatism. Uncompromising traditionalism. "Free market" dogma. Reagan-worship. Militant homophobia and systemic sexism. Never-ending war. Consolidation of corporate power. Secret money influencing politics. The erosion of the New Deal and slashing of the social safety net with the neoliberal machete. Is American fascism so unrealistic a possibility? Or are there already undercurrents of it in mainstream, establishment politics?

It bothers me to think that there are people that think that war is justified. Are we going to continue to think that needlessly killing countless human souls is necessary because two parties can't come to a resolution over a socially-constructed ideological conflict? No, we should never think that war is an appropriate solution to anything. It only generates more animosity, more hate, more hostility. Bombing for peace, drone-striking for democracy, and imperially colonizing for liberty - these are all contradictions. War will never be able to be a means through which one can bring about lasting, genuine peace.

War is the most fundamental symptom of capitalism because material scarcity pits parties against one another, and reduces all human relations to violent jealousy. It (and all the social constructs that attempt to justify it) strips humanity of any chance for productive co-operation and tells everyone that *some other* demographic is to blame - and then, when that group is an oppressed minority struggling to survive inside a structurally abusive system, the oppression will not even be noticed because it will have been phased in gradually over time. It will be normative, accepted, and part of everyday culture.

Since the fascist experiments in Europe during World War II (and those outside Europe that tried to emulate them - Pinochet in Chile, etc), mainstream American debates have been tainted with their hyper-patriotism. One is no longer allowed to critique the government; to do so makes one "un-American". One can no longer oppose their country's war (or, in the case of the U.S., "wars") without being called a spineless traitor. And one certainly cannot propose even moderate economic reform without being called an anti-capitalist parasite.

We may not have a political system that is as openly totalitarian as the fascist police-states throughout the 1900s, but have do have something much worse: a strict, puritanical culture that does not tolerate open philosophic dissent. We have allowed the ruling political and financial élite to place a boundary around what is allowed to be said - anything that even questions the structural integrity of the system is thrown out the window! Fascist nations need war to feed and drive their military-industrial complex. War is the means through which fascists drum up a nationalist fervor via "rally around the flag" rhetoric - it only serves as tool through which power can be increasingly removed from democratic, publicly-accountable institutions and centralized in inaccessible corporate boardrooms.

There has been a perverted marriage between corporate CEOs and politicians ever since the disastrous *Citizens United* Supreme Court case; indeed, it bares a disturbing similarity to the famous Mussolini quote wherein he said that "fascism should more properly be called corporatism because it is the merger of state and corporate power". What is even more disturbing is how

Mussolini's views are part of the American mainstream - think of the 2012 DNC, wherein President Bill Clinton said that the country should "focus on the future, with business and government working together." The spirit of fascism is alive and well in American politics, but it lies hidden just beneath the surface.

Or maybe it's beginning to shift from being hidden - think of the establishment of Golden Dawn offices (the Greek nationalist and neo-Nazi party that arose in response to their crushing public debt) in New York City, Chicago, and Washington, D.C. The fact that there far-right institutions explicitly stating their racist jingoism growing across our country worries me daily.

Open your eyes and realize that there are hegemonic power systems all around you. There are totalitarian cultural values that mentally enslave each and every one of us, all of which need to be resolutely cast off in order to create a political environment that is conducive for progressive growth and creative development. Do not be afraid to point out totalitarian power structures and call for the revolutionary abolition - we must do everything we can to crush the fascist embryo growing in our country before it's too late and we wake up in a dystopian police-state.

Jesus, Socialist Extraordinaire
Originally, "Jesus, Le Socialiste Extraordinaire"

Jesus can accurately be considered to be one of the fathers of socialism. The religious right-wing distorts an overwhelming majority of what Jesus says - abandoning material possessions, common ownership, universal solidarity, limitless compassion, and railing against the anti-progressive Pharisaic establishment of the time. He was outstandingly revolutionary. There is nothing "conservative" about Christianity, when you look at its actual teachings.

There is nothing in our Christian religion for justifies a system based on human exploitation. There is nothing holy about capitalism: it is a system that ignores the needs of the poor and homeless, rejects the foreign, forgets about the sick and hungry, and rewards the greedy over the compassionate. Capitalism is a cruel and inhumane system that places short-term profit and corporate interests over those of the working class; it is not something that Jesus Himself would be able to support. Catholic Bishop Thomas Gumbleton of Detroit acknowledged that "the system doesn't seem to be providing for the well-being of all the people. It is almost, in its very nature, contrary to the Jesus who said 'blessed are the poor, woe to the rich'."

Father Dick Preston, a Michigan-based priest, agreed and even went on to say that "capitalism, in its present form, is an evil. It is contrary to all that is good ... Capitalism is precisely what the Holy Book reminds us is unjust and, in some form of fashion, God will come down and eradicate. It is wrong, and therefore needs to be eliminated." So did Father Peter Dougherty, who went so say that "it is immoral, it is obscene, it is outrageous. It is really radically evil ... It's radical evil."

Gumbleton, Preston, and Dougherty are absolutely correct. Capitalism does need to be eliminated, but what should take its place?

On what grounds, then, can the bourgeois élite and corporate aristocracy argue that Jesus is on there side? Christ would not come to modern-day America to ring the daily bell at the New York Stock Exchange. Christ would not argue that obsessive deregulation will provide healthcare for everyone, and He would certainly not support any war, even those under the faux-guise of humanitarianism and democratization. Jesus would charge into Stock Exchange, denounce the moneylender for disregarding the well-being of the whole community, and stand in unwavering solidarity with the poor, sick, diseased, socially-outcast, and brokenhearted - the very people that capitalism refuses to help.

My Savior is one who stands with the working class and the needy, not one who rejects them.

The Jesus Christ that we, as Christians, worship is not the same Jesus that the rich and powerful have claimed for their own; our is a loving God, one of that heals the sick and houses the poor, not one that shakes His finger in righteous anger at them and tells them to work harder, for longer hours, for less pay. The bourgeois power structures that exist in our society - the banks, energy producers, pharmaceutical corporations, venture capitalists, and the lobbying industry - have a vested interest in wrapping naked greed up in Christian rhetoric, because as long as they do so they'll have an illusion of legitimacy. The ultra-rich have claimed Jesus for their own in an attempt to make it look like their existence has meaning - even though their overly parasitic nature is becoming increasingly obvious as they continue to wage class warfare against the working class.

Religion holds a very important place in our society - it in intimately tied in with our federal government, prominent Church leaders hold political clout in the lobbying industry, and Church teachings dictate morality in our supposedly-secular culture. At what point are we going to stop lying to ourselves and pretending that we live in a modern, post-medieval society, when our entire economic system is modeled off of the unholy alliance of the Church and aristocracy that characterized our previous mode of production? At what point are we going to be honest to ourselves, and admit that the "religion" that capitalists adhere to has absolutely no correlation with the teachings of Jesus Christ - the same teachings that gave birth to numerous collectivist, agricultural communes between the first generations of Christians helped establish?

Or what about the oh-so-famous line that Christ said in Matthew 19:24: "Again, I tell you, it is easier for a camel to go through the eye of a needle than for a rich man to enter the kingdom of God". Christianity is not a religion for the wealthy to justify their greed; it is a philosophy of hope for the working class, a form of inspiration to help them deal with the truly lethal climate that laissez-faire capitalism spawned. A position that I found to be especially interesting is the story of Sodom and Gomorrah. Of course, the literalists and fundamentalists are going to tell you that it and the over-used quote from Leviticus 18:22 ("Thou shalt not lie with mankind as with womankind; it is an abomination") justifies and inequality and homophobia, but will ignore the context in which it was said regarding negative population growth in the midst of waring country. One cannot argue with the people who are so dead-set and close-minded in their beliefs that they are unwilling to have an intellectually honest discussion.

It is time to stop lying to ourselves about what Jesus said and what He stands for, and realize that he championed the poor and denounced the rich, not the other way around. Jesus Christ is the hero of the working class and one of the principal fathers of socialism.

Living Wage, not Minimum Wage, is the Answer

There are numerous proposals on how to increase the minimum wage. Some, as President Obama proposed in his State of the Union speech to Congress last January, would increase it to just over $9 an hour and then index it to inflation - meaning that, as the cost of living rises over time, the minimum wage would rise proportionally to make up for the increased costs. This isn't the only one, however; Senate Democrats have introduced bills to bring it to $10.10, and Seattle City recently saw Kshama Sawant - a member of the Socialist Alternative, one of the many fragmented socialist parties in the country - win an election with her campaign based on a $15 an hour minimum wage.

Does a jump from $7.50 to $15 sound like a lot? Yet it's not even as much as workers technically should be making. If wages had always increased at the rate of inflation, and taken aggregate national economic growth into account as the value of the dollar rises, the minimum wage would be hovering between $21-22 per hour. What does this mean? It means that, although the total value of your labor is equivalent to that, the difference is being re-distributed upwards to the ruling class through a backwards tax and wage system that does not give the everyday worker the full value and product of his work.

There is a systemic parasitism running through capitalism, but the consequences are even worse when one takes into account the impact that such exploitative business entities have on local communities when they serve as mass employers. There are numerous studies that have come out over the past several years - from economists on the Left and Right - showing that for every 100 employees Walmart hires it costs the city just over $2 million in taxpayer funds to provide public services for the employees because they do not have a high enough income to obtain them in the private market. These things include food stamps, subsidized and public housing, low-income health insurance via Medicaid, and municipal services.

If the minimum wage was increased to Kshama Sawant's proposed $15 solution, that would give working-class families the economic buying-power to lift themselves out of poverty and reduce strain on the public safety net. This reduced strain would allow for taxpayer funds to be reallocated into programs that would directly benefit the infrastructure and economic interests of the local economy. Yet, because this is $15 dollars an hour, it would still not be the total net worth of one's labor; the difference between the $21-22 "real" wage and the $15 "minimum" wage would still flow to the upper class in the form of direct profit. In the end, a $15 wage would still be a means through which there is systemic exploitation of workers and would still be the means through which the ruling class could accumulate extraordinary amounts of wealth over time.

To those who say that an increase in the minimum wage would cause a reactionary spike in inflation, I would direct them to the reports put out by both public agencies (Treasury Department, Congressional Budget Office, etc) and private entities (the majority of the D.C. based conservative think-tanks) that say that, at most, prices would rise up to an approximate six cents in certain sectors of the economy, and that other sectors would potentially be untouched.

Of course, raising the minimum wage to $15 and indexing it to inflation is not the end goal; the end goal is the construction of an economic system wherein those who contribute as much as they can are able to survive. Those who work a full work-week should be able to earn a living wage - a wage conducive for them to pay their rent, put healthy food on the table for their children, cover their energy and transportation bills, and allow for enough recreational time and discretionary buying-power. Having working-class families have the economic power to move markets is good, because it introduces a level of democratic decision-making into an unfortunately centralized, corporate-based economy. Currently, the market controls and direct people; instead, the people should control and direct the market.

Open your eyes and look at the reality of the situation - we live in an economy wherein decision-making power and wealth accumulation only happens to those at the top. A prime example of this is the university in which we now sit. Despite its rich traditions and fact that our departments are filled with brilliant educators and doctorates, there are those executive managers that sit atop our university's ivory towers that spend our hard-earned tuition money on things that are not directly related to our educational experience. The new UNH logo is a prime example because it shows how completely out-of-touch the university executive is with the material wants and needs of the student body - the body that cares more about how much it makes in work-study paychecks (which many students are financially dependent on!) and dining hall choices than on wasteful, cosmetic nonsense. If the university executives truly wanted to spend $100,000 effectively, it should have asked the students what it they could do to improve our education here.

  We need an immediate increase in the minimum wage to $9, followed by a gradual increase to $15 over several years that is then indexed to inflation. This is an economically sound and politically realistic way to improve the living standards of the working class, when done in conjunction with other progressive reforms - single-payer healthcare, mass infrastructure repair, green energy investment, and increased education funding. Do not be afraid to be principled and demand the liberation of the working class - always be dedicated to liberty, not sensationalized "compromise" that acts as a veil for perpetuating bourgeois rule.

Section Three:
Exegetical and Thematic Papers

Republic Revisited:
A Marxian Critique of Platonic Justice

"Democracy ... is a charming form of government, full of variety and disorder, and dispensing a sort of equality to equals and unequals alike."
Plato, *Republic*, book VIII, *Decline of the Polis*

Many believe democracy to be the greatest political system conceivable - that is, Western-American capitalism. Such representational democracies, defined by their majoritarian tendencies, codify the will of the plurality, regardless of whether that will is either right or wrong, into law. The democratic tradition considers 'right' and 'just' to be whatever the majority of hands say that it is[1], rather than holding true to an perfect and unwavering definition of the two. The Greek philosopher Plato is deeply critical of this, and makes a poignant case in his revolutionary text *Politeia*, often translated as the *Republic*, that 'justice'[2] is not merely an abstract concept: it has a concrete definition, and once that definition is realized, it should be adhered to with an absolutist fervor. Written as a Socratic dialogue between Athenian philosophers, *Republic* seeks to discern the true definition of 'justice' and a way to apply it both to one's life and to the community. It is Socrates, in the end, who provides us with the conclusive definition, but we should not listen his words without a lens of willing skepticism: we should question and debate 'justice', and perhaps even critique it.

---

[1] Thus we see the 'tyranny of the majority", as French historian Alexis de Tocqueville puts it. This can be exemplified in the democratic elections that brought the Nazi Party to power to Germany. We will explore democratic thought throughout this essay.

[2] I place *justice* in quotations to signify how vague and ambiguous it is. As this essay progresses, however, its definition may become clearer to us.

Our investigation into the definition of 'justice' will take place with a brief overview of Platonic philosophy vis-à-vis the *Republic* and an explanation as to why Socrates' eventual definition is correct. After this, we will also adopt a Marxian[3] outlook to attempt to bring its well-known scathing criticism of power structures into the debate and challenge Plato. In an almost Hegelian sense, our proposed thesis and antithesis will meet, and we shall try to see if there is a subsequent synthesis or if one of the two proves to be the stronger argument and will win out.

But let us dispense with this and commence with our primary thesis, that Platonic 'justice' is absolute, righteous, and true. To begin, we will assume *a priori* that a component of 'justice' is freedom, and must therefore investigate the definition and meaning of freedom in an attempt to understand the whole concept of which it is a constitutive piece. Yet while this seems a logical place to begin, it leaves us with an equally difficult starting point: the definition of 'freedom 'is just as ambiguous and subjective as 'justice'. When confronted with the opportunity to define 'freedom', however, there will be varying answers from different people - some may argue that freedom is the ability to act on one's own accord, or the right to voice their opinion and choose for themselves; others still will bring quasi-intellectualist responses in the debate of "freedom to" and "freedom from" in an attempt to differentiate different types of freedoms. All of these are both correct and wrong at the same time - a concept as complex and dynamic as 'freedom' cannot possibly be summed up in a single sentence, but if it was to be, it could logically be considered that *freedom is a slave to desire*. Freedom is multifarious and momentary: if one has the ability to do anything at any time, he or she will be dragged in various directions by momentary impulses and desires. Yet our presumed definition is contradictory and mutually exclusive in that, if

---

[3] I do identify with the existential Marxism of Jean-Paul Sartre, but let us dissociate any revisionism or any 'post-Marx' Marxism from this essay. It is appropriate enough for us to view Platonic theory as vulgar Marxists.

being free also makes one a slave, then one is not free, for being a slave is inherently 'un-free'. It seems that our original starting point that a component of 'justice' is freedom, and that we can begin our study with an examination of that component, is not as reasonable as we thought, and that we must observe it from another angle.

When addressing the *Republic*, we mustn't merely discuss freedom, however. If anything, it is about education and *dikniosyné*; that is, the abstract concept that is a blend of 'justice', objective morality, honor, righteousness, and order. *Dikniosyné* does not simply refer to these in a legal sense - it refers to universal, cosmic, and moral justice, something that transcends such mundane definition and is inscribed in Greek culture as an aspirational thing to obtain. In order to be properly educated and attempt to understand *dikniosyné*, the Athenians turned to two sources of wisdom: the poets, who were said to be inspired by the gods, and the old men, who had lived long, full lives and could share their experiences. Perhaps an appropriate place for us to begin, then, is by studying these sources of wisdom.

The *Republic* opens with several Athenians - including Socrates, the famous philosopher; Cephalus, a wealthy metic; Polemarchus, the son of Cephalus; and Thrasymachus, a Greek sophist - discussing their theories as to the meaning of 'justice' down by the Piraeus, the lower edges of Athens that are close to the waters. Cephalus, an old man, would logically be considered to be one of the sources of wisdom that the others could use to define 'justice', and is even described as being "keen to things of the mind". However, when he explains that he believes that a good and 'just' life is one of good character and that "money for the right-thinking man can pay debts to the gods and men" via donations and social aid, the others see that the justification for his noble behavior is not one of altruism or an adherence to 'justice'. Cephalus is merely acting as he does because he hopes that, by living an upstanding life, he will be secure in the afterlife after death. Thus we see that he is motivated by fear, not 'justice'.

Polemarchus dismisses his father's definition and cites Simonides[4], arguing that 'justice' is the rendering "to each his due", which he later clarifies and says is exemplified in one's ability to help their friends and harm their enemies. However, we should join the others in the *Republic* by stating that Polemarchus' definition is inherently flawed: as potentially bad judges of character and imperfect human beings, one cannot always tell who is a "friend" or an "enemy" in a truly objective sense. Breaking the community down into these two groups, and defining what those groups consist of, is subjective and open to debate. Not only is Polemarchus imprecise, but he also forgets that 'justice' is never able to harm. 'Justice' only supposed to make things better, and an action that results in social or physical damage or corruption cannot be labeled as 'just' in any sense of the word.

Thrasymachus attempts to pick up where Polemarchus leaves off and states that justice belongs to the stronger and is the interest of the stronger. 'Justice', he argues, *is* self-interest. It is from this idea that we derived our earlier claim that 'justice' is not determined by a majoritarian state of hands. As the strong or the majority in power may not be in power forever, and will eventually be replaced by another person or class of individuals, plurality-based rule is fickle, irregular, and subject to quick change. This is unstable and wrong, they argue, because self-interest is socially fragmenting and "the strong" may result in a tyrannical leader[5], but Thrasymachus rebuts them by stating that by "the strong" he refers to a "ruler in the strict sense", not an ambitious politician.

The idea of a "ruler in the strict sense" is something that we must look at. This "ruler" will not be one who was elected to

---

[4] That is, Simonides of Ceos. He was a Greek lyrical poet that was born at Ioulis on Kea, an island amongst the Greek archipelago. The Hellenistic-Alexandrian scholars consider him to be one of the most influential of poets, and he is credited with inventing several letters in the Greek alphabet (ω, η, ξ and ψ).

[5] "Tyranny" is described by Socrates, Plato's student, as a "perverted state" in which a single individual rules in his own self-interest.

office with the ambitious desire to exercise and acquire power. He or she[6] would act with the best intentions of the community, using wisdom and foresight to do the best good that he or she was capable of. That person would be able to apply his or her knowledge of 'justice' to be build a 'just' society, and would not be selected from the community at random: the "ruler" would be an effective and destined ruler because of his or her *techné*[7] would make it so. The concept of *techné* is something that is used quite often in Platonic theory - it represents an intrinsic quality or talent that one has that makes a person suited for a particular task or occupation. In this sense, a person would be an effective "ruler" because their *techné* has given them the aptitude necessary to do so.

Socrates refutes Thrasymachus and offers three critiques to his idea of 'just' self-interest. He states that "justice is a harmony" and the result of communal cooperation. An effective example of this is the idea that no member of an orchestra can be an individual: each must work in harmony with one another and do their part, and that equal, collective action brings about cooperation and peace. Socrates also believes, should self-interest rule the day, there could be no group action. If each person was to be an ardent individualist, there would be no unity[8]. There would be constant social chaos and constant competition between people. The rise and rulership of self-interest would result in an equally proportional fall and death of social collectivism. He argues that self-interest is dividing and is

---

[6] I say "he or she" in the attempt to be as non-sexist and non-prejudiced as possible. While I do believe that men and woman are equal (although the modern capitalist market has prevented them from being so) the Athenians did not, and any "ruler" would most likely have ended up being male.

[7] Greek, "τέχνη". Generally translated as "skill", "craft", "art", or an "application of knowledge".

[8] The "individualist vs collectivist" debate is one that permeates politics when discussing freedom and liberty. Indeed, Plato's statement here (said through Socrates in the dialogue) is still relevant today.

not beneficial for the community - it does nothing other than fragment it.

The third and final critique that Socrates offers to Thrasymachus is that of proper behavior, of being in *psyché* and living an ordered life. The *psyché* is the Greek concept for the soul: to tend to one's *psyché* is to "tend to one's breath", to be aware of their existence and life. Those that are not aware of their breath and existence are not in *psyché* and are not truly living, and will spend their time chasing momentary desires and living an unordered and perverted life. The *psyché* has a function in one's life, and it gives orders and injunctions, and must be acknowledged and tended to.

So far we see that 'justice' is not merely freedom, nor is it good character, aiding one's friends and harming one's enemies, or advocacy for self-interest. Socrates, held at the Piraeus and unable to leave by his inquisitive peers, argues that if one is to look for 'justice', one must look at the State: it connects individuals to the entire community and is easier to observe on a larger scale than it is when simply examining a particular individual. An individual cannot be self-sufficient, he says, as one cannot be both 'just' and alone at the same time. 'Justice', it would seem, includes not just an intrapersonal dynamic, but also a communal one. There must be 'justice' in both. He points out that the Sophists, those Greek educators who would charge money to the wealthy so as to teach them to happy and successful, were "educators for money" rather than "educators for truth", and were not furthering a 'just' cause in the State. He challenged their teachings by asking them what happiness is, and they were unable to give him a definitive answer.

'Justice', Socrates said, is a social contract agreed upon by the political community - but this statement does not elaborate to explain specifically what that contract is. We are not self-sufficient because our freedoms, which many of us take for granted, are "born on the backs of countless millions" who fought for their existence and for the material environment in which we can exercise them. The community is connected, not only to each other through mutual cooperation, but through history - and members of the community should be divided up through an ontological[9] division of labor; that is, by delegating certain occupations and tasks to certain people based on their *techné*. Those who were born with a love of farming should farm; those with a talent for weaving should make clothes; and those who are upstanding, moral people may be inclined to be a "ruler in the strict sense", as we saw earlier. Does this not make sense? Do people not have certain talents and skills that give them a particular inclination or interest in a certain occupation? There are those that say that they feel drawn towards a particular career; there are those that do what they love for their work. Perhaps a *techné*-based and ontologically divided community would not only produce a happier population (as people are engaged in a trade that they enjoy) but also a more skillful one (as they excel in the craft of their choice). Indeed, a society in which its citizens take up occupations they love - rather than those that they have to based on economic or financial situations - seems to be much better.

Although, in order to the State to obtain the resources necessary to sponsor these occupations and secure a high standard of living, it must procure them - and the most common way to secure resources, land, and labor is to go to war. The expansionistic tendencies in any State will eventually encourage it to push outwards, consume the surrounding materials, and better itself. Going to war can be argued as a way to fund an ontological division of labor, guarantee a safe State, and allow the State to produce luxuries for its citizens. Because of this potentially necessary militarism, there needs to be a social class devoted to doing so. This class - divided ontologically, based on *techné* - is known as the *Guardians*, who members are characterized as being spirited, courages, philosophical, physically fit, and quick to passionate responses over perceived injustice. The Guardians are to be educated in both *musiké* and *gymnastiké* - that is, the "measured thing" (as in rhetoric, poetry, and language arts) and physical training, respectively. The

---

[9] Derived from *ontology*, or *ontos-* ("being", "that which is") and *-ology* ("the study of"). Literally, "the study of being" or "the study of reality".

Guardians are to be the "kin" of the philosophers, associating with them and sharing their interest in objective ideology so as to temper their militant tendencies.

The formation of ontological classes in Platonic theory involve more than simply delegating specific tasks and traits: it involves a fundamental change in social roles to establish *techné*-based positions. In order to reinforce this and create such a mindset, the stories that are told and taught in the Athenian educational system need to be managed - specifically, it needs to be censored. It needs to be altered to so that the fundamentals show a civil society, not a war-mongering one. It also needs to teach piety, and the idea that the gods are responsible only for the good, are perfect, and are unchanging. This last concept is in direct opposition to what was classically taught in Athens: that the gods were often mercurial, wily, greedy, overtly sexual, incestuous, quick to anger, and the bringers of unpredictable intervention. Plato proposes in the *Republic* that it be taught instead that they are not victim to such petty and simple human emotions, and that they have instead transcended past all of these. The populace should also be taught *sophrosyné*, or *moderation*, so that they are not subject to excessive laughter or lamentation. This temperance is a key aspect of Platonism, as we will see shortly.

This drastic education reform - this sweeping censorship for the good of the community - is eloquently described in the phrase "lying is like a poison". Although some poisons are deadly, others, when used correctly, can be helpful and used as the bases for certain medicines; censorship, while altering history, can be advantageous in that it removes the negative aspects of society and reminds us of the good ones. It is what we can call a "noble lie".

In the new, *Republic*-based society, art, Plato argues, must be an "expression of the good", not of the self. When forms of moral quality - such as 'justice', courage, and temperance - are realized, they should be firmly adhered to They should be expressed in art, so that that art can enrich and reaffirm the 'just' society instead of showing the fragmenting self-interest of individualism. One might not consider modifying the arts to be a particularly important element when discussing a fundamental restructuring of society; however, it is important for us to realize the dramatic effect that this would have. Everything in our physical environment had some degree of aesthetic thought and design go into it during its creation - during production, both appearance and function are taken into account. Changing the arts would not merely move the focus from the self to the the good, but also impact our entire material environment.

Socrates extrapolates upon the idea of a *techné*-based society by invoking the allegory of the metals, in which states that a gods mixed a certain metal into one's soul. The type of metal that is inside someone is indicative of what kind of person he or she will be. Those with gold souls are naturally inclined to be philosopher-kings, those with silver to be the Guardians, those with bronze to be the common tradesmen, and those with copper to be the lowest members of society. The philosopher-kings, Guardians, and tradesmen are the three social classes that, Socrates postulates, will emerge in a 'just' society. Platonic theory visualizes society in the shape of a pyramid, with a large base and a small tip, whose top and bottom are roughly indicative of the size of the upper and lower classes. There are social gradients and classes in-between the two, of course. At the top will be the philosopher-kings, who rest above the Guardians, who in turn will sit atop the larger tradesmen group. This 'Platonic pyramid', as we shall call it, is justified by by the four virtues: wisdom, temperance, courage, and justice. The philosopher-kings will understandably be the holders of wisdom, who are prudent in council, and are an upstanding representation of every value that society holds dear. Whatever positive trait society deems is desirable will be embodied in the philosopher-king; he will be the most upright member of the community. Courage will be exemplified in the Guardians who are, as we have discussed, spirited, philosophical, fit, and quick to passionate responses over perceived injustices. They know, as the *Republic* states, "what is truly fearful" and that "moral evil is the only evil". Their steadfast and preservative nature is to protect and preserve what is morally good. The tradesmen, however, have multifarious appetites, are mercurial, and are subject to momentary desires. They are not embodiments of one of the four virtues other than temperance, though each of the three classes is said to contain this. Temperance includes order, harmony, and consensual government and popular democracy.

Yet this is only three of the four virtues - the philosopher-king's wisdom, the Guardians' courage, and everyone's temperance - that are shown in our Platonic pyramid. Where in the pyramid is 'justice' present? The trait around which our whole investigation hangs isn't as simple to locate as the others. Socrates gives an interesting answer as to where to find it: he argues that 'justice' is not a trait that is held by a single person or a single class; it is larger than this. He defines 'justice' as living within the Platonic pyramid: by knowing one's place in society, remaining dedicated to it, minding one's business and living his or her life in accordance with what he or she can and ought to do. This is in accordance with the ontological division of labor, that certain people are born to do certain things and have innate tendencies, and that they should honor those tendencies by devoting their lives to them and recognizing their occupational niche in society. Social order and living in accordance with one's *techné* is 'justice'.

Justice cannot exist only in the State, however. If it is to exist, it must be present in both the State and the souls of its citizens. Not only can we construct a pyramid to illustrate a just state, but also one for a just person. Our second Platonic pyramid should look very much like the first: a small tip and large bottom, orientated upwards. The top represents the *reflective*, which holds wisdom, forethought, and caution, and corresponds with the mindset of the philosopher-king. The middle represents the *spirited*, which demonstrates courage, is "aroused by indignation" and injustice, and is "kin to the reflective." This is shown in the Guardians. The bottom is the *appetitive*, which, like the tradesmen on our previous pyramid, has multifarious desires and is driven by momentary needs. Each of the three parts of the soul holds temperance, and knowing and living according to the triangle - that is, tending to one's *psyché* and their breath - is what makes an individual 'just'.

This sounds perfectly reasonable to us, does it not? Can we not agree that an ordered and stable society wherein everyone is naturally inclined to their occupation and nurtures their soul to be the most perfect system? It seems that Socrates' definition of justice, while elaborate, is much truer than that of Cephalus, Polemarchus, Thrasymachus, or Glaucon. Yet there is something that must also be pointed out if we are to conclude that Platonic justice has been effectively codified by Socrates: that while Plato's *Republic* illustrates a utopian society, it is, and will potentially always remain, utopian and idealistic. Socrates himself admits that its construction is implausible - it is perfect, yes, but it is only a theory, and attempting to systematize that theory into a concrete, existing system will always fall short of the ideal which it hopes to aspire to. While the *Republic* may tell us the absolute definition and application of justice, actualizing that justice may be much more difficult than we originally thought.

Does this de-legitimize Platonic theory? Not at all. Just because something is theoretical and idealistic does not mean that it is not worth striving towards. Just as communism is considered by many to be utopian[10], it is also considered to be a "perfect" society, and thus is worth working for, even only if slight reform and improvement are actualized, instead of a fundamental change to the perfect form. Perhaps Marxism and Platonism are oriented much closer to one another than could originally have been thought, if they share this same trait. Seeing as they do, it might be effective for us to use Marxism as a tool through which to critique Plato's theory of justice to reinforce our own understanding by it.

If we are going to adopt a Marxian outlook, we must first recognize that communist ideology was not effectively codified into a single manuscript until 1848, when Karl Marx

---

[10] Those that say this clearly do not have a sufficient background in Marxist theory. While Marx does explain the historical dialectic that will result in communism, he gives few details as what that sort of world will truly look like, other than simply labeling it as a "worker's state". Those that do know Marxism, though, often point to this vague ending as one of its chief flaws.

and Friedrich Engels' *Manifesto of the Communist Party* presented a damning critique of capitalism. Not only did it prophesies its eventual downfall and transformation into a socialist dictatorship of the proletariat, but it also sought to demystify the socio-economic dynamics that constituted society at large. Religion, morality, ethics, cultural norms, group psychology, rhetoric - nothing was safe from Marx, and it can be argued that it, like *Republic*, stands out amongst all other political writings.

Neither communism, socialism[11], nor Marxism represent an authoritarian or statist system. Those who perceive them as being ideologies that advocate a large, centralized, or bureaucratic government only do so because they have been conditioned to by the systems that are threatened by them. That is, capitalism has a vested interest in teaching the populace that it is the proper and 'good' system, and teaching that all opposing theories are 'bad'. Doing so perpetuates its existence. If the people believe that capitalism (or whatever the prevailing system may be) is the best possible system, then they will not stray from it.

Marx offers an interesting critique of capitalism and proposes a new worldview. It is important, though, to begin a Marxian exegesis with an understanding of Marxism[12] itself. Therefore, it seems appropriate to elaborate on one of its most basic tenants: the existence of the base and superstructure.

The dialogue in *Republic* looks at many things: the role of religion and the gods in society, social norms, the dynamics between different classes of people, and difficult ethical questions. Each of these represent narratives that act as different

---

[11] "Socialism" and "communism", in the context of this essay, will refer to decentralized and cooperative-based worker's control, rather than any form of collectivist statism. It does not refer to Third Way politics, contemporary social democracy, or either Soviet or Chinese influenced authoritarianism.

[12] By "Marxism", we will refer to the classical theses set out by Karl Marx. We will not focus on any extrapolation or interpretation of Marxism, such as those of Lenin, Bernstein, DeLeon, or Chomsky,

ways for one to study the world, which can be used to study by observing religion, social interactions, the media, or morality. Each of these narratives, when connected together, form a complex culture. This culture, as a whole, can be referred to as the *superstructure*. The superstructure, in its totality, is what conditions and defines people in a society. Socrates, Thrasymachus, and others spend their time analyzing its various components. Rather than look at the superstructure and its constitutive narratives, though, one must look at what defines it; that is, one must look past the existing culture and question where that culture comes from and how it was created. One must look at the foundation that the superstructure sits on.

This foundation is the *base*. The base is the political economy - the existing economic system of production, how products and commodities are generated and distributed. Economic relations determine how each of the superstructure's narratives are created and how they act - both in relation to one another, and to society at large. As sad as it is, those economic relations have come to define religion (by commercializing holidays and transforming religions into a bureaucratic businesses and political lobbyists), morality (wherein greed, says Ayn Rand, is "man's highest virtue"), and politics (where business' and oligarchs' money speaks louder than a citizen's voice). Even education, as respected as it was in Greece, has become, as mentioned in class, is now a means of "maximizing profit to increase profit", wherein "all the seats are orientated to a truth inscription machine". The entire superstructure, we can see, is economically determined by the base.

Yet we can deconstruct this system even further - *Republic* is a dramatic dialogue about justice in society, and we have agreed that that society is the product of the superstructure, which in turn is a product of the base. However, to fully adopt a Marxian outlook, it is necessary to understand what constitutes the base. The base is the foundation for all of society - but what is the basic component of the base? What singular item is the driving influence behind everything in history, and why does it have that power?

The answer is called the *means of production*, the things in the community that generate goods, services, commodities, and capital - that is, the things that gives rise to all of components that, when added together, create a dynamic economy. Examples of the means of production include factories, corporations, large businesses, and mass employers[13]. Each of these create commodities that are bought, sold, and exchanged; together, they form the base. Those that work with the means of production are, as Marx calls them, the *proletariat* (derived rom the Latin word *"proletarius"*, or "citizen of the lower class"), and are employed by the *bourgeoisie*[14]. With its root being the Old French *burgeis*, meaning "walled city", the bourgeois are the owners of the means of production and the chief owners of property, who do not perform any labor but simply make money off of the exploitation of the proletariat. They often make philosophical and ideological justifications for the established order so as to rationalize their position to the proletariat, however, and retain their status. This oppressor-oppressed dynamic, referred to in Marxist theory as the *relations of production*, is the driving force behind history. This friction and class antagonism, with both classes pursuing different socio-economic agendas, is critical to Marxism. Indeed, the *Manifesto* opens with the *a priori* statement that "all hitherto existing society is the history of class struggle". To Marx, all peoples fall into (or will eventually fall into) either the bourgeoisie or the

---

[13] As Greece is still a pre-capitalist society at the time of *Republic*, it is best to look at the means of production as an abstract concept and understand them in a Marxian sense, rather than view them as concrete, communal buildings and items.

[14] The bourgeoisie and proletariat do not exist in Athens in the traditional Marxist sense, as there are no industrialized means of production to control. For all intents and purposes in this essay, the "bourgeoisie" and "proletariat" will not refer strictly to *ownership* or *lack of ownership* of the means of production, respectfully, but rather the existence of a *ruling* and *subordinate* class (that is, oppressor and oppressed) in the spirit of Marxism. The Athenian aristocracy could be considered an example of a pre-capitalist bourgeoisie and the general populace could be the pre-capitalist proletariat.

proletariat, and although their forms and relationship have altered throughout history, it is appropriate to focus on the relations of production in our discussion of Plato, as *Republic* deliberates human relations. This will be the focus of our Marxian analysis.

A Marxist would argue that Plato's arguments in *Republic* are profoundly structuralist. There are heavy elements of authoritarianism, wherein personal freedom is not valued: the good of the State, and that of the whole community, takes precedence over that of the individual. The rigidity of social classes (that is, the philosopher-kings, the Guardians, and the tradesmen) does not take social mobility into account, and keeps them contained in their class by an almost enforced caste-based system. It is logical to say that Plato reinforces classism in his argument.

There is an objection to this in the text, though, when it's stated that each person would enjoy their status because it matches their inherent nature - that each person was destined to be born into that caste because of their innate qualities. One can ask the existential question of the existence of a truly inherent (or conversely, a universal) human nature, but for the sake of simplicity, we will not go into this[15]. We will simply adopt a skeptically Marxist approach, and view people in the abstract, as a class, rather than reify and deconstruct such a complex topic. The purpose of our Marxian lens is to view the *Republic* in term of the relations of production, rather than what constitutes each class itself.

Marxism says Plato's structuralist and classist views emphasize and greatly exacerbate class antagonisms. By reinforcing class-based rule and social immobility, Plato is indirectly enforcing bourgeois supremacy, and thus its oppression and rule. As Thrasymachus so eloquently puts it, justice is the "rule of the strong". Such a system, based on class antagonisms, cannot be just. Justice, by definition, can do no harm, and a class-based system is inherently harmful to those

---

[15] Existentialism and its synthesis with Marxist theory will be the topic of another paper.

that are part of the strong, ruling class: the petit-bourgeoisie[16]; the proletariat, trapped in the exploitative chains of wage-slavery; the entire State, prevented by bourgeois ideology, from progressing into a more equitable and 'just' form; and the sick, chronically unemployed and unproductive, the non-Athenian, the slaves, and the social delinquents[17], all cast by the élitist Greek aristocracy into servitude or the forgotten slums in the cities. Plato's advocation for a structuralist "proper order' can merely be perceived as bourgeois ideology intended simply to retain the established power of that class.

When viewed at with this Marxian perspective, Thrasymachus' "rule of the strong" and Plato's ordered society take on an entirely new meaning. The relations between the Athenian bourgeoisie and proletariat do not seem to be more 'just' if *Republic*'s principals were applied to them. Instead, their antagonistic tendencies would be inflamed. Perhaps Platonic justice is less desirable than originally thought?

Let us also examine another point of Thrasymachus: the idea of self-interest. He is given three strong critiques by Socrates, who argues that "justice is a harmony". The example that we gave - that no member of an orchestra can be an individual: each must work in harmony with one another, and that equal, collective action brings about cooperation and peace - seems to echo of the egalitarian classlessness[18] of Marxism can be heard here.

The second critique is that, should self-interest rule the day, there would be no group action. If each person was to be an ardent individualist, there would be no unity; there would only

---

[16] Or, those that work alongside the bourgeoisie, their employers, or be self-employed, and live a modest 'middle class' living, but do not control the means of production.

[17] What Marx would identify as the "lumpenproletariat", the marginalized, lowest, and least productive layer of the proletariat. Derived from *lumpenproletarier*, or "rag proletarian" in German.

[18] The elimination of social classes and the equality of all peoples is an eventual goal of Marxism. Marx postulates that communism would eventually result in the dissolution of both government and class.

be social chaos and constant conflict between people. The rise and rulership of self-interest would result in an equally proportional fall and death of social collectivism. Socrates argues that self-interest is dividing and is not beneficial for the community - it does nothing other than fragment it. However, with our sufficient understanding of Marxism, we can point another similarity between it and Platonism: not just the idea of a theoretically perfect world, but also their agreement on having anti-Thrasymachus stance.

Platonism states that morality, like justice, has a concrete definition and is entwined in the concept of *dikniosyné*. We can offer an interesting critique to this concept of morality. "Good" and "bad" are wildly difficult to define, as their definitions vary throughout time and from one culture to another. What is honorable in one period of history may be considered a taboo in another; what is once noble can eventually become improper. We can theorize that the belief in a 'moral' and 'just' person or system is both unwarranted and unobtainable: morality is a product of one's historical moment, physical environment, and ancestral bias. It is a learned condition; morality is something that is taught by a culture to its own subsequent generations in order to perpetuate its own existence. Professor Thomas Docherty, a prominent professor at the British University of Warwick who specializes in both Marxist and post-modern theory, eloquently describes the power of history to define morality when he states:

> *"Writers do not write in a vacuum: writers are always located in history,and in a specific historical conjuncture or position. They are, quite simply, situated, and their situation determined what it is possible for them to think ... The texts which these authors write, we Marxists would say, are thus determined ... by their*

social and historical moment of their production"[19]

Cultural relativity prevents morality from having a true, objective definition, and makes it inappropriate to consider when trying to discern a universally applicable and 'just' political system. We can conclude that Plato only speaks of morality in a way that he has been conditioned to at his point in history, and, in our critique of *Republic*, we can point out that any attempt he makes to insert morality (or base his definition of 'justice' on it) is inherently flawed and cannot stand up to the test of time. A political system that is rooted in a concept that changes with the rise and fall of new historical epochs is not one that will last or function.

Yet let let us leave these investigations for another day. We now have a basic foundation on which to continue our Marxian critique of Plato: of both the superstructure and the base, how the *Republic*'s structuralism exacerbates class antagonisms, how self-interest fragments society, and why morality should potentially be dissociated from the definition of 'justice'. A basic premise of our argument is that the social classes in Greek in Plato's time stood in opposition to one another, and many ideas in the *Republic* make that opposition all the more stark and hostile. A component of this thesis that we must also consider is how the bourgeoisie would retain power if Plato's *Republic* was to actualize itself and become a legitimate government. Would the bourgeoisie be able to retain their power if their domination is legitimized into an actual government? Would such a system be as ideal as Plato believes, or would it fall prey to many of the problems that we have seen? Platonists argue that there would be no such class antagonisms because everyone would willingly and joyfully engage in their occupation due to their *techné* and a desire to hold true to the concept of living a 'just' life. They dismiss the entire idea of

---

[19] This excerpt from Professor Docherty's lecture "*Marxism*" was given at the University of Warwick on December 11, 2008. It can be found online and downloaded from the University's website free of charge.

classism by stating that class rank is inherent and natural, and not the result of any form of exploitative gain.

Censoring the stories of the previous generations to show civil society and not war is a means of re-writing history. There are few, other than perhaps the most ardent imperialists or expansionists, that would say that war is a desirable thing[20]. However, it is part of history, and one must study and understand history lest it be repeated. Erasing any part of history, no matter how undesirable, is wrong, Marxism would argue; selectively choosing what parts of the past to teach and reject will only breed ignorance, not a 'just' utopia. We should encourage the understanding of war so as to better ourselves as a people and avoid it, rather than forget it.

We should also take a moment and look around us: how many of the objects around us are artistic? The answer is, quite simply, everything. Someone had to conceptualize the form of an item and work to make it aesthetically appealing. A certain degree of self-expression, imagination, and creativity went into the construction of everything that we know[21]. Encouraging people to only create what is "good" promotes a certain mindset, and the wide-spread distribution of that art will cause many people to adopt that mindset, too. The *nomenklatura*[22] of the

---

[20] Many strands of Marxism view war as a large-scale competition between the bourgeoisie for control of territory, resources, and property, This begs the question: is the reason that the Athenian bourgeoisie want violent war to erased from the history books because it would prevent the proletariat from recognizing the extent of their power and rule, and to keep such class antagonisms hidden?

[21] Just because something is creative does not mean that it is useful and contain use-value. Marx defines use-value in *Das Kapital, Kritik der politischen Ökonomie* (abbreviated as *Das Kapital* or *Capital*) as fulfilling some practical purpose. With this definition, the use-value of art can be brought into question.

[22] That is, the apparatchik and other bureaucratic élite in the Communist Party that became the *de facto* ruling bourgeoisie under Stalinist rule.

Soviet Union[23] encouraged the Stalinist cult of personality, and all the art of the previous system (that is, the Tsarist) was swept away and replaced with pro-Bolshevik artwork. Art, media, and advertisement has become a key tool used under authoritarian regimes. This can be exemplified by Hitler's Reich Ministry of Public Enlightenment and Propaganda, which oversaw literature, music, the visual arts, and theatre. Control of art is a way to subtly control thought: Plato's theory of selectively enforcing "good" art is classist propaganda. Is this a recurring trend, this argument of classism? Indeed, it seems to be a key one that Marx would make.

The *Republic* makes a startling point when it says that in order for their to be gain, there must be war and expansionism. The extrapolation that war requires the Guardians and that the Guardians require an ontological division of labor and applied philosophy is what leads Socrates to present the "four virtues" and what constitutes his beliefs. Let us examine this more closely, however, because Socrate's definition of 'justice' - located nearly half-way into *Republic* - is the key theme in the book, and something that we must address.

Plato's *Republic* depicts an ordered, structured, and harmonious society; when viewed through a Marxian lens, though, we can see it for what it could truly be argued to be: a fully class-based system, with the bourgeoisie using Athenian-era ideology to justify their powerful status and prevent the populace (that is, the proletariat) from climbing the social latter and challenging their position. The concepts of morality, metals in one's soul, rule of the strong, and the Platonic pyramid can all be examples of this ideology. As all of this is occurring in a pre-capitalist society, formal means of production and more evolved relations of production have yet to come about. But this

---

[23] It is plain to those who are well-versed in socialist and communist theory that the Soviet Union did not subscribe to either philosophy. A point made by American democratic socialist Michael Harrington as to why it was not is because its economy did not pass through capitalism; that is, its attempted jump from agrarian feudalism to socialism skipped industrialization, modernity, and the ability to overcome scarcity. He referred to it as "bureaucratic collectivism".

situation, this historical moment of Athenian pre-capitalism, makes a heavy assumption that innate traits are what defines individuals. The unskilled, the slaves, the non-intellectuals, the handicapped, and the unproductive people who lack a *techné* would be considered unimportant and insignificant members of society. They would be easily brushed to the side and exploited by those who *do* have a productive *techné* , and this thinking that people's inherent worth and class is determined by what they can do might suggest that it is the foreshadowing of a sophisticated means of production and exploitative relations of production.

In essence, the Platonic view of 'justice' might be the precursor to a complex bourgeois-proletarian dynamic and lead to a starker, more Marxian definition of the classes.

Allowing the base of either the State's Platonic pyramid or the self's 'unjust' and considered to be an 'un-life'. Having either of the pyramids inverted and their rulership transposed is disorderly and wrong.

Yet while we have now pointed out the follies of Platonism, it is time that we recognize our own shortcomings. Even through our Marxian lens, we can see that there are parts of our theses that could be debated. Just as we have argued against the absolutism in Plato's theories, we must acknowledge our own. The chief problem that lies within Marxism is also its greatest strength: its ability to criticize. While it has given powerful critiques against the bourgeois-proletarian relation, morality, the rule of the strong, self-sufficiency, and Plato's final definition of 'justice', that seems to be all that Marxism is able to do. It can rhetorically denounce something, but it does not often give an alternative proposition to put in that thing's place. It does identify definitive socio-economic trends throughout history, but can not absolutely define where that arc will eventually end; it promotes a dialectic of inevitable communist transformation, but is supremely vague on that society's actual structure and implementation; and it overlooks the creativity and individuality of each person in its relentless determinism.

This is often the flaw that is pointed out in Marxian theory by its opponents: that it can only destroy and not build, and that it can only critique and analyze a system rather than propose a legitimized, functional one. Is our fate, then, simply to denounce Plato's theory of 'justice' without proposing an alternative? Are we, as Marxists, simply limited to analyzing the Platonic supposition without offering our own?

We have, up until this point, been regarding the *Republic* through the eyes of a classical Marxist, with our lens situated the same as Marx himself had his at his historical moment in time. We have been trying to view Plato through the perception of an 1800's German philosopher, who's own ideology was still blooming and had yet to encounter any definitive attempt at being put into practice. Yet, in order to fully propose a Marxian alternative to Plato's 'justice', it is necessary that we alter our viewing ever so slightly. For the time being, it is necessary that we tint the frame of our lens with a certain 'post-Marx' version of Marxism; that is, *analytical Marxism*, a synthesis of logic-based philosophical study and late-1900 Stalinist-influenced Marxism[24]. Agreed by many self-identified analytical Marxists to have been codified in the late 1970s by Gerry Cohen's book *Karl Marx's Theory of History: A Defense,* it became a prominent school of thought amongst English philosophers and social scientists shortly thereafter.

If we, as classical Marxists, were to attempt to define 'justice', we would most likely scorn it instead, calling it a bourgeois-ideological construct to justify exploitation and maintain the class-based system. It would be impossible, we would argue, to objectively define 'justice' because it cannot be seen as independent form any historical moment or conjuncture, or from the other sociological questions at a moment in history. However, if we were to adopt the mindset of an analytical Marxist instead in an attempt to offer a solid, objective, and concrete definition (as it often attempts to reify many philosophical concepts), we would dramatically shift our

---

[24] To be clear: analytical Marxism does not advocate Stalinism. There are indeed Stalinist tendencies in it, as the dominant strand of Marxist thought at that point in time of its founding was intimately connected with the Bolshevik-Leninism of Soviet Russia, but it still holds true to many of the liberating ideals that classical Marxism does. It is highly logical, and focuses on the objective reality of the individual and State.

argument. 'Justice' has, we would say, a definitive connection with egalitarianism, free of bourgeois coercion; this means an engagement with both political and moral philosophy so as to demonstrate the profound injustice of the political economy, and the need to construct a more appropriate egalitarian metric in its place.

Analytical Marxism would argue that 'justice' would be freedom from exploitation and control. Thus we see that it - with its social mobility, freedom to choose an occupation or art, fair economic system, and advocacy for equality - runs in direct opposition to the Platonic pyramids that we studied earlier. Which, then, is truly 'just' - a system based on social rank, or social mobility? A freely chosen occupation, or an innate, *techné*-based one? An absolute and unwavering definition of morality, the soul, and society, or one that is completely self-interpreted and existential?

These two philosophies appear to be in constant opposition to one another and are irreconcilable. Which are we to pick? The structuralist 'justice' of Plato, or the liberating 'justice' of Marxism? Should we simply say that the former is profoundly flawed and the latter is not? After all, how 'just' can a society be when that 'justice', by definition, involves a class-based system and and hierarchical control? How can its unwavering absolutism compare to the unconditional emancipation from all forms of coercive structuralism? How can one objectively say that Platonic 'justice' is superior to Marxist 'justice', when the later is an explicit advocate for freedom?

But then, conversely, why would one want to subscribe to a definition of 'justice' that holds such a profoundly negative view of society and has an aggressive stance that pits Athenian against Athenian on the basis of class? Why should we state that Marxism more accurately defines 'justice' when it so pessimistically looks at any provided alternative, and there is plenty of room for its own criticism?

It seems that, even though we have moved from the ideas of Cephalus, Polemarchus, Thrasymachus, and Glaucon to that of Socrates and then criticized him via Marx, Socrates' definition seems to have a stronger foundation on which to rest.

Is this surprising? Not truly. Socrates' dialogues have proven to be so profound and enlightening that - even thousands of years later - they are still regarded in awe.

Perhaps we can see that our Marxian lens has not given us the clarity necessary to critique Plato's *Republic*. Perhaps we are not any closer to understanding 'justice' than we were when we began this journey, and, rather having learned the answer to the question, perhaps we have merely learned how to ask the question in new ways. Marxism and Platonism may hold differing worldviews and using each as a filter through which to see the world may only highlight issues rather than solve them. Understanding such a concept as 'justice' is not something that will ever truly be completed by a single text or author, and neither Plato nor Marx are able to provide a universal definition that is without any criticism. It seems that, now that our Marxian examination is complete, that we will have to begin anew and approach the question from a new angle. Perhaps with a deeper understanding of history's philosophers and their ideas will give us the opportunity to articulate and discuss the definition of 'justice'. For now, though, we must conclude that our primary thesis of the validity of Platonic justice has been proven to be, at least to a degree, correct.

Socialist Economics: the Cure for Cap

Although Karl Marx gives a dan
capitalist mode of production[25] in his m
Manifesto of the Communist Party, he actua..,
numerous commentaries regarding the contradictions .
inhumane aspects of capitalism. Many of these were articulated
in his *magnum opus Das Kapital*, wherein he defined capitalism
wherein there are "an immense accumulation of commodities",
and studying the economic system "must begin with the analysis
of a commodity". Others, such as the *Economic and Philosophic
Manuscripts of 1844*, contain a series of essays that lay the
groundwork for much of his larger writings. In *Estranged
Labour*, Marx effectively counters the insult that is too often
thrown at him: that is is just as dehumanizing as the bourgeoisie
themselves - that while they turn man into a commodity with
quantifiable financial value, Marx does the same in discussing
'the proletariat'. He effectively uses sight of humanity, some
argue, and begin to see men and women as concepts rather than
flesh and blood. *Estranged Labour*, however, argues against this
and is one of the few times that the wall of harshly anti-capitalist
rhetoric is dropped and the humanitarian, caring Marx is seen.

Marx posits that there are four modes of estrangement -
although, one could make the very plausible argument[26] that
there is only one form of estrangement (that is, estrangement
itself) and there are simply different manifestations of it that
become apparent in different settings and at different times.
Estrangement represents alienation: a sense of disconnect from
one's environment that is brought about by the economic
climate; specifically, capitalism. The four modes that he puts
forth are *product estrangement, process estrangement, species-
being estrangement,* and *estrangement of man from man*, and
each has a distinct and powerful impact on the role of man in

---

[25] I make the assumption that the reader has sufficient understanding of Marxist theory to read this paper.

[26] I agree with this argument quite strongly.

pitalism. Indeed, man is ultimately reduced to the status of the commodity that Marx so readily attempts to understand.

When asked what legacy one would like to leave behind, man[27] will quite often say a child, something that will be fondly remembered by other men, or some great accomplishment that will give him a semblance of being remembered after he is gone. Marx describes this when it was stated that "my creative energies objectify myself in nature" and "I congeal myself": to bring into physical manifestation something that, out of one's imagination and personal labour, physicalizes that desired legacy for others to see and experience. However, man is estranged, as his work does not lead to such fruition. Instead, it leads to the creation of a commodity that is utilized by, and profited for, his superior; he is trapped in and endless cycle of working so as to live, and living so as to work, and so on. This - the source of food, shelter, clothing, and the means of actualization of such - prevents man from creating what is necessary to live and leave behind a piece of himself.

Process estrangement can be sufficiently summed up in the statement that labour has been altered by the economic system so that it is no longer satisfying in and of itself, but rather a means to satisfaction. This is illustrated in that one works so as to accumulate capital[28] so as to be able to afford to engage in an activity that will bring a modicum of satisfaction to one's labour-centered life.

The estrangement that a man feels as a result of *species-being*[29] *estrangement* is more abstract than the previous two: because of the development of the means of production - which

---

[27] From this point on, I will use the term 'man' to refer to both 'man' and 'woman'. It is being used in the place of 'mankind'.

[28] That is, currency, money, and the means used in a society with which to exchange one product for another. In *Das Kapital*, Marx describes capital as M in the equation C = M = C, wherein a commodity (C) is sold for money (M), which is then used to purchase a new commodity (C). It exists simply as a medium of exchange.

[29] Derived from German, also means "essence" or "nature".

have only existed only in a sophisticated form since the emergence of capitalism from the ashes of feudalism, wherein the caste-based system evolved into a class-based one - man cannot hand down humanity to man. That is, the commodification that is characteristic of capitalism has dehumanized man to such an extent that he is no longer able to sufficiently relate to the rest of the peoples in the world, and he cannot have a fully emotional connection with others.

Capitalism has placed an impenetrable barrier between one human and the rest - as teacher cannot properly show affection and genuine, human sympathy for others in the class at their time of need, the constitution of the system has established a short of bubble around each person, alienating them each other by constructing so called "professional behavior" and "work-space ethics" that, in the end, only perpetuate the system itself when carried out.

This view of other human beings as productive objects[30] effectively leads to the fourth and final form of estrangement - the *estrangement of man from man*. This alienation could be what conservative and libertarian philosophers colloquially refer to as the "profit motive", wherein competition between individuals forces each person to engage in an unspoken war with one another, fighting for limited and finite resources[31]. There is an almost perceptible, but not quite fully tangible, sense of animalistic competition between humans in this regard.

Even without knowing someone else, being estranged from others creates an unconscious desire that they fail so as to ensure there is one person who is able to gain at the loss of others.

---

[30] What Marx refers to as the "forces of production", or the ones who engage in labour with the means of production.

[31] Although, capitalism is described by Marx as being necessary before one reaches socialism (and eventually, communism) because the capitalist mode of production is capable of generating such a high number of commodities that scarcity will be effectively overcome and "no one will go wanting".

This is one of the greatest problems that I have with capitalism: the concept that, in order for one person to gain and move ahead, it has to be done at the detriment of others. I simply have a hard time understanding why one would support and advocate for - let alone even tolerate - a system whose very foundation is the alienation of one human being from another, the splitting up of mankind into groups whose sole glue that holds them together is their distrust and ill will towards *other* groups. I cannot conceive what kind of human being would willingly chose to spend their time and energy perpetuating such a harsh, dehumanizing system instead of looking for, and indeed, fighting for, a much more humane alternative.

It is very logical to argue that the four modes of estrangement that Marx puts forth are simply one; rather than assume that there are four, it makes more sense to group them as a single form ("estrangement") that readily leaps forth from a single source ("capitalism"). As supportive of Derrida's deconstructionism[32] as I am, I do not think that it is necessary to break down estrangement any farther than this. Doing so only over-complicates the discussion and, when discussing something as elaborate and sectarian as Marxism, increasing the degree of complicity in the conversation does little good.

Perhaps the best way to go about constructing a system wherein estrangement no longer a factor would be to move past capitalism and construct an economy with profound socialist tendencies: namely, through economic democracy. The working class should own the means of production so as to reduce a modicum of the estrangement that is a result of bourgeois ownership. When Noam Chomsky famously declared that capitalism is a "faceless tyranny", he eloquently hit the nail on the head by illustrating it; the corporatist system that masquerades as the 'free market' needs to have its economic

---

[32] That is, Jaques Derrida, the post-modern French philosopher that was active in the later half of the twentieth century. He is credited with developing the critical theory known as deconstruction, which, while applied to political philosophy, is more commonly associated with literary theory.

control wrestled form it and transferred to those who actively engage in the day-to-day labour.

Marx makes a very compelling case for the existence of alienation as a result of the capitalist workplace; indeed, such estrangement is a symptom of how diseased the system truly is, and why it needs to be ripped up by the roots and replaced with something else that, instead of glorifying the 'job creators' that are the criminal bourgeoisie and turning members of the working class against each other by telling them that *others* are the problem, places the infinite preciousness of every human being before any economic action. I am not making a revolutionary call to arms - no, I am simply stating that, if we truly want to tackle so many of the chronic problems that we have (including estrangement) as a result of capitalism, that we cannot focus on the symptom: we have to focus instead on the condition of which that symptom is a symptom. In this case, that would be capitalism. It is time for peoples of all color, gender, and nationality to look at the workplace and realize that estrangement is something that one must deal with: it is something that can, and has to be changed.

What is Freedom?
An Inquiry into the Possibility of Absolute Freedom

"The illusion of freedom will continue as long as it's profitable to continue the illusion. At the point where the illusion becomes too expensive to maintain, they will just take down the scenery, they will pull back the curtains, they will move the tables and chairs out of the way and you will see the brick wall at the back of the theater."
-Frank Zappa

    The definition of 'freedom' is very much an ontological question; it is something one can describe, but not define. As numerous philosophers have discovered when trying to discern the true nature of many of these difficult topics, one can go about discussing them: they can name traits that 'free' countries have, can describe revolutions and wars fought for the sake of 'freedom', and differentiate with relative ease between individuals who are 'free' and those who are not. They cannot, however, give a simple, accurate definition: when describing 'freedom', the majority of what we, as philosophers, can do is approach the issue from an ontological standpoint. It is quite difficult - if not impossible - to give a fully ontic, absolute definition.

    But let us try to confront this with the information that has been presented to us: let us try to give a fully ontic answer to the time-tested and unanswered question as to the definition of 'freedom'. Can we successfully accomplish this task when others, such as the Platonists, Aristoteleans, and the contemporary social contract theorists have all had relative difficulty in positing an unwavering definition? Let the past history not dissuade us from our task: let us attempt to answer the question as to the meaning of 'freedom' by approaching it from an entirely new angle, one that has been generally forgotten and left to the dusty pages of history.

I am speaking, of course, of the utilization of Marxist theory to aid us in our endeavor[33]. Many have disregarded Marx and his subsequent disciples as extinct, being lost in the 'proven' failure of communism by the fall of the Soviet Union. To many (particularly those on the American Right), the collapse of the USSR and the expansion of a middle class in China *vis-à-vis* economic liberalization provide evidence as to the failure of the implementation of Marxist policies, and serve as a stark example as to how Marxism is, by and large, a system of oppression and totalitarianism rather than liberation and 'freedom'. Let us move past this and ignore the historical implications of the governments who have claimed to have acted on behalf of Marx's theories, and instead focus on Marxism as a purely conceptual item.

This paper does not serve as an attempt to persuade one to subscribe to Marxist theory, nor is it trying to justify the atrocities committed in the name of its founder. There is no justification that one can give for the human rights violations attributed to the Stalin's regime in the Soviet Union, or by the Maoist guerrilla-revolutionaries in China. That is not our goal: our goal is to delve into the heart of classical Marxist theory, to the original writing of Karl Marx, and attempt to discern what form legitimate Marxian liberation would take.

The answer is, I think, not one that we would suspect. The anticipated answer to our inquiry as to the nature of 'freedom' is not a revolution: it is not a proletarian uprising wherein the working class revolts against its bourgeois oppressors to liberate itself from the exploitative chains of capitalism. This would simply change the political economy, changing the means of production from being capitalist to being socialist instead. We do

---

[33] As much as I disagree with much of Adam Smith (mainly, for being a theorist for the contemporary capitalist mode of production), his argument towards the 'deliberalization of the soul' and the 'narrowing of mental faculties' very much applies to me: as a firm Marxist, much of what I see is unconsciously through a Marxian lens.

not want to change the base[34]: we want to bring about a dramatic, liberating altercation of such magnitude that we could consider everyone[35] to be 'free'.

I submit to you that the truest definition of 'freedom' that we can possibly conceive would be the separation of the superstructure from the base[36]: the removal of the political economy so that it does not act as an economic determinist that dictates the makeup and function of all aspects of society. A society whose cultural fabric is constituted by something other than productive forces, material distribution, exchange-value and use-value, and rampant commodification is one wherein people would be able to existentially imbue the subjects around them with relative value, as opposed to a value dictated by the political economy.

We can to postulate that 'freedom' is allowing one to chose the course of one's life without a form of economic determinism, and that - while this 'freedom' is not absolute or even possibly attainable - that it is indeed plausible to move along a gradient to a reality that is *more* 'freer'.

We cannot eliminate the political economy's influence: we can only reduce it. Indeed, the base has considerable power in forming the superstructure. Think of the many ways that it has determined things that we would consider non-economic: religion (by establishing for-profit fronts, governmental lobbying, and utilizing Lutheran theology so as to reinforce

---

[34] I use the terms 'base' and 'political economy' interchangeably, as Marx does. He simply refers to the political economy as the base to linguistically illustrate that it is the foundation of the superstructure.

[35] An all-inclusive and universal 'freedom', rather than a proletarian 'freedom'. When I say 'freedom', I mean a 'freedom' that applies to everyone, not a specific, oppressed demographic.

[36] I make the assumption that the reader is sufficiently familiar with Marx's base-superstructure theory. It's text can be found in the preface of Marx's *A Contribution to the Critique of Political Economy*.

productivity[37]), art (by cutting away at its place in society by declaring to be non-productive and having no immediate economic value), and the family (by having "reduced the family relation to a mere money relation"[38]).

However, at this point, we must ask ourselves an important question. We are agreed that the capitalist mode of production that is the current base is a very strong influence on the value and worth of all things in society[39], but is it possible to truly separate that base from the superstructure? Can one exist without the other, or are they required to live together in a mutually symbiotic relationship that gives each other meaning?

One could argue that something can *only* have being and meaning so long as there is something that is equally opposed

---

[37] I do no think that Max Weber accurately portrays Protestantism in his book *The Protestant Work Ethic and the Spirit of Capitalism*. I believe that religion is independent of a particular mode of production; however, established and institutional religion, such as the Catholic Church, has very much turned it into a business and commodified something that, instead, should remain priceless. In the *Manifesto*, Marx argues that capitalism "has converted ... the priest ... into its paid wage-labourer" and that "all that is holy is profaned". There is a difference between institutionalized religion and a personal, spiritual religion, which is a distinction that I do not think he articulates.

[38] Marx, the *Manifesto*. He argues that the capitalist means of production and their owns have "torn away the sentimental veil" of the family. Indeed, the fact that many marry for health insurance, immigration purposes, and financial benefits illustrates this. Some strands of feminism view the family as the fundamental unit of capitalism, rather than the means of production.

[39] Exemplified in the commodification of *human beings* under capitalism. The concept that a human's inherent worth is intimately tied to their productive value and material contribution to society reminds one of this famous quote spoken by Gillian Tett:
"Most societies have an elite, and the elite try to stay in power - and the way that they stay in power is not merely by controlling the means of production, to be Marxist - i.e., controlling the money - but by controlling the cognitive map: how we think."
The altercation of our perception regarding human value illustrates the profoundly deep hold that the capitalist mode of production holds over the citizenry's psyche.

and is polar opposite to it so as to give it definition. Black is black, and white is white because it lacks black; one cannot exist without the other, as they each represent the starkest opposites. Their being defines each other's being.

Does the base have to exist to give the superstructure meaning, and, inversely, does the superstructure have to exist so as to give the base definition? Are they each required to give each other being, or can one possibly exist without the other?

This is a very important question that we must ask ourselves, because the nature of existence is something that is very fundamental to our inquiry as to the nature of 'freedom'. We could take the traditionally Sartrean stance that existence precedes essence, and that one could possibly exist without needing the other to grant it definition; just because something is in existence does not mean that it has to be imbued with any significant or clarifying essence. Something that is can simply be - it is arguably possible to have either the base or the superstructure but not the other, as it does not need its opposite component to give it essence because its existence is not dictated by whether or not it has any essence to begin with.

It seems that we are at a crossroads, then. Which path should we take? The one that says that these two pieces cannot exist without each other, or that they can exist completely independently of their symbiotic essence-definition?

If we were to argue the first, then we would say that the base and superstructure need to be connected to give each other meaning. Yet if we cannot remove the base, is it possible for us to change it? Marx argues that it is. The capitalist mode of production could be modified so as to become a socialist[40] or

---

[40] Marxian socialism; after the proletarian revolution, of course, granted that the society in question has the productive forces necessary to overcome the problems of economic scarcity. I do not consider the bureaucratic collectivism induced by a Leninist group surgically inserting itself into the motor of history to encourage the revolution, and then assuming a 'dictatorship of the Party' so as to forcibly push the nation into modernity, to be socialism in any sense of the word.

even communist[41] one, but it will still be the supporting foundation of the superstructure. It may change[42], but its position stays constant; we may obtain a post-capitalist base, but it will still act as an influencing political economy of sorts.

Changing the base does not correlate with 'freedom' in an absolute sense of the word: it does not liberate one from its economically determining effects, but merely changes the type of influence that is there. Yes, it does remove the human commodification and production-oriented mindset that is characteristic of capitalism, but it replaces it with a use-value and collective-oriented one. Our inquiry is not to find an 'alternative' form of 'freedom', which is based exclusively on the absence of capitalism. We cannot declare this to be our final point: we cannot say the transition to a socialist mode of production (or any one that is post-capitalist) would be simply enough - it is not a true, absolute definition of 'freedom'.

The movement away from capitalism would be a purely relative and specific[43] 'freedom', and that is not our goal. We need to describe as pure and absolute a 'freedom' as possible.

It is plausible to continue this argument by stating that the two cannot exist without the other: that the superstructure exists because it is both defined by and supported by the base, regardless of whether it takes a capitalist or post-capitalist form. The state of the means of production are the most determining

---

[41] That is, the post-dictatorship of the proletariat 'withering away of the state'.

[42] On a side note, I side with Eduard Bernstein (the founder of revisionist Marxism and the intellectual father of my socialist identity) in his argument that a 'society built in blood cannot stand'. His argument that socialism should be brought about through reformism and *evolution* as opposed to *revolution* is something that strikes me strongly.

[43] 'Relative' in that the ardent Ayn Rand-worshipping Objectivists and others would disagree; 'specific' in that it does not remove the base, merely changes it. This changing, though, has far-reaching consequences, if one takes a country's full productive capacity and citizens' mindsets into consideration.

force of the makeup of the superstructure - if they are taken away, there is so little left in the material world that is not economically determined that it would not be given sufficient definition to exist. By this extrapolation we can say that the only reason that the superstructure exists is *because* the base is there: it is truly needed to bring the superstructure, as a whole, into being. So will our changing of the means of production from capitalist to post-capitalist make one 'free' in the absolute sense, or simply make one 'freer'?

The answer, unfortunately, is the latter. Altering the means of production so that they are no longer capitalist will indeed bring about a fundamental transformation in society, but it will not bring about as fundamental a change in the nature of freedom as we wish.

The realization that changing the means of production will not bring about what we desire means that we must continue on to our second postulation: that we must discuss[44] the constitution that society would have if they were. What would that look like? What would a world wherein the economy is no longer a determining factor appear to be? The entire conceptualization that we - as human beings, born and raised into a capitalist society with the veil of bourgeois ideology still acting as wool over our eyes - have about culture, religion, fashion, technology, and so many other pieces of the superstructure involves them being tied intimately to money.

What could our culture look like, if we removed the political economy? Would consumerism still be as rampant as it is now? Would religion still have organized institutions that construct for-profit fronts and engage in political lobbying? Would any of the things that we recognize as constituting our society still be the same, or would their be a transformation that

---

[44] Theoretically discuss, that is. We have stated that it is impossible to truly separate the base and superstructure, but let us wonder what reality would look like *if they were*. Thus we move past reality into the conceptualization of the nature of a perfect reality. This is very reminiscent of Plato theorizing the perfect form of 'justice'.

is so fundamental that it would bring about an unrecognizable change?

We cannot say that it would not; the separation of the base from the superstructure would indeed bring about an unrecognizable change.

I do not mean simply dissociating the two, separating them so that a gap of space lies between them and so that they do not connect: I am referring to the *removal* of the base so it no longer lies in existence, a complete erasure of it so that it no longer has any being.

What would be the determining factor that would dictate the behavior and constitution of the superstructure, if there was no base? What would give it definition and supply it meaning? The answer, I think, is far simpler than one would expect it to be: ourselves. The granting of an existential value to all things - the imbuing of everything with the use-value and exchange-value that we perceive to be socially necessary, rather than economically necessary - would grant mankind the freedom to construct whatever sort of reality that he or she wishes.

Now, it is quite logical to argue against this and say that a supremely subjective, self-constructed reality would be impossible: if everyone was to give everything different value and meaning, and view the world differently, than there would be so many conflicting worldviews that people would not be able to integrate seamlessly into a society. There would be too much friction between everyone, as every person would be the most ardent of subjectivists.

I posit this against that argument: that a truly subjective reality with an existential superstructure would have numerous people with fairly similar conceptions of reality. These people would be able to group together into loosely-associating serial collectives that, when becoming large enough, create a *de facto* society. The grouping of like-minded subjectivists would create a complex system with identity politics, interest groups, and ideological communities - in short, subjectivism would eventually result in the creation of a dynamic political system. This system, free of the base, would be able to be run by the will and views of the *people* rather than the invisible hand of the capitalist marketplace[45].

This would leave every person as an existentialist, as the supreme arbiter in the meaning and value of his or her own life, and able to live their life by their own choosing rather than by the dictations of economic trends.

However, we must return from our state of conceptualization to that of reality: because we acknowledge that we cannot possibly separate the base and superstructure and can only do so in theory, we must tackle the question of how 'free' one can become by moving along the aforementioned gradient of being 'freer'. One is either 'free' when the two are separated or not when they are together. To move along that gradient, we must do two things, each of which we will discuss in turn: recognize that we are not 'free', but work to be so.

By the first, I mean this - that we realize that the capitalist mode of production has utterly commodified everything, establishing a dehumanizing and for-profit system wherein everything that does not have immediate productive use or capacity is callously thrown to the wayside. We have to realize that it prevents us from truly being 'free', and from exercising whatever 'freedom' we desire because our own wishes have been conditioned by, and supplanted with, economically determined ones whose fulfillment would only lead to the perpetuation of the system itself. We must recognize that we are not 'free' because the base and superstructure are inseparably linked and that they cannot be separated. So does our journey end in hopelessness? Does it end with the final realization that we cannot be 'free', and that 'freedom' is simply an over-romanticized concept rather than a real?

---

[45] The existence of a marketplace is not inherently bad: there are many strains of socialism that include a market that is subject to regulation and strict boundaries to prevent the cyclical depressions that are typical of the capitalist business cycle. An example of this 'market socialism' could be the single-payer healthcare system of Canada: using public, tax-funded revenue to supply all citizens with universal health insurance, but leaving the hospitals and healthcare-providers privately owned so that they have to compete for the government's service.

Perhaps: it ends with the recognition of what reality is, and how we are always going to be determined - to some degree and to some variance - by the base. So an understanding of this is the first step towards liberation.

The second seems profoundly contradictory at first glance - how can one work towards 'freedom' when we have so blatantly stated that an absolute 'freedom' is not completely obtainable? The answer, though, is simpler than what we might expect. By being 'freer', I mean taking the next step past the realization that the base and superstructure are irreversibly joined by doing one's best to strain the link between the two until the breaking point by rejecting consumerist conditioning.

We cannot adopt this fully, however. We cannot make the sudden jump from being influenced by the base and not being 'free' to suddenly 'free' and independent of the means of production simply because we will it. One cannot make such a rapid and dramatic transition simply because one wants to.

The best that we can do to be 'free' is to recognize the for-profit system that exists around us and work to do what we can in a non-profit way - by placing consumerism to the side and acting out of altruism, by doing what is right *because* it is right, not because an external force is dictating that we should. We cannot pull the base and superstructure apart: but we can do our best to act as if the former was not there, or as if it was not connected to the latter.

This, in the end, is the highest form of freedom: the will to be independent of the political economy, to reject it and all of its modes as a form of psychological and behavioral determinism, and to do what one can out of a genuine sense of selfless altruism. Does this take any higher, cosmic order to incentive into consideration when discussing this 'freedom'? No, it does not. The 'freedom' that we are discussing is purely of the mundane, material variety: a 'freedom' that is rooted in the here-and-now and the immediate, physical world.

Yet if there is no cosmic drive behind doing what it takes to be 'free', than why push for that 'freedom' anyway? The answer is very simple: for the sake of 'freedom' itself. One works towards 'freedom', regardless of how far along that gradient one can move, because, by doing so, one *becomes* freer. One needs to pursue that goal of being 'freer' for sake of incrementally working towards an ever-freer state of being.

There are many - particularly, the classical liberal and libertarian philosophers - who would romantically invoke images of a harmonious state of nature, independent of the strong arm of the central government wherein self-determinism is the supreme dictator of all action, to try to illustrate their own opinion as to what 'freedom' is. They ignore the impact that the political economy has on the superstructure, and hold fast to an outdated, colonial definition of 'freedom' that is rooted in a time period wherein the world had not fully entered modernity. It simply strikes me as interesting that many white, privileged, educated, middle-class[46] Americans who identify as 'libertarian' believe they they, in their mightily fortunate situation, believe that they understand 'liberty' and 'freedom' in the truest sense of the word. Who are they, waiting expectantly for a continuous, never-ending stream of luxurious products constructed from the exploited labor of Third World slaves, to claim that they understand 'freedom'? It is a gross insult to *all* freedom that they do so. Libertarians are only able to advocate 'freedom' in that they are free of the labor necessary to survive; the people who believe that they are fully self-sufficient have anesthetized themselves to the plight of those whose sweat constructed the affluent nation in which they sit. I have no desire to present a disagreement with libertarianism through a Maoist lens, wherein the bourgeois-proletarian dynamic has been replaced with those

---

[46] I use the phrase *middle-class* loosely. It is entirely plausible to argue that there is no middle class anywhere in the world, in that the capitalist bourgeoisie, under the protective aegis of the 'banking sector' (which, in reality, is little more than a central committee to manage the financial affairs of the transnational bourgeois), has spun an elaborate illusion of the existence of one. The introduction of payment plans, credit, deficit spending, loans, and other means of 'stretching one's money out' give the working proletarian the illusion that he has more money than he does in reality; this illusion that one is not truly in poverty prevents a proletarian uprising, because the proletariat *do not realize* that they are proletariat.

of the exploitative First World and exploited Third World, respectively; one must realize, though, that it is only the ruling class that preaches the doctrine of 'freedom' so as to create a false state of consciousness over the masses. If the masses think that they are 'free', then they will not revolt against the system: the political system has a vested interest in its people believing that they are free so that it can perpetuate itself.

Can any of us even discuss 'freedom', though? We could very easily argue that language is just as oppressive as any dictatorial government: that, try as we may to describe and articulate 'freedom', our words will get in the way of what we are trying to say. That is, the whole issue of "what I meant to say, not what I did actually say" presents itself rather effectively - our limited vocabulary and rudimentary understanding of the linguistic origins of each of the words that we use prevent us from efficiently articulating what is truly on our mind. The only way to transmit our perception of 'freedom' to another would be to do so without language, to somehow project the meaning through space without speaking. But then, does Smith not argue that speech results in trunk, barter, and exchange, which then results in a division of labor? So, can we follow this train of thought and say that the oppressive nature of language eventually grows into an oppressive and commodifying political economy? Making that argument is certainly plausible, but it is not our goal[47].

There are probably many critiques that Plato and Aristotle, Luther, Rousseau, and even Marx himself would give to our base-superstructure theory; as it is only partially articulated and has not stood up to rigorous critique, there are certainly many points in it which can be addressed and argued as wrong or not fully explained. However, we must look at the question of "what is freedom?" the same way that we do with so many others that can be seen in the aforementioned philosophers' writings: the definitions of 'freedom', 'justice', 'reality' need to be continuously asked and are so very ontological that, in the end,

---

[47] Foucault eloquently discusses this and is known for his controversial aphorisms, one of which is that "language is oppression".

we may not have come to a sufficient conclusion. Our journey for an ontic and absolute definition of 'freedom' has ended in a conceptualization rather than a reality, and we have acknowledged that, despite all of the work and effort that we put into defining 'freedom', that we cannot possibly reach it regardless of the net altruism that flows forth from us to the world. In the end, though, we have have relatively solid conclusion of what 'freedom' is and how to become 'freer' than before: to be 'free', we must recognize that we are not, and do what we can, individually, to reject the political economy.

State and Polity:
Man and His Relation to the Political Ultimate

Depending upon both the historical moment and material conditions that one lives in, one may view the Ultimate - that is, the cosmic meta-narrative that justifies of how a given society is structured - different than someone else. The given economic conditions in which one operates has a profound effect on the one's political and sociologic development; some have taken this a step further and proposed a type of radical economic determinism, wherein all sociology is reduced to being the public reflection of a hegemonic mode of production. Although this interpretation of base-and-superstructure theory is vulgar and reductionist, there is a modicum of truth to it. Social relations are significantly determined by economic conditions, perhaps more so than by anything else[48].

Modes of production are characterized by the relationship that humans have to the means of production (and contingently, with each other as a result) that exist at that point in time, and that relationship dictates those conditions' location in the overall historical dialectic. Because Marxian class has yet to be abolished via socialist revolution, the existing (and predeceasing) classes are in a state of violent sociologic conflict and have competing economic interests. Leninist theory argues that the hegemonic organ that arises out of these class conflicts to facilitate the perpetuated supremacy of one class over the other(s) is referred to as the State in Marxist discourse.

---

[48] But the relation is dialectic: just as the base can exert structural change in the superstructure, so too can the superstructure exert changes on the base, to a degree. However, any fundamental change from one mode of production to another is most likely going to have to be brought about by a revolutionary re-orientation of the economy, not by simple social progressivism.

In Sophocles' tragedy *Antigone*, Kreon [49] makes the emphatic declaration "Gentlemen, the state!". By doing so, he asserts that the guiding narrative for society for society should be devotion to, and unity with, the state. Kreon declares that the Ultimate is the state in response to Antigone's assertions that familial loyalty is of greater importance. One of the key underlining themes throughout *Antigone* is man's relation to the Ultimate, and the debate as to whether that Ultimate is Kreon's state or Antigone's familial love exists as a constant undertone as the plot develops.

It is not surprising to see Sophocles penning a tragedy that contemplates the relation between man and the Ultimate, as theoretic absolutism was prominent in ancient philosophy. An example of this can be seen in the Platonic notion of the spheres[50], which exist as the theoretically pure, metaphysic embodiments of the "essence" of an object.

It is important for us to deconstruct the nature of the State in order to understand what Kreon means when he asserts that the state is the Ultimate. However, before we do so, it should be noted that there is logocentric difference between my writing of "State" and "state". I make a conscious effort to distinguish between the two while writing. The fact that one has a upper-case letter and the other does not has profound metaphysic and

---

[49] Attic Greek: Κρέων, *Kreōn,* or Creon. In Greek mythology, he was the ruler of Thebes in the legend of Oedipus, whose son Haemon is betrothed to Oedipus' daughter Antigone.

[50] In Euclidean geometry, the "world of the spheres", or the theoretic dimension whereon only Platonic spheres exist, is expressed mathematically. These spheres (despite their name) take geometric shapes that are regular, convex polyhedra. Each has the congruent faces of regular polygons, and have the same number of faces meeting at the vertices. By these standards, there are four solids: tetrahedron (pyramid), hexahedron (cube), octahedron, dodecahedron, and icosahedron.

politico-economic ramifications; a slight change in the spelling gives it a wildly different meaning[51].

Let me try to explain why I think that the "State" and the "state" are two radically different political concepts before discussing man's relation

It is not appropriate to think of the state as the dynamic, civil politic that arises out of the sociologic relations of a given community; the state is not merely the intangible social relations that unties people into a secular institution. To think of the state as a non-politicized sociologic collective is crude - I would call such a thing a polity. When Kreon famously cries "Gentlemen, the state!", he uses terminology that I consider politically inappropriate because he assumes that "the state" and "the polity" are synonymous. The truth is that they are not. There is an irreconcilable difference between the two that makes them mutually exclusive.

I put forth that so long as a State exists, the polity (that is, Kreon's "state") cannot. And so long as the polity exists, there is no State in any way, shape, or form. A polity without a State would a system of direct democracy without the hierarchical, sociologic castes associated with capitalism; it would be an anarchic experiment that would incorporate profound socio-political liberation with the socialist ethics of co-operation and solidarity. However, in order to discuss the potential existence of a polity with a State, we must first address the conditions upon which it appeared.

---

[51] I do this with several other terms. An example of this would be the fact that I refer to the aggregate non-heterosexual population as LGB't and not LGBT, if only to illustrate the radical alterity between those who are transgendered and those who are not. In the LGB't liberation movement, advocates and activists are disproportionally white, upper-class cisgendered males. Deconstructing and abolishing sexual and gender binaries are often not the goal of LGB't activists - generally, the goal is to institutionalize the movement itself, thus granting it monetary and sociologic power. It is not a genuine "liberation" movement but rather a reformist "incorporation into the establishment and capitulation to capitalist conformitivity".

At particular point in the distant anthropologic past, the vaguely egalitarian hunter-gatherer societies had an increase in population and material abundance of such proportion[52] that there became a dynamic relationship between one's sociologic position in the community and the aggregate material abundance. Of course, at this specific point in historic development, the total amount of material goods available to the rudimentary society was extraordinarily low, and net scarcity was one of the most potent stumbling blocks to societal progress. Because scarcity existed, there could be no universal abundance for everyone; it was only logical that differences in material ownership and productive contributions would develop a sociologic connotation.

The simple social position occupied by the primitive peoples that existed that that time laid the foundations for the complex social status of "haves" and "have-nots" that would arise as history progressed. Effectively, those with greater control over production would have greater social power than those that did not; in this we see the embryo of the complex political relationship between the "rich" and "poor". These primitive "have" individuals that occupied a place of sociologic and economic power, contingently, found themselves also occupying a space of profound political power as well. The two stand in diametric opposition to one another based upon their competing economic interests, and thus do we see the evolution of the modern bourgeois and proletarian classes.

Political power is nothing other than the ability to make decisions regarding the usage of finite materials in the face of net scarcity. Politics is the management of scarce resources and the sociology of economic conflict, and the State is the politicized organ through which that management if facilitated. The constituent elements that constitute the State political

---

[52] This may be attributed to the domestication of animals (wolves, etc), the development of rudimentary agriculture (which allowed fixed, non-motile villages), or a combination of the two.

Friedrich Engels puts it aptly in the 1984 6th-edition of his *magnum opus* work, *The Origin of the Family, Private Property, and the State*:

"The state is, therefore, by no means a power forced on society from without ... Rather, it is a product of society at a certain stage of development; it is the admission that this society has become so entangled in an insoluble contradiction with itself, that it has to split into irreconcilable antagonisms which it is powerless to dispel. But in order that these antagonisms, these classes with conflicting economic interests, might not consume themselves and society in fruitless struggle, it became necessary to have a Power, seeming standing above society, that would alleviate the conflict and keep it within the bounds of 'order'; and this power, arisen out of society but placing itself above it, and alienating itself more and more from it, is the State."

The State is the hegemonic organ that naturally arose as the economic "haves" historically asserted their authority over the "have-nots". It is not something that represents the collective social identity, as Kreon thinks; the complex sociologic polity that units all of the people in a given geographic area is not the state, but rather that State. The Marxian State cannot exist in concordance with Kreon's - his is a dynamic, transcendent polity-like collective that encompasses the entire society, while Engels' is a profoundly classist tool to assert economic rule.

Engels' State is above society while Kreon's state is level with society. Kreon assumes that the people together constitute the state, that the political and social relations that manifest in a given society *is* itself the state. Aristotle reaffirms this line of thinking when given the opportunity to flee in *The Apology*. To leave the polis, he argues, is to reject the civic institutions that have raised him, allowed him to grow, and provided him with education. One cannot be part of the state when it is convenient and distance one's self from it when it is not convenient; to do so, he continues, flies in the face of civil, participatory democracy. This is an example of Kreon's state: level with society because the people themselves, with their collective sociology, constitute the state in its most pure form. It sounds, if one is intellectually honest, like genuine socialism[53], and there is a great degree of philosophic similarity between Kreon's state and a communist society.

The State does not rest on the same plane as society - it hovers over it, alien, subject to a radical alterity that leaves it as a foreign, distant organ. As Engels said,

"Because the State arose from the need to hold class antagonisms in check, but because it rose, at the same time, in the midst of the conflicts of these classes, it is, as a rule, the State of the most powerful, economically dominant class, which, through the medium of the State, becomes also the politically dominant class, and thus acquires new means of holding down and exploiting the oppressed class."

Thus do we see the primary difference between the theoretic concepts of Kreon and Engels. To the former, the state is the collective polity; to the latter, the State is the facilitator of socio-economic supremacy.

It is possible, however, for a State to become a state. Just because a given society is the way that it is does not mean that it cannot be structured and politicized in a different way - and the exponential increase in technologic development, when combined with the infinite creativity of the human spirit, has opened literally infinite doors to possible ways of structuring society. A prime example of a real-world possibility is the revolutionary abolition of the State by a class-conscious proletarian movement that works to replace it with a de-politicized, egalitarian "administrator of things".

---

[53] I use the term "socialism" in the same way that Marx and Engels did: interchangeably. A philosophic justification as to the difference of the two did not rise until Lenin's seminary works *What is to be Done?* and *State and Revolution*, wherein he labeled the "lower" stage of the post-capitalist society as "socialism" and the "higher" stage as being "communism".

Engels describe the transformation of the State into depoliticized economic management system at the closing of *Socialism: Utopian and Scientific*:

"The proletariat seizes the public power and turns the means of production into State property. But, in doing this, it abolishes itself as proletariat, abolishes class distinction and class antagonisms, abolishes also the State as the State ... When, at last, it becomes the real representative of the whole of society, it renders itself unnecessary. As so as there are social class to be held in subjection; as soon as class rule and the individual struggle for existence based on our present anarchy in production, with the collisions and excesses arising from these, are removed, nothing more remains to be repressed, and a special repressive force, a State, is no longer necessary."

There are several things that need to be pointed out in regards to the preceding paragraph. Primarily, it should be noted that the seizure of public power by the proletariat has been a topic over which sectarian feuds have fragmented the left. The majority of socialists favor an electoral programme wherein a populist, revolutionary people's party[54] democratically seizes control of the State political apparatus and uses its immense legal, political, and economic authority to re-orientate the economy in the direct material interests of the proletariat as a whole. This constitutes the basis of what has since become

---

[54] The notion of the "party" has been a subject of particularly fierce debate. In Marx's time, there was no legitimate example of contemporary bourgeois parliamentarianism, so the communist "party" that he envisioned was not that of an electoral political organization. Instead, it means the most revolutionary strata of the proletariat that exists as a class for-itself (that is, that is aware of its revolutionary potential and the economic space it occupies under late-stage capitalism) which organizes to institute democracy in all spheres of life (political, economic, social, communal, etc). How this "vanguard party" may be structured and how it may operate during the revolutionary period is a topic of further debate.

known as democratic socialism[55], which has been particularly influential on the political philosophies of western European labour parties. However, since the hard-lined statism of the post-Stalin USSR during the Cold War, most have abandoned this explicitly socialist rhetoric and instead argue for socially-progressive Keynesian welfare-states. The primary democratic socialist experiment was when Salvador Allende, an open Marxist in 1970 Chile, assumed control of a minority government and worked to institute programs that improved working conditions, public healthcare access, literacy, and basic infrastructure and mass sanitation. This, coupled with his national liberationist foreign policy, earned him the ire of wealthy American-based political reactionaries, who organized a military coup d'état against him that installed fascist dictator Augusto Pinochet to serve their economic interests. This historical experiment shows that democratic socialism, while able to improve the living conditions of working-class families, does not have the emancipatory power necessary to establish a genuinely socialist mode of production without being attacked by the bourgeoisie whose hegemonic power begins to wane as the working class' rises.

   I do consider democratic socialism to be a necessary tool in the conversion of a State into Kreon's de-politicized polity. The capture of the State by a genuine people's party, and its orientation towards working class needs, is one of the first things needed to transform it from a hegemonic organ of class rule in an egalitarian manager of the economy.

---

[55] I consider democratic socialism to have impacted my own philosophy, although one must be intellectually honest and realize that the bourgeois class is not going to be willingly relinquish control of the State and allow for a fundamental change in the mode of production. Any structural change to the system will be met with resistance, and potentially even reactionary opposition. As a result, systemic change is likely going to have to be violent. Whether that violence is politico-economic (mandated transition of mass private enterprises into worker co-ops) or physical (damaging the means of production directly) in character will ultimately be decided by the material conditions at the time of the revolution.

Of course, no vanguardist State is going to be able to use federal authority to create socialism (that is, the spirit of Kreon's polity state), and no government administration is able to dictate the exact structure of the economy; the revolutionary transformation of the economy will come about through the expropriation of the workplace by a class-conscious proletariat, not State decrees. However, this does not change the fact that the State - armed with incredible legal, economic, and political authority - can use its powers to support the endeavors of the proletariat. Under the dictatorship of the proletariat (wherein the working class seizes control of the State political apparatus and uses it to assert its classist hegemony over the bourgeoisie), the proletarian-controlled State can enact fundamental, systemic change by altering the legal code so that the workplace can be easily and effectively transitioned into collectively-owned, worker-managed co-operatives. If nothing else, the usage of the State's right of eminent domain - something that, dialectically, is decried as the most unholy of bourgeois property relations - is exceptionally useful when that right can be seized and utilized by the proletariat correctly.

Would that not mean that the economy would then be organized along the lines of state capitalism, where a single entity takes up the role of being the "national" and "collective" capitalist, rather than the "private" and "individual" one? That is, would not rampant nationalization under a proletarian State simple be the substitution of the bourgeois by the collective? Would the economic authority of the individual "private" bourgeois capitalist be replaced by the "national" proletarian State, and property (that is, the means of production specifically, at least in the commanding heights of the economy) would now be the "collective" property of the proletariat proper when under the control of a proletarian State?

Would such economic collectivism be socialism, or would it be state capitalism? Then again, is there necessarily a difference between the two?

Is that the end product in our search to discern whether a contemporary State can be transformed into a democratic, socialistic polity state? To end up with an economic system of intense centralization under the control of a proletarian State, which, after the relations of production have been fundamentally altered, will be nothing more than an "organ" to facilitate the continued operation of state capitalism? Is our socialism polity simply analogous to worker-managed state capitalism?

Engels does seem to suggest that a proletarian State, complete with the full nationalization of the economy, represents the ushering in of socialism. Lenin continues this train of thought when he argues the that implementation of socialism in Russia required the establishment of state capitalism. Indeed, he argued that a period of state capitalism is necessary to lay the economic foundations of socialism, at least for the overcoming of material scarcity by inducing rapid industrialization. If we extrapolate, we can assume that "socialism" is related to nationalization by a proletarian State. By having the workers of a particular country rise up and seize control of their government, they seize it in the context of a national government; the transfer of power from the bourgeoisie to the proletariat does not abolish the State, borders, nationality, etc. They all continue to exist, but the capture of the State by the proletariat foreshadows its gradual withering away, which in turn will cause the withering of related power structures.

During the revolution, organic parallel structures will work to take up much of the local and regional (and, perhaps, even "national" or "international") responsibilities of their mirroring bourgeois one. These can include local peoples assemblies, town-hall style meetings, democratic community councils, co-op management councils, and the like. As the revolution progresses and bourgeois power wanes, organic parallel institutions will spontaneously arise to take over the responsibilities lost by the bourgeois State. The grouping of citizens into local assemblies is the natural political order, as people are be definition structural animals: the tendency of animals to group themselves into packs, engrained into them by the evolutionary understanding of power-in-numbers, is a political extension of a natural, biotic tendency.

By doing this, they will be revolutionarily expropriated authority from the bourgeois domain to the proletarian one; that is, the "State", the hegemonic organ, will be fundamentally transformed so that it no longer be the manner of bourgeois elections; a profoundly apolitical and spontaneous town-hall assembly councils will replace the majority of what the State once dictated over. The seeds of Kreon's de-politicized sociologic state are planted and the stage is set in a manner that is conducive for its full maturation.

The bourgeois State is manifest in the forms of oppressive government institutions and political structures; the proletarian State will be manifest in decentralized and democratic organs that are run exclusively by the proletariat itself. These proletarian organs will eventually replace the State in numerous economic spheres. These town-hall, community assembly, and workers' council institutions that will arise during the revolution will be the new political organ that will replace bourgeois political structures and "elections"; they will serves as the decentralized means through which the state capitalist economy, built out of State centralization, can be locally and democratically managed. This will allow a form of decentralized, councilist organs to manage the common affairs of the proletariat and preside over a form of councilist anarcho-syndicalism.

Thus, the transformation of businesses into co-operatives is something that socialists should fully support because it provides the Luxemburgian "germs of socialized production" to also become "germs of socialized exchange" if they are networked together into an ever-expanding matrix of worker-run enterprises. One of the great problems with co-operatives is that, while they act as the first seeds of socialist economics, they are seeds that have been planted amongst a capitalist economy. They do not exist in an environment that is conducive for their growth and development - power structures, particularly the reining financial multinationals, have a vested interest in crushing co-operatives before they can arise as a genuine economic alternative to their own hierarchical, top-down management.

Often, they are bought out and purchased by corporations[56] so as to minimize the danger that emanates from them; corporations can also use their vast economic power to out-compete and out-spend co-operatives, thus driving them into financial ruin and out of the market completely. Co-operatives are destroyed by capitalist powers before they have a chance to fully thrive and develop. However, if they are able to opt-out of the market and remove themselves from competitive capitalism, then there is a great deal of potential in them. Co-operatives that form stable, long-term business contracts with each other and with public agencies, and which continuously grow to incorporate more and more co-operatives, can form a powerful economic network that will be able to use inter-network planning avoid the damaging market mechanisms that corporations use to crush them.

Large networks of co-operative enterprises, other worker-owned and worker-managed businesses, and local, decentralized community councils can help set the foundations for a new economy, and a proletarian State can use its immense authority to help do so. As private institutions are democratized and genuine community decision-making is actualized, then councilist anarcho-syndicalism (that is, economic organization of Kreon's socialist polity) can be actualized. The political ramifications of this new economy, and the host of socio-economic and cultural power structures that it will topple, will potentially set the basis for real-world communism - or, in other terms, be the politico-sociologic conditions necessary to have Kreon's polity state that is level with society.

This appears to suggest that there will be a succession of events that will occur in a cascading fashion in order to transform a classist State to Kreon's state: firstly, that the bourgeois State will be captured by a proletarian party, who will

---

[56] This is what has happened, to a degree, to the Mondragón Corporation of federated workers co-operatives in Basque, Spain in the wake of the civil war between the republican socialists and Franco's fascist government in 1956. Although inspired by the socialists' anarchic principals of workers self-management, it has hired *private* executives to manage the co-ops' and workers' financial affairs.

use its immense economic and legal authority to orientate the economy in the direct interest of the working class by facilitating the transition of private-hierarchical businesses into worker-managed co-operatives and by nationalizing key sectors of the economy (banking, healthcare, education, transport, energy, etc); and secondly, the revolutionary expropriation of the workplace by the workers themselves, either in concurrence with the first event, or shortly thereafter, after which the new proletarian State has laid the legal framework for private-to-cooperative business transition. Both of these will be accompanied by the networking of co-operative businesses with one another - in the same industrial sector, in the same geographic region, with other co-operatives in associated and secondary sectors, etc - in order to maximize production, minimize waste, democratically manage the workplace, and provide long-term business contracts between co-operative enterprises in order to set the foundation for decentralized economic planning.

But this still presents numerous problems. Primarily, the transition from a bourgeois State to a proletarian State, and from privately-owned workplaces to worker-owned workplaces, does not abolish wage-slavery, capital, classes, nations and borders, etc. It presents a fundamentally altered economy: the contemporary neoliberal situation is gone and a co-operative and syndicated economy has been established, but it does not eliminate many of the structural problems that are present under capitalism. It does improves the situation for the working class, but it does not establish socialism or communism.

To this, we can say several things.

Firstly, that the proletarianization of the State (that is, the dictatorship of the proletariat) means that the hegemonic class is no longer the bourgeoisie, and that the bourgeoisie has lost its traditionally dominant political power. This has fundamental and far-reaching consequences, because the "withering away of the State" throughout this dictatorship will cause the class character of numerous power structures (economic, social, cultural, etc) to wither along with them. This will cause a cascading change in social relations in society that will gradually transform the entire social superstructure - as the landscape changes economically, so will the social phenomena that they create. Numerous things will be subject to change.

And, as one power structure after another begins to loose its class character, so will others. The primary power structures that are defined by their relationship to the State will wither along with it, and the secondary power structures that are defined by their relationship to the primary ones will slowly begin to transform. The withering of the State, primary power, and secondary power will all occur as the proletarian State facilitates the creation of a co-operative economy. All of the individual socio-economic narratives that, collectively, constitute the superstructure will gradually loose their class character.

Secondly, the capture (and subsequent usage) of the State political apparatus by the proletarian party will not be the only action engaged in by the proletariat. Concurrent with democratic and electoral procedures, parallel institutions will spring up organically in communities and will assume control over many spheres that once belonged to the bourgeois State but were removed from the jurisdiction of the proletarian State. That is, local town-hall assemblies and community councils will assume authority over things that the State no longer controls: management of communities and local social relations, for example, will fall under their control while the proletarian State concerns itself with the establishment of the networked co-operative economy. We cannot assume that the transformation from capitalism into socialism will be dictated by the decrees of a "socialist" government, but rather through the revolutionary action of the proletariat itself. A surge in democratic involvement (which will culminate in the seizure of the State by the proletarian party) will go hand-in-hand with a surge in civic involvement, causing organic peoples assemblies to grow in concordance with the State's proletarianization. Political proletarianization will happen at the same time as the hatching of organic socialist councils.

Thirdly, the withering away of power structures and the establishment of parallel institutions presupposes, logically, that the two will be connected. As bourgeois power increasingly withers away, proletarian power will increase proportionally; the eventual "abolition" of the State (that is, the historical moment where its withering has been completed and the last vestiges of class character in the State have been fundamentally removed) will be the specific point wherein socialism has been established. As power structures and the State continually wither away, the authority of parallel institutions will grow and assume control over the spheres of authority that originally fell under the jurisdiction of the bourgeois State.

The conclusion that can be drawn from these three events (the withering away of power structures, the birth of parallel institutions, and the assumption of authority by them) will represent a potent transformation of society. In essence, democracy will be moved from just the purely political sphere to include economic, cultural, and social matters.

What I am currently thinking is that the abolition of the State will mean the newfound hegemony of the democratic peoples assemblies; this historical moment represents the terminal death of capitalism and the ushering in of socialism. The economy will be orientated along councilist anarcho-syndicalism and democracy will saturate every aspect of society. I see this as being the logical chain of events necessary to turn a classist State into an polity level with society, as Kreon considers his state to be the constitutive sociology of the people. While he argues that the state is the Ultimate meta-narrative, I argue that his state's sociology can only be actualized after the State has been de-politicized and brought level with the working majority.

Kreon's state is not something that I would argue exists today, in any shape for form. However, it is something that should be strived for because doing so would be conducive for the expansion of human freedom.

Nietzsche, and the Intersectionality of Continental Philosophy and Radical Humanity

*"Was aus Liebe getan wird, geschieht immer Jenseits von Vut und Böse.
That which is done out of love always take place beyond good and evil."*
- Nietzsche, *Beyond Good and Evil,* Aphorism 51

Paul Strathern[57] put it aptly when he says that "with Nietzsche, philosophy becomes dangerous, because you have the riveting feeling that philosophy really matters". Even though this statement is crude and reductionist, it effectively encapsulates Nietzschean theory because of its ability to act as a deconstructive paradigm[58]. Utilizing this perspective, Nietzsche de-legitimizes social, religious, and political norms and concludes that there is no apodictic human essence, let alone one that can be governed by "objective" reason. This "liberation unto a terror", as it has been referred to, is a chasm of nihilistic possibilities wherein the only value that anything (be it material or metaphysic) is completely existential.

The fact that reality is valueless and gains definition only through subjective assertions has horrifying possibilities, because it effectively throws all structuralist, liberal-democratic, and normative ethics out the window. To believe such has profound psychological implications, because a fundamental re-structuring of the understanding of "good", "evil", and "value" contingently means that one's own internal sociologic and

---

[57] Born in London in 1940, later studied at Trinity College in Dublin, Ireland before serving in the Merchant Navy for two years. Strathern was a lecturer at Kingston University in both philosophy and science, wrote several books on economics and medicine, and currently still resides in London.

[58] "Deconstruction" in the sense of metaphysic analysis and social criticism, not in the specifically post-structuralist sense of Jaques Derrida.

phenomenologic interaction with the world will be different. Nietzsche argues in *Thus Spoke Zarathustra*[59] that the individual who would be able to rise above the moral structuralism of conventional Christianity and be able to establish, and live by, subjectively-defined values that would be conducive for personal growth and liberation. This individual is referred to by Nietzsche as the *Übermensch,* the literal German of which can be translated as "super-human" or "over-man". As the name implies, the *Übermensch* would be able to pass "over" normative morality and consciously impose his or her own.

Nietzsche argues throughout his works that many of the social structures that are taken for granted - such as, but not limited to, morality, religion, politics, sociology, ethics, psychology, philosophy, etc - are superficial constructs that have no legitimate material foundation. The superstructure[60] is an sociologic meta-narrative that was established at a particular anthropologic moment to serve the direct interests of the ruling authority that existed at that point in time. As such, Nietzsche's declaration that the various constitutive sub-narratives are illegitimate power structures needs to be taken into account, and any proper understanding of Nietzschean theory must be grounded in a radically historicist perspective that pays extensive attention to the specific anthropologic events that were occurring at any given time, and how those events contributed to the rise of

---

[59] That is, *Also Sprach Zarathustra: Ein Buch für Alle und Keinen*, composed between 1883-1885. It is often considered to be his *magnum opus* work, despite the fact that many of its ideas are drawn from his previous writings (ie, the anthropologic development of morality in *the Genealogy of Morals*).

[60] As is referred to in Marxist discourse. The *superstructure* is the collection of social narratives that are created, perpetuated, and given value by the *base*, or the particular structure of a mode of production at a given moment in the historical dialectic.

the hegemonic power systems that the *Übermensch* must overcome.[61]

An potentially illustrative way to show that irreconcilability of conventional morality with anthropologic reality, and why that morality needs to be abolished by the *Übermensch* to ensure greater human freedom, can be to look at the contemporary "science versus Creationism" debate that unfortunately still rages in our legislatures and school. Society needs to develop a post-moral consciousness wherein all individuals are "over-men" that are able to pass "over" this systemic hegemony.

To effectively explain Nietzschean theory, some time should be taken to address the "science versus Creationism" argument and use it as a microcosm for the larger *Übermensch*-based revolution against superstructural authority, in order to use it as an example to explain the anachronistic existence of antiquated morality.

As evolution progressed and animals were being pushed into ever-populating communities, a general sociologic ethic developed in order to facilitate co-operative behavior that served to perpetuate the group's survival and reproduction. The habituation of this ethic over the course of human development resulted in its become a normative convention whose existence remained but whose purpose did not. This allowed power structures that existed at that specific anthropologic moment to radically politicize them and turn them into immortal tools of moral coercion.

Morality is not a set of fixed, unchanging principals handed down by some Great Being that is being eroded by teachings of biotic evolution. It is an anthropologic construct created by the natural historic process, a set of artificial social

---

[61] It is interesting to note that there are particular strands of Marxism (including the Situationist International, an organization of communist intellectuals and avant-garde social critics that was active from 1957-1972) that refer to "*Übermensch* theory", or "Great Man Theory", wherein a "great man" would be able to impose his will on history and control its direction, rather than have it be regulated by dialectical materialism or natural economic forces.

principals with no legitimate foundation now that reproduction no longer needs to be encouraged to the point of self-perpetuation.

Thus it is not possible to say that teaching organismal evolution causes moral degeneration, because morality does not exist. It is nothing but a manufactured sociologic ethic whose original biologic purpose has long since expired - it exists only as a meaningless hologram that cannot interact with science due to its own non-being. Morals cannot be violated by teaching evolution because "morality" itself does not exist in the absolutist, divine manner that religious power structures describe it as.

As Nietzsche said[62], "an idea which arises from a true and healthy instinct may survive long after this instinct itself, in consequence of the changing conditions of existence ... This survival of ideas we call morality. By its operation, the human race is frequently saddled with the notions of generations long dead and forgotten". He also made the point of stating that "a code of morals was nothing more than a system of customs, laws, and ideas which had its origins in the distinctive desire of some definite race to live under conditions which best subserved its own welfare". This provides credible philosophic support for the postulate that morality is an antiquated facilitator of reproduction and community growth. It is, as he put it, the "consensus of instinct" and "the herd morality", not a divine ethic[63].

---

[62] *Before* passing away from tertiary syphilis. Although there are some critics of continental philosophy who will argue that Nietzsche's contributions are illegitimate due to his contracting of syphilis - and that his philosophic works are simply the eclectic ramblings of a man suffering from intensive neural degeneration - he should not be subject to such rampant reductionism. Syphilis aside, Nietzsche was able to produce a penetrating system of philosophy.

[63] These terms re-appear throughout Nietzsche's works, as do others that are bluntly dismissive of mass psychology. Principally, they can be found in *Beyond Good and Evil* and *On the Genealogy of Morals*.

Morality as a sociologic ethic was necessary at a specific point in time because it encouraged co-operative behaviors amongst humanoid animals in rudimentary communities, which helped facilitate the perpetuate of the particular group in question. The complex sociology of "morals" was nothing more than a collaborative mass-psyche that promoted material abundance and sexual reproduction. Nietzsche is not the only one to repudiate the existence of morality; history is abundant with philosophers that questioned moral epistemology. Friedrich Engels, the co-author of the 1848 edition of the *Manifesto of the Communist Party*, wrote that "the conceptions of 'good' and 'evil' have varied so much from nation to nation and from age to age that they have often been in direct contradiction with each other", which only reinforces the idea of morality being a product of specific historical and material conditions; as different communities are faced with varying degrees of scarcity and population growth, each have grown their own relative "morality". He[64] and Karl Marx continued to expand on 'moral' conduct until they formulated the classically Marxist view was that "morality is a form of ideology, that any given morality arises out of a particular stage of development in productive forces and relations and is relative to a particular mode of production and particular class interests".

Thus is "morality" not only a false construct, but false construct whose particular make-up is determined by the specific material and anthropologic conditions around it at a certain historical moment. It is a historical creation, not an objective, divine, and timeless ethos; it is an artificial social construct the grew out of the natural anthropologic process. This has a profound impact on our thesis, because the postulation that objective morality does not exist places it in a new light. If

---

[64] Besides being the fellow co-author of the *Manifesto*, Engels was also the author of numerous other communist dissertations, including the influential *Socialism: Utopian and Scientific* that attempted to differentiate materialist "scientific socialism" from pre-Marxist "utopian socialism". He was born in 1818 in Trier, Prussia and died in 1883 in London from a catarrh, which brought on both terminal bronchitis and pleurisy.

morality does not exist, what ramifications does that have on the Creationist argument that teaching biotic evolution corrupts moral fortitude?

The only reasonable conclusion is that morality, as a natural sociologic outgrowth of an evolving, mature civilization, cannot be something that corrupts science because it, like science, is a material phenomena. Science cannot be corrupted by morality because they are both "natural" - rather than be considered mutually exclusive, "science" and "morality" are radically connected in that they are both expressions of human development. There could be no modernist society without prior historical development, and such development implies the creation of a complex sociologic ethos to maintain, perpetuate, and grow that society.

Science cannot corrupt morals because they are not at odds. Morality was a necessarily anthropologic development because it encouraged human development, and science serves as a means through which material reality can be more properly understood. They are two sides of the same coin; they are both two different manifestations of civil progress. In time, as an understanding in science grows, the mass subscription of the public to religion will wane and society will become increasingly secular. Until that point, the barrage of insular anti-intellectualism by Creation fundamentalists will continue, and it is the duty of scientists to inform the public about the nature of material reality and its history.

Thus do we see that Creationism, as a "scientific" movement, is a product of particular hegemonic power structures that existed at a given anthropologic moment. It has no rational, material grounding and is one the superstructural narratives that needs to be passed "over" by the "over-man" in order to obtain both philosophic enlightenment and intellectual honesty. It serves as an effective example of the illegitimate social narratives that need to be overcome by the *Übermensch*.

Marx vs Marcuse
Aesthetic Theory and the Campaign for "Revolutionary" Art

Since the recent advent of post-modernist theory, there has been a drive to re-evaluate the legitimacy of semiotics and aesthetics. While this drive has manifested primary as hermeneutic analyses, it also includes art theory and art analysis. Despite being part of the political Left, both Karl Marx and Herbert Marcuse have dabbled in aesthetic commentary and provided philosophic contributions to the greater artistic tradition. The praise and criticism that they have received for their work has, unfortunately, been tainted by the anti-Left propaganda campaign that was launched in the early 1900s to discredit the revolutionary movements in the wake of the Russian Revolution. As a result, a significant portion of what Marx and Marcuse wrote has been misinterpreted and this misinterpretation has become the normative interpretation. The goal of this essay is to serve as a discussion regarding the nature of art, its production, and its politicization as the two originally spoke of it.

However, in order to discuss the relationship between Marxian and Marcusian art, we must first discuss each in turn before we address the intersectionality of the two. Despite its unorthodoxy, the manner through which we analyze the two will be in regards to the notion of estrangement, and the dynamic relationship between the observer of the art and the art itself.

When Marx speaks of estrangement, he means it in both an intangibly metaphysic and radically materialist sense at the same time - there is a profoundly dialectic relationship between the two, in a deconstructionist sense. That is, in order for their to be a metaphysic issue at hand there must be something material (say, a given anthropologic-economic moment in the history; or a single, materially-concrete object) to analyze. Yet in order for there to be something material, there must be a notion of metaphysics with which to analyze it. Thus we are caught in a convoluted loop: in order for one thing to exist, there has to be an exact polar opposite so as to grant it structural definition. Just as black requires the existence of white so as to grant black its defining apodictic non-white-ness, the existence of that white is contingent upon the existence of black in the first place! Here do we see the philosophic inadequacies of a binary system, because the existence of one pole pre-supposes the existence of the other when, in reality, neither can exist without the other already being present. Binary systems are false constructs that are intellectually belittling because they serve as reductionist mechanisms for shoving complex, multi-faceted concepts into reified, absolutist "either-or"s. This structuralism is violent in that it de-limits metaphysic possibilities by establishing a rigid, authoritarian framework.

However, for the sake of intellectual honesty, we must admit that binary structuralism has provided mankind with a great service - by institutionalizing absolutism, it has provided man[65] with a linguistic reference upon which to build an understandable and perpetuate-able language. Without a totalitarian binary, contemporary language would not have have able to have been formed because the binary itself provides the foundation on which linguistics is possible. There are numerous literary theorists and linguists that postulate that binary opposition provides the basis for comparison (that is, "what something is" or "what something is not" in relation to the two binary poles), which contingently allows for the establishment of a communicable understanding.

I agree with Derrida[66] when he argues that contemporary society is subject to a "structuralist invasion" in his *Force and Signification* essay. He rejects reductionist philosophies and

---

[65] That is, "mankind" or "humanity" - not "man" in an anatomic sense, nor in the patriarchal hetero-normative sense, as I consider such a concept of "man" to be an illustrative example of a totalitarian binary system that is serves to enforce a domestic division of labor.

[66] Jacques Derrida (1930-2004), the French Algerian philosopher that was intimately involved in literary criticism, post-modernism, and semiotic analysis. He is considered to be one of the major fathers of post-structuralism and gave the famous 1966 "Structure, Sign, and Play in the Discourse of the Human Sciences" lecture that set the foundation for modern deconstructionist theory.

defends existential subjectivity by saying that "by the very act of considering the structuralist invasion as an object he would forget its meaning and would forget what is at stake, first of all, is an adventure of vision, a conversation of the way of putting questions to any object posed before us - to historical objects - his own - in particular; and amongst these, the literary object."

However, for the sake of simplicity, let us lay aside hermeneutic deconstruction and proceed with the assumption that estrangement is both legitimate and present.

Marxian estrangement manifests in four different manners, although it would not be incorrect to assert that all four are contextual manifestations of one kind of estrangement. These four types are referred to as "product" estrangement, "process" estrangement, estrangement from "species-being", and estrangement from "others". I assert that they *are* four constituent pieces of one whole meta-estrangement that actualizes in response to a dehumanizing economic system. I put forth that a revolutionary re-constitution of social and economic relations, ultimately culminating in the establishment of a genuinely alternative mode of production, will de-politicize the division of labor (both in the domestic family and the occupational work-place) and thus render estrangement obsolete.

I postulate that the construction of a socialist economy - rooted firmly in a Marxian analysis of the nature of capital, and of the sociology that it generates - will herald the end of estrangement in all of its forms, and that art will serve as a mechanism through which revolutionary consciousness can be induced in the mass public. However, this postulation is rooted on several fundamental pre-suppositions and internal contradictions, all of which need to be adequately addressed before a revolutionary, artistic programme can even be discussed.

Let us begin with an analysis of the nature of estrangement.

"Product" estrangement is the result of systemic division of labor, wherein proletarian laborers are forced into specialized tasks in the workplace that make them only yet another cog in the industrial process of churning out a commodity that they have no viable control over. Being an "employee" now means to be a niche-specific task-worker along a great conveyer belt, to be reduced to labor over a single remedial task before passing the commodity on the next laborer. This radical alterity between the specific productive task that one performs and the commodity that it yields is referred to as "product" estrangement, because the labor that the proletarian engages in does not result in the "self-congealing" or "self-objectifying[67]" of his or her voluntary, creative work

However, the economic scheme that exists at a given anthropologic-historic moment[68] may not necessarily be conducive for encouraging such voluntary, creative work. As a result, there is a structural coercion to engage in economic activities that are necessary for survival. This pits humans against one another in a perpetual[69] state of violent competition

This contingently follows with the conclusion that, because certain labor is forced, there is "process" estrangement. This form of estrangement is manifest in the organizational framework of a given economy.

An economic system that *does* promote constructive, volitional activity may be conducive for extensive physical, intellectual, or artistic development, and thus produce outstanding athletes, scholars, and artists. These people serve as

---

[67] "Objectifying" in the sense that the voluntary, creative work that takes place results in material production that (in some way, shape, or form) illustrates the essence of the worker.

[68] That is, a mode of production in the historical dialectic. It is not illogical to argue that a pre-capitalist mode of production would not have had favorable conditions for self-congealing work (if even for the reductionist notion of material scarcity), and that capitalism is necessary to establish a post-scarcity economy conducive for providing genuine opportunities for diverse, voluntary, creative work.

[69] Only "perpetual" so long as the means of production are not industrially sophisticated enough to effectively overcome net material scarcity. Once scarcity has been overcome through industrialization, mankind will be able to enter an economic epoch characterized by democratic, co-operative management (that is, socialism).

the "concrete universal" example of what other humans have the potential to achieve, given that there are favorable conditions. Hence "product" and "process" estrangement overlap to produce an socio-economic intersectionality referred to as "species-being" estrangement - it is referred to as such because difference of potential between the concrete-universal individual and the proletarian worker is so great that it has a de-limiting effect on the ways in which he or she is able to engage with the world.

Not only is there a "species-being" estrangement between humanity's potential and proletarian reality, but there is also an estrangement from "other" humans. Due to the fact that the means of production are not sophisticated enough to overcome material scarcity[70], resources are finite and limited; thus, proletarians are forced to compete with one another to access and use those resources. This forces each proletarian to view every other proletarian as an economic competitor, dissociating all public solidarity and reducing human relations to feuding rivalry. This de-humanizes proletarians by causing each one to view every other as both an opponent and an object, causing a profound estrangement from "others".

Thus do we see that four inter-connected forms of "estrangement" are contingent upon the existence (or the non-existence) of each other, signifying that they are arguably one, universal form with differing contextual manifestations.

A distressing majority of those on the Left[71] reject existential subjectivity and view art as simply another superstructural narrative that exists only because of the economic

---

[70] "Not sophisticated" in certain areas of the world - i.e., indigenous Africa and South Amcrica. I would argue that the advanced, industrial countries in the West have effectively overcome scarcity, but lack an efficient political system that can manage such complex material allocation.

[71] Generally, orthodox Marxists that subscribe to a form of radical economic determinism, who drain both humans and their sociologic relations of any creative individuality and reduce them all to cold, mechanical economics and dry materialism. I am strongly opposed to this dehumanizing reductionism, and think that existential subjectivity is an integral part of any legitimate political narrative.

base that defines it. Art, these purist argue, exists only as the materialized ideology of the ruling class at at given anthropologic-historic moment. It is materialized either as a legitimate illustration of hegemonic authority (either directly portraying superstructural normativity) or as an illusionary tool to redirect social orientation and distract from revolutionary consciousness. That is, art can have propagandistic characteristics that reinforce cultural hegemony[72] if it portrays images that are in line with superstructural narratives; it can also be a mental diversion from material woes that prevent the growth of a revolutionary zeitgeist.

Thus do we see that art has profound social and political characteristics that can be orientated towards a particular end. The fact that art has both public (mass sociologic) and private (personally psychologic) qualities is reminiscent of the socio-psychologic reflex instigated by symbols that Göttner-Abendroth refers to as "magic". If this "magic" could be orientated towards an end that does not reinforce superstructural values, it has the potential to be the means through which the seeds of a non-normative consciousness can be planted.

There are several manners through which art could be a tool through which one builds revolutionary consciousness. Primarily, the "magic" socio-psychologic response to art must be such that it runs contrary to the values put forth by the superstructure. Doing so give it the characteristic of being anti-establishmentarian and socially revolutionary, but the question that arises in response is how to go about mass-producing such "revolutionary" art without institutionalizing it as being

---

[72] "Cultural hegemony" as put forth by Antonio Gramsci (1891-1937), a founding member and leader of the Communist Party of Italy. It asserts that the ruling class dominates a culturally heterogenous population by forcibly making its worldview normative, thus institutionalizing mental domination and "social" class. It is a form of modernist "social" oppression, as opposed to the strictly "economic" oppression of capitalism.

artistically normative; to have it be institutionalized[73] would drain it of all of its revolutionary potential. Any art that is only "revolutionary" so long as it is contrary to superstructural narratives would no longer be so if revolutionary sentiments were normative narratives in and of themselves.

In the end, for art to have a revolutionary function, it must be able to engage in what Sartre[74] referred to as *le revolt perpétuelle* - the "perpetual revolution", wherein the anti-establishment movement must be structured in a way that is conducive for its own constant change and internal mutation, thus rendering it unable to be homogenized or institutionalized. In order to do so, the art would most likely have to be Dionysian in character.; that is, it would have to be a non-static art rendition, such as dance or music, because the temporal unfolding of the media in question would allow for an extended engagement, as opposed to the fleeting glance at an inert, finished painting. Such a protracted interaction with an amorphous art (for lack of a better term) would arguably be conducive for conveying a more complex - and potentially revolutionary - message.

Explicitly revolutionary art may not be neither popular nor mainstream, but there are elements of it that are buried in contemporary capitalism. This art would most likely include: post-modern cinema, with its superstructural narrative-bending themes that incorporate politically controversial or socially taboo

---

[73] What is referred to in Marxist discourse as *embourgeoisment*, wherein anti-establishment sentiments and movements are incorporated into the establishment itself so as to render them impotent and non-threatening.

[74] Amongst others, such as his contemporaries Maurice Merleau-Ponty and Simone de Beauvoir. Sartre (1905-1980) was one of the principal fathers of existentialism and is argued to be the first to publicly accept the label. He is associated with the French Communist Party, the Maoist-inspired Proletarian Left, and the Revolutionary Democratic Rally. He occupied a unique political space at the intersectionality of anti-Soviet Marxism and anarchism. The influence of his works on my own political development cannot be over-stated, and I consider him to be one of my primary philosophic influences.

components (such as non-hetero-normative and non-cisgendered romance); political propaganda, with its government-sanctioned or seditious ability to reach a mass public audience (such as the Soviet Union's omnipresent workerist art, or the popular Maoist literature of the Naxal revolutionaries in India); and symbolism the is universally recognizable and evokes Göttner-Abendroth's "magic" (such as the swastika, crucifix, or peace sign, which have profound social power).

The production of revolutionary art must be done in a manner that is independent of bourgeois support, meaning that it has to be produced completely free of the determinist conditions set upon it by the élite who established the cultural framework wherein it is produced. Revolutionary art is profoundly proletarian in character because it exists as the material embodiment of a desire for an alternative reality - the temporal unfolding of music and dance allow for the conveying of a message that, in some way for form, calls out the structural failures of the existing system. These Dionysian arts may be able to participate in *le revolt perpétuelle* if the messages and themes they share are always unapologetically critical of the base and superstructure that exist at their time, and if they serve as means of deconstructionist criticism rather than a proposal for specific new social narrative.

That is, for Dionysian art to be revolutionary, it must be a form of emotional, violent critique rather than a dogmatic proposal for a new, "progressive" social norm. "Revolutionary" art must not be politicized and advocate a specific change in the superstructure[75]; rather, it must be unabashedly deconstructionist and push for the thorough dissection of the entire superstructure, ending all normative narratives in order to establish a political environment conducive for voluntary, "self-objectifying" work based on one's own creative development, rather than due to structural conformitivity.

---

[75] Say, by normalizing the aforementioned non-hetero-normative and non-cisgendered relationships, thus being a mechanism through which to actualize progressivist agendas.

Revolutionary, Dionysian art must not be "anti-establishment" and campaign for a progressive sociology, but rather be "non-establishment" and promote human development independent of the superstructural narratives that exist. The wide-spread dissemination and popularization of this "non-establishment" art may be such that it persuades enough of the proletariat to recognize the illegitimacy of the superstructure as a whole, and this has the potential to lay the groundwork for a socio-political movement that ultimately results in a revolutionary re-constitution of social relations. A change in social relations, contingently, will have an influence on the economic base that supports the superstructure[76], and thus the seeds of structural change will be planted in the present system.

The production of revolutionary art will not herald the end of Marxian estrangement, but it does lay the foundations for a movement that has the potential to do so. Revolutionary art is a means, not an ends; the goal is not to produce non-normative and socially-progressive art, but rather art that questions structural normativity *in order* to deconstruct the system and promote the construction of socialism. However, capitalist powers structures that exist have a vested interest in curbing such budding revolutionary tendencies, if for nothing else than to perpetuate their own hegemonic authority; this is why revolutionary art has to push for superstructural deconstruction, not simple progressivist change, because "change" can easily be incorporated into the establishment and "progressivism" can be institutionalized.

The over-arching meta-estrangement, and its four contextual manifestations, will only be relegated to the dustbin of history when the proletariat is able to engage in labor that is voluntary, creative, and conducive for personal development. This will only be possible via the conscious construction of a

---

[76] To a degree. Despite the fact that the base and superstructure have a dialectic relationship and a change in the former will result in a change in the later, a change in the later will have a less pronounced change in the former because the base is arguably more determinist. Any alternative mode in production will only be established by a revolutionary change in the economy, not in that epoch's sociology.

post-scarcity and non-capitalist mode of production[77], whose manufacturing will only be possible due to the revolutionary potential of art. The mass "magic" of wide-spread deconstructionist art has the potential to be the catalytic instigator for a revolutionary social movement that will end estrangement, the division of labor, and proletarian serialization[78].

Despite the stereotypic notion amongst academics that Marx was "anti-art" due to its being a product of a classist mode of production, I would argue that the genuinely Marxian view of art is far closer to that of Marcuse's revolutionary art than not. Those who view art in such a simple, vulgar, and reductionist way are (possibly unknowingly) engaging in a gross violation of humanist principals by de-valuing human activity and regarding it as subject to cold economic determinism. Existential subjectivity and an extended personal engagement with revolutionary art is fundamentally necessary for building socialism - as a result of this pseudo-nihilist radical subjectivity, every proletarian will come to conclusions about the art that have enough difference that it will generate an amorphous, ever-changing matrix of social narratives. This may be be enough to build the dynamic, post-structural environment that is necessary for *le revolt perpétuelle* required for a socio-political environment that is consistently conducive for creative work.

---

[77] The exact structure of socialism has been debated *ad nauseam* by sectarian dogmatists. I do not see it as being akin to Soviet-style hyper-centralization and the consolidation of governmental power by the "people's" party, but rather the voluntary association of co-operative business, workers' councils, and decentralized organic units in tiered, federated structures that can be regional, national, or even international in character.

[78] As described by Sartre in his *magnum opus,* "Critique de la Raison Dialectique", wherein he postulates that the bourgeois class has a vested interest in identify politics (women's rights, racial rights, etc) because it fractures the proletariat into interest-specific demographics that care more about their own serial group's agenda than that of their class as a whole.

In the end, I would argue that there is far more intersectionality between Marxian and Marcusian notions of art than not, and that a reconciliation of the two is fundamental for art's usage in establishing a mass revolutionary consciousness orientated towards ending estrangement, proletarian serialization, and structural conformism. Art has the potential to be an outstandingly revolutionary tool, if used correctly, and that usage is imperative in the coming years as the "structural invasion" continues.

Existential Subjectivity as Radical Humanity

There have been numerous philosophic movements that have gained the intellectual prominence necessary to leave a firm mark in history. The philosophic tradition generally referred to as "continental philosophy" - which incorporates phenomenology, existentialism, nihilism, and its derivative traditions - seems to have the most persuasive argument as to the genuine nature of humanity. It is necessary to see all of them as constituent components of the same philosophic meta-narrative, which, when integrated with the tenants of post-modernist deconstructionism, offer a uniquely insightful look into what the fundamental essence of humanity is - of what a "radical" humanity is.

To be a "radical" human is to be many things. It is to have a profoundly Nietzschean view of morals and recognize them as illegitimate power structures that, having served the interests of a hegemonic demographic at some point in the distant anthropologic past, need to be abolished to be "flown over" in order to expand human freedom. It has a ontologically Sartrean notion of bad faith and the drive to live an authentic life independent of determinism from superstructural narratives. It is Husserlian in that it derives metaphysic meaning from direct engagement with the material world. It is Marxist in that it recognizes the mechanistic economism that generates sociology. It is reminiscent of Pannekoek in that it supports organic, democratic organizations that arise out of natural human sociology. It evokes Heidegger in that it accepts that *Dasein*'s[79] being-in-the-world-ness gives it the responsibility of making meaning out of its being in absurd, chaotic social conditions. It resembles Derrida in that rejects either-or absolutist binary systems and their exclusion of entities that do not conform to one

---

[79] That is, the physical "being" that consciousness occupies. It is the German vernacular for "existence". It was originally used by Hegel to mean *being-there* or *there-being*. It stands opposed to *Sein* ("Being"), the transcendental, existential spirit that directly experiences subjectivity.

its polar values. And it echos Descartes in that it places *cogito ergo sum*[80] as being of the only metaphysic certainty.

There is no fundamental, universal nature to man and the value that each person subscribes to another (or to his- or herself) is, like everything else, completely existential. If we accept the thesis that morality is a product of the anthropologic process[81], we must also accept that any of the values that we give to things are illegitimate because they are derived from an artificial social construct. Thus we must acknowledge that social values and morals, being illegitimate power structures that serve as behaviorally determinist systems and means of de-limiting human potential, need to rejected and revolutionarily abolished so as to expand human freedom.

Yet the abolition of morals and the recognition that reality is genuinely valueless has terrifying potential. It has even been referred to as a "liberation unto a terror" because such radical, existential freedom leaves one with a sense of profound angst over their limitless ways to engage with the world and the direct responsibility that each engagement carries. In an attempt to protect itself, the psyche engages in a convoluted practice of adopting social narratives to define itself, willing accepting Sartrean "bad faith" labels to give itself meaning so that it does not hang in the void of valueless nihilism. Doing so is psychologically self-destructive, an act of profound personal self-negation, an act of voluntarily abolishing the self and replacing with a social construct because of the "terror" that the "liberation unto terror" brings.

---

[80] That is, *je pense donc je suis* ("I think, therefore I am"). Descartes postulated that, when doubting the nature of reality, the only thing that he could be sure of was the fact that he was doubting. This lead him to suppose that the only metaphysic certainty was that there is a subjective consciousness that *can* doubt.

[81] As I put forth in a previous essay. I argued that morality is an antiquated social construct that was instituted in a distant, long-ago anthropologic period to facilitate a socio-economic need; chiefly, I posited that this need was material abundance and population growth.

There are terrifying possibilities that can potentially arise from such radical individualism. At first glance, one would think that it is translated politically into a form of viscous social Darwinism, into a form of radically anti-collectivist singularity that prevents cohesive, co-operative social relations. Sartre[82] addresses this in his October 1945 lecture "Existentialism is a Humanism".

"One group after another censures us for overlooking humanity's solidarity, and for considering man as an isolated being. This, contend the Communists, is primarily because we base our doctrine on pure subjectivity - that is, on the Cartesian I think - on the very moment in which man fully comprehends his isolation, rendering us incapable of re-establishing solidarity with those who exist outside of the self, and who are inaccessible to us through the cogito."

A society wherein existential subjectivity reigned would not necessarily be one of perpetual violence, of a radical individualism so comprehensive that it prevented any mass sociologic co-operation. Rather, an adherence to the existential ethics of Simone de Beauvoir's[83] *Ethic of Ambiguity* - wherein all people act as if their decisions were reflective of the value of all of humanity, and as if all humanity was to make that decision

---

[82] Jean-Paul Charles Aymard Sartre (1905-1980), the French playwright and anti-Vichy political activist who was intimately involved with Hussserlian phenomenology and was the first to allegedly adopt the title of "existentialist". He is associated with the French Communist Party, the Maoist-inspired Proletarian Left, and the Revolutionary Democratic Rally. He won (and rejected) the Nobel Prize for Literature in 1964.

[83] Simone-Lucie-Ernestine-Marie Bertrand de Beauvoir (1908-1986), the French feminist theorist, existentialist philosopher, and socialist activist that was Sartre's on-and-off lover. She also penned *Le Deuxième Sexe* ("*The Second Sex*") in 1949, which later became one of the central tenants of second-wave feminism. Her ethics are reminiscent of Kant's categorical imperative.

- leaves one with a social responsibility to do what is right in a public context.

It is important to note that a public context is the only thing that gives political actions their characterization as political. This is because every action that a person takes has economic consequences, and the economic structure is the base on which the social superstructure sits; as a result, every action is translated through an economic impact into a sociologic one. This means every action wherein one engages with the world, via economics, is brought forth *already tainted* by the sociologic narratives that the economic base generates. One cannot give an action value without placing it in a sociologic context; all actions are public and political because they take place in an economic, material framework[84].

One cannot engage in a non-political action: every time that a person engages with the world, metaphysically or physically, he or she is engaging in actions that are relatively pre-determined by mass sociologic values. *Every* action is political. When a person chooses a course of action, that action is being chosen at the intersectionality of numerous social and economic power structures that have already given it a connotation and worked to de-limit its possibilities[85].

Even consciously choosing to do nothing is a profoundly political act because it is, in the end, the decision made in relation to one's fully aware rejection of the situation. One cannot escape the radical politicization of his or her actions - the mere fact that a person exists in a material world with other

---

[84] I have repeatedly postulated that the sophistication of the means of production to the point wherein net material scarcity is overcome will set the preconditions that allow for the de-politicization of society at large, and facilitate the transition to a co-operative society.

[85] The fact that hegemonic power systems (and the totalitarian sociology they generate) are able to set a framework around what is possible shows that, as a de-limiting determinant, the State political apparatus needs to be violently abolished so as to allow a truly determinism-less existential authenticity. The revolutionary abolition of the State is grounded in the supposition that doing so will be conducive to expanding life-defining possibilities for the existential subject.

people renders all actions (and non-actions) as having a constant political undertone.

Yet, if actions are always political in nature, that does not mean that one should shift focus from the primacy of the *individual* to that of the *social collective*. The recognition of reality as completely valueless, and of finding value only in a politico-sociologic context, does not mean that one should fetishize the social collective over the individual self in a desire to induce contextual meaning. To do so means that there is a sacrifice of the self. It is not the self-negation of bad faith, but rather the voluntary negation of the personal "I" in order to generate the social "we". And this - the defining of one's self based on the sociology of the collective group - is the gravest violation of the human spirit because it effectively erases individuality. It destroys the "self" to make the "group". It is a psychic action of terrible self-destruction when one believes that he or she should voluntarily hand over their existential freedom, adopt bad faith, and adhere to social narratives in order to gain meaning and value in society. Instead, everyone should grant their own life meaning and merit through ontologically authentic actions, not through the desperate search for approval from bourgeois superstructural meta-narratives.

Any engagement of the existential subject with the world is going to be profoundly phenomenologic in character. That is - because the only thing in which one can be certain is that the *cogito* is the central subjective object that perceives reality - all interactions with material reality are the means through which one can gain understanding about the self and reality. As a result, the physical and psychic relationship between the "radical human" and the world works to generate meaning for each. The subject and the object both work dialectically to grant each other meaning and value in relation to one another. This occurs even both the physical realm (that is, understanding of the physical boundaries of subject and object via world engagement) and the metaphysical one (wherein engagement breeds experience, and experience generates existential value). A phenomenologic relation with the world translates simple physical actions into profound metaphysic ones.

Thus there is no such thing as "radical humanity", except in the radical absence of all ontological matter other than the existentially subjectivist *cogito* that has the ability to mentally evolve in response to psychic stimuli. The only thing that can be reasonably assumed to exist (with any degree of philosophic certainty) is the *cogito*; everything else is in a state of perpetual metaphysic uncertainty, and this - when hand-in-hand with a nihilist abandonment of values - has the potential to leave one teetering on the border of a destructive, reality-negating solipsism. It has the potential to take the subject-object duality[86] to the extreme and leave one questioning whether or not the only thing that actually exists is the subjective consciousness, and whether everything else is merely valueless matter that exists so as to give the subject metaphysic definition.

The fact that the world is so absurdly valueless (and that all values are the product of antiquated, hegemonic power structures that determine and de-limit choices) leaves one with the responsibility to consciously and soberly reject the superstructure and give reality subjective value instead. This is the only possible alternative to the nihilism that results from the "liberation unto a terror": to boldly confront the valueless and give it value. The granting of value to things isn't limited strictly to the metaphysical and physical things that populate the existential subjective's experience; one must also give *one's self* value through authentically deciding which political actions to take. The actions chosen are going to have a sociologic result, a socially-observed "projection of the self" that others will see rather than see the existential subject as a genuine individual with full agency. That is, because of the subject-object duality, every person is going to objectify everyone else and give them value in accordance with superstructural narratives *and* the life choices that they choose (be they authentic or inauthentic). Thus

---

[86] Wherein every human questions whether he is the metaphysic subject that engages with the non-subject material objects in the world. This causes every individual to question whether they are the subject in a subjective experience or merely manifest objects that populate some else's subjective experience.

does our political engagement with the world result in a social "projection of the self" image that the world can interact with as we are mutually objectified by others, rather than have each person interact with the legitimate, individual subject beneath the "projection" mask. People interact with each others' socially-constructed "projections" rather than the sovereign individual underneath[87].

The value that an existential subject has - and the value of their "projection" as interpreted by others - is self-granted. As a central tenant of the existentialist tradition, the subject must realize that he or she, through conscious and independent action, has the burden of building one's one value through one's own choices.

In "Existentialism is a Humanism", Sartre adds:

"No doubt the thought of this may seem harsh to someone who has not made a success of his life. But, on the other hand, it helps people to understand that reality alone counts, and that dreams, expectations, and hopes only serve to define a man a broken dream, aborted hoes, and futile expectations; in other words, they define him negatively, not positively. Nonetheless, saying 'you are nothing but your life' does not imply that the artist will be solely judged by his works of art, for a thousand other things also help to define him. What we mean to say is that man is nothing but a series of enterprises, and that he is the sum, organization, and aggregate of the relations that constitute such enterprises. In light of this, what people reproach us for is no essentially our pessimism, but the sternness of our optimism."

The value that the existential subject has is only the result of the actions that he or she has taken in the world, and the value given to the choices that he or she has made. People are

---

[87] This is reminiscent of Karl Marx (1818-1883), who posited the theory of *entfremdung* ("estrangement") wherein all individuals are radically separated from one another (socially and metaphysically) as a result of an economic division of labor and capitalist sociology.

defined by their actions, and this leads further support to the notion of existential ethics being conducive for socialistic co-operation, because (if we adhere to Kant's categorical imperative and de Beauvoir's universal humanist ethics) every action taken by every person should be done consciously, soberly, with the consideration of all of humanity making the same choice, and with full awareness of one's life-building choices free from the inauthenticity of bad faith. This would lead all human actions to being conducive for the advancement of the greater good and of egalitarian co-operation.

Fully authentic and existentially self-aware choices by the existential subjective can only lead to the development of profoundly Marxian political tendencies. This is because one quickly learns that, while he has the power to define himself sociologically based on chosen actions, there is a structural framework around what choices and actions are permitted by the system. That is, the capitalist mode of production generates a superstructure of such incredible potency that it places a de-limiting boundary on the possible areas of existential freedom that one can act in. Awareness of superstructural hegemony, and of its power to restrict the boundaries of practical free choices, should led one to develop revolutionary political stances that propose a radical re-structuring of social and economic relations, if for nothing else than to abolish the determinist State to allow greater existential freedom.

Marx's words from the *Manifesto of the Communist Party* are as pertinent today as they were in 1848:

"In place of the old bourgeois society, with its classes and class antagonisms, we shall have an association in which the free development of each is the condition for the free development of all."

A reality governed by existential subjectivity would be one wherein a socialist, humanist ethic would preside over a State-less society of co-operative individuals that are aware of the decisions that they make. It is imperative that society adopt such a stance if it wishes to be metaphysically honest and true to the rudimentary ontology inherent in humanity.

Section Four:
Hermeneutics, Notes, and Thoughts

On the Existentialism of Political Vanguardism

Material scarcity causes proletarians to adopt bad faith in order to escape the socio-political struggles they are subject to under capitalism. When confronted with de-humanizing estrangement, they associate with stereotypes, labels, and social demographics in order to give their lives meaning. Yet, the proletariat is not a single, homogenous unit; it is ever-aware of its heterogenous demographics because identity politics have served to fracture it and prevent it from forming any social group more complex than those that serve its immediate demographical aims. These heterogenous "serial collectives" serve the socio-psychologic mechanism through which mass-populace bad faith is adopted. In these serial collectives we see the unfortunate thesis of "public" existentialism.

Let us take a Hegelian approach and extrapolate to see the social consequences of this in context of the proletarian movement. As the thesis is offset by its dialectic antithesis, the serial collective is offset by the "fused group", wherein a homogenous group of people transcends its seriality and is united in solidarity as a fraternal enterprise in order to achieve a common goal. In this we see the theoretic "the" proletariat. To maintain its existence and justify its fusion, such a group must give itself some type of functional specialization - the fused group must legitimize itself as being greater than its constituent serial collectives by giving itself a formal definition. However, in the process of such self-legitimation, it turns itself into a structuralist, conservative, and hierarchical system that neglects the individual for the sake of constituting the collective.

Yet, because every individual is radically unique and existential subjectivity is the basis of the most fundamental elements of humanity, there cannot truly be a fused group proper. It cannot be truly homogenous and unified group because to assume so would neglect the creative individualism of each of its constituent pieces. The fused group is intimately aware of this, and and it tries to make its relations all the more intimate and cohesive by trying to establish a mass-group consciousness - that is, it explicitly defines itself, states its objectives, and engages in existential self-definition that puts the group identity before personal identify. This functional specialization that it gives itself results in the sacrifice of the individual in order to form the collective.

Thus we see that the proletariat in-itself is serialized by identity politics but - through the political alliance of the various social serials - is not able to form the theoretically pure "the" proletariat for-itself without sacrificing human individuality. Establishing the collective annihilates the individual.

It must be said that the corporate, financial, and political élite have a vested interest in identity politics because they work to fracture the proletariat. Gay rights, women's rights, black rights, senior rights, ethnic rights - each and every one of these fragment the working class into sub-groups that, rather than strive for political supremacy as a class, strive for demographic-specific goals. These competing political interests cause each demographic inside the proletariat to fight against one another in a never-ending politico-sociologic struggle wherein each fights for political supremacy; they are arrayed against one another instead of uniting for fight for their common interests.

The goal, then, of those involved in both continental philosophy and revolutionary politics is to formulate a programme wherein the proletariat is able to institute a socialist mode of production that serves the direct material interests of the working-class majority *collectively, as a class for-itself and acting out of its own volition, without abolishing individuality in the process*. How do we go about doing so? I postulate that the means through which we can do so begin with a proper understanding of the relationship between the *individual* and the *collective*, as well as between the *proletariat* and the *State*. Let me explain.

The State is the hegemonic organ that arises out of irreconcilable class antagonisms, and works to facilitate the supremacy of one class over another as they have competing economic interests. Those bourgeois class that currently controls the State is not a heterogenous class like the proletariat - it is homogenous, united, and dedicated to perpetuating its political supremacy. Even the social narratives that justify the serialization of the proletariat - race, gender, religion, sexuality, ethnicity, age, and so on - do not carry the same heavy sociopolitical connotation for the bourgeoisie as they do for the working class. The bourgeois are independent of age, of race, and of gender: they care for none of the biologic or social serials that uses to fracture and weaken the working class. It cares only for the accumulation of capital so as to further its own politico-economic agendas. It is for this reason that any fundamental conflict between the two that results in a revolutionary re-constitution of society is not going to be social in nature - that is, a revolt against capitalism cannot simply be a culture war against antiquated, feudal-, and colonial-era traditionalism and morality. The class war between the bourgeoisie and the proletariat must be fought on purely economic grounds, because any sociologic culture war is not going to be sufficient for laying the foundations of a new mode of production. Sociology can influence economics, but it does not generate new economies. Only a populist, proletarian revolution has the power to radically transform economics in the direction that we wish.

Any confrontation between the homogenous bourgeoisie and the heterogenous proletariat is not going to be taken up by the whole proletariat. Entire sections of the working class are not currently ripe for revolution. Whole segments of the proletariat have - via the generations-long State-sponsored propaganda campaign that we call the mainstream media - internalized bourgeois morality and have existed amongst superstructural narratives for so long that they have forgotten how to question their structural integrity. As a result, only a particular strata of the proletariat is in the mindset necessary to develop revolutionary consciousness. This section, the vanguard party, is the one that is going to have to instigate the first elements of fundamental change and inspire the overwhelming majority of the proletariat to join suit.

The vanguard party will be the strata that works to take the first step toward seizing control of the State political apparatus and orientating it and its immense legal, economic, and political authority in the direct material interests of the working class. As this democratic revolution continues and the vanguard is able to use State media to have its message be heard, its size will grow to the point wherein the number of revolutionary proletarians outnumbers the number of non-revolutionary proletarians. At this point can we consider the proletariat to be a class for-itself rather than simply a class in-itself, and it will be able to assume its historic responsibility of establishing a genuinely alternative mode of production.

The heterogenous proletariat will not be able to form a homogenous, unified vanguard to oppose to the bourgeoisie. But, it will only be able to stage an effective proletarian revolution when it realizes that the vanguard that initiates the process will be a heterogenous association of revolutionaries dedicated to social and economic justice that operate in a democratic fashion, not Blanquist-inspired democratic centralism. This seems to suggest that, once the vanguard has assumed control of the State, a multi-party system will exist wherein all are dedicated to justice and liberation but approach such on different terms.

Yet, how does the vanguard come about? If the proletariat cannot form a homogenous fused-group vanguard, then how shall socialism be instigated? And does not its establishment of any fused-group vanguard annihilate individuality to establish collectivity?

This is the problem which we must overcome. We must sketch a means through which the proletariat for-itself can be de-serialized so as to give it the opportunity to form a fused-group vanguard intent on socialist construction *without metaphysically destroying the individuality of its constituent proletarians in the process.*

If the problem is reduced to the impossibility of heterogenous serials uniting into a homogenous vanguard, then we must ask what the cause of that serialization is, and if overcoming and negating it would facilitate any successful homogenization. There is reason to think that it would, intuitively; if serialization is induced by bourgeois narratives of identity politics, then de-serialization could be brought about by establishing an environment conducive for the abolition of the narratives themselves. That is, do what needs to be done to de-legitimize the functional specialization that defines each serial.

This needs not be done by violently annihilating its individuality, but rather by raising the serial to a position wherein it has the political power to exert definitive decision-making influence on the State.

Doing this would mean that the political programmes of each serial (racial justice for ethic groups, legal equality of non-heterosexual relationships, social and financial equality between the genders, etc) would have to be completed to such a thorough degree that the serial itself would loose its functional specialization - that is, it would loose the thing that defines it as a serial and, contingently, be de-serialized and rendered non-demographic.

This means that only the comprehensive institutionalization of all the social, political, and economic demands of each serial would effectively de-serialize them and establish conditions conducive for the formation of a homogenous vanguard of for-itself proletarians. Given that de-serialized conditions are met, the proletariat would be able to act as class for-itself and overcome all of the anti-revolutionary narratives that justify serialization by forming an effectively (yet not necessarily "fully", as some lumpenproletariat may hold anti-revolutionary tendencies) homogenous proletariat. Only after de-serialization can the proletariat be prepared to take up the historic task of constructing international socialism - given the means of production are sophisticated enough to overcome material scarcity. Only through overcoming scarcity will the economic preconditions for a legitimately socialist mode of production be set, and only a de-serialized proletariat has the potentially to seize control of the State political apparatus and fundamentally re-orientate it towards that goal.

On Sartre's "The Ghost of Stalin"

"Socialism in a single country", or Stalinism, does not constitute a deviation from socialism; it is the long way around it that is imposed on it by circumstances. The rhythm of and evolution of this defensive construction are not determined by the consideration alone of Soviet resources and needs but also by the relations of the USSR with the capitalist world, in a word, by circumstances external to socialization that oblige it constantly to compromise its principals."

In this excerpt, Sartre lays out the foundational differences that separate Stalinism from Marxism. Due to the fact that the West was, predictably enough, hostile to the Soviet Union because the "socialism" it allegedly represented was a legitimate political threat to systemic capitalism, the USSR was forced to undertake its economic industrialization without any international aid. The result was not merely national isolation, but a contingent perversion of its governing philosophy which, from its very inception via Marx and Engels, was profoundly internationalist. The internationalism of socialism was warped and became a distorted form of nationalism: a bizarre, patriotic devotion to the construction of socialism that vilified the capitalist powers who had a vested interest in impeding it.

One cannot expect the Soviet experiment to have turned out anything other than an amalgam of collectivism and nationalism, especially when the internationalism - one of the fundamental, core tenants of socialism - was violently removed and the Russian populace was forced to undertake the task of constructing industrial modernity on its own.

Despite the fact that I agree with Sartre on many an issue, this is one where he and I do not. Let me clarify: despite the fact that many on the political non-Left have equated

Marxist-Leninism with Stalinism[88], I think that it is important to dissociate the two from one another. There are significant areas wherein they overlap, but the distinctions between the two have enough philosophic subtly that, in my opinion, justify a separation between the two. Sartre views "Stalin-ism" as an manifestation of Marxist-Leninism appropriate for the material and economic conditions that existed in the Soviet Union, and I do as well; however, the difference between him and I is rooted in his belief that Stalinism "does not constitute a deviation from socialism". I am firmly convinced that, while Stalinism was born out of the Marxist-Leninism doctrine that presided over the newborn Soviet Union after Lenin, it was a profound deviation from it. The principals of Stalinism - "socialism in one country", socialist patriotism, the cult of personality, the "aggravation of class struggle under socialism", and anti-revisionism - are all profoundly anti-socialist in character and use convoluted Marxist theory to justify economic systems that are anti-worker in character.

Despite the fact that I disagree with the majority of Marxist-Leninism, credit must be given where credit is due: as an managerial system, it was able to induce rapid industrialization and bring a backwards, feudal-agrarian culture into relative economic modernity, even though its succession of

---

[88] Including some of those on the Left as well, although it is not difficult to understand why: due to Marxist-Leninism being the official philosophy of the Soviet state, and Stalin being the *de facto* head of all Soviet affairs, the two have become intimately connected. At this point in history, the distinction between the two is generally only a matter of debate for academics, as the two are generally considered to be synonymous by the general public.

Five Year Plans resulted in politically-engendered mass famines[89].

The idea of "socialism in one country" was borne out of the desire to pursue the construction of socialism without international aid. As mentioned, the stripping of internationalism from socialism de-values both, and turns socialism into a mockery of itself: it reduces it to a contradictory hybrid of nationalism and egalitarianism, whose development over time only results in the exacerbation of these contradictions, resulting in a complete collapse of any and all socialism that hides under the moniker of "socialism". The support for this "socialism" is justified by socialist patriotism, a dedication to "socialist" construction within the bounds of "socialism in one country". Dissociating internationalism from socialism only results in a isolated, progressive nationalism.

It is thus important to view Stalinism not as a form of socialism proper, but rather as a deviation from traditional Marxist-Leninism that was caused by both international isolation *and* pre-scarcity economic conditions - the two of these resulted in a failure of socialist construction, and any future attempt to build socialism must take the historical implications of Stalinism into account.

The "cult of personality" that was established under Stalin - and to other extents, the ones under Mao in China, and under Hoxha and Tito in the East Bloc - was not politically designed to further his social and economic agendas. It was not an intentional movement created by the Party to manufacture mass adoration of the Party, and leaders, or the State. Instead, it was an organic movement that was produced by the specific material conditions that existed in Russia at the time. In order to perpetuate the Soviet government, grant Stalinist "socialism" a

---

[89] Of course, the economic calamities in the Soviet Union that resulted in the deaths of numerous peasants and workers were caused by more than more political management (a centralized decision-making body far removed from the local areas their decisions impacted; a Party whose democratic centralism marked alternative view points as "counter-revolutionary"; etc), because the economic pre-conditions of post-scarcity where not met.

sense of public legitimacy, and illustrate the public's support for domestic "socialist" construction, the Russian populace rallied together against perceived Western imperialism[90]. This "rally around the flag" phenomena did not result in mere support for the newfound Soviet government, but also support for the head of the government. Thus the "cult of personality" under Stalin was less about Stalin himself and more about the mass support for whoever happened to be the leader at that perilous time.

Rather than refer to a Stalinist "cult of personality", we should refer to mass public support for the office of "socialist" leadership itself, regardless of the individual who occupied that space. Therefore, the Stalinist "cult" could have easily been a "cult" in support of whoever else may have historically have had the opportunity to lead the Soviet Union instead of him, and the "cult" was thus the product of historic and material conditions and not of a conniving Party.

However, it should be noted that - once this "rally around the flag" phenomena did organically manifest - the Party and its leaders were able to co-opt and influence its development and direction. The Party did not create the "cult", but they did co-opt it for their political purposes.

The Stalinist conception of the "aggravation of class struggle under socialism" is rooted in a fundamental misunderstanding of the Marxian notion of historical materialism, and of the nature of class relations at different points in the over-arching historical dialectic. A socialist mode of production is going to be one wherein there are no classes; the bourgeoisie will be liquidated as a class via the socialization of the means of production by the revolutionary dictatorship of the proletariat. This dictatorship represents the terminal end of

---

[90] "Perceived" in that the Soviet government had a vested interest in demonizing the liberal democracies in the West, just as the West demonized the Soviets. Despite the fact they did engage in open political, financial, and military conflict, the Soviets did exaggerate the extent of the conflict to aid in Western demonization.

capitalism: while imperialism[91] is the final period wherein capitalism is governed by commodity-production, the dictatorship of the proletariat will signify a conscious re-direction of State power by the proletariat which - as a class not merely in-itself but also for-itself - will contingently coincide proportionally with the State's "withering" de-politicization. This dictatorship will only take place when the means of production are sophisticated enough to overcome aggregate material scarcity.

This has profound implications, because it means that that a successful proletarian government can only be established at a specific point in the historical dialectic. It cannot happen *before* that point because the economic preconditions which define the specific point's specificity have not yet been established.

Stalin argues that there will be an "aggravation of class struggle under socialism" because he equates socialism with *being* the dictatorship of the proletariat. I dissent and argue that socialism will commence at the historical point wherein the dictatorship of the proletariat will have succeeded in liquidating the bourgeoisie as a class, thereby ending class relations and contingently ending the proletariat. There can be no "aggravation" of class relations under socialism because classes themselves would not exist. Thus I think that Stalin's theory shows a misunderstanding of the historical dialectic because he equates socialism with a historical phenomena (class) that will be antiquated and abolished at that point in the over-arching historical process. It would have been more appropriate for him to refer to an "aggravation of class struggle under the dictatorship of the proletariat" because there would be a period

---

[91] It does not matter whether "imperialism" is violent military aggression to seize land and natural resources or the opening up of hyper-active foreign markets. In the end, they both serve the same economic function: staving of one culture's internal economic collapse by exploiting the resources of another abroad. This is what Lenin describes in his book *Imperialism, the Highest and Final Stage of Capitalism.*

of intense class conflict while the proletarian-seized State liquidates the bourgeoisie.

Anti-revisionism is something else that continues to plague Stalinism. It represents a dogmatism so intense, so fundamentalist and unwilling to engage in self-analysis, that it renders itself static and unable to adapt to material conditions. While this does allow for the preservation of original teachings, it does so in a way that violently rejects any modicum of modernization that might render it more effective. Stalinism's anti-revisionist tendencies make it intolerant to change, differing interpretation, or circumstantial application.

Each of these political phenomena that are unique to Stalinism - "socialism in one country", socialist patriotism, the cult of personality, the "aggravation of class struggle under socialism", and anti-revisionism - are what I consider to be the things that define it as unique perversion of Marxist-Leninism born out of unique economic conditions, and not as Marxist-Leninism proper. Stalin's legacy was not only politically-induced famines, mass famines, centralization of power, and expansive thought-control - it also includes the poisoning of Marxist-Leninism and of socialism as a whole.

On Luxemburg's "Reform or Revolution"

I have taken a firm stance for and against reform at different times. This is not because my opinion regarding the political nature of reform has changed, but rather than different answers were required at different times because the parameters of the questions were circumstantially unique. The value that reform has should not be determined by the fact that it is or is not reform; that is, one should not support reform *over* revolution *because* it is reform, and one should not *oppose* reform *for* revolution. The value of reform is only proportional to the degree of change that it brings about to class relations, given that the change is directly conducive for proletarian de-serialization and explicit politico-economic hegemony.

This means that reform is a means, not an end. The goal of any political movement should not be simply to enact progressive legislation, but rather to challenge the structural integrity of the mode of production itself as a whole, thereby setting the preconditions upon which a success revolution can be carried out. These preconditions must fundamentally overcome both scarcity and serialization before the political vanguard can re-orient the economy in the direct material interests of the working class. Reform is not the means through which socialism can (or will) be enacted, but it does have the potential to be a tool through which a revolutionary environment can be fostered given that it addresses structural class relations.

Reform must deconstruct the bourgeois dictatorship and construct the proletarian one. However, the consideration, implementation, and expansion of each reform must be analyzed in relation to the class relations at that specific historical and material moment. Does the reform upset, reverse, or instigate the reconstitution of the relations of production? Does a legislative change in property law have the potential to impact real-world class relations? Does the expropriation of one party's property by another party have the potential to make that property work in the interests of its expropriator? Does the economic reform have the potential to introduce elements of democratic decision-making and local management in the means of production?

There are indeed reforms that socialists should support because they can improve the immediate material living-standards of the working class. These reforms are going to differ from one liberal democracy to another because the material and economic conditions in each nation are going to be unique and different, but there are general ones that would be applicable, in some form or fashion, to them all. These can include: universal healthcare via a non-profit single-payer program; investment in, and development of, domestic "green" energy that is conducive for ecologic sustainability and the preservation of biodiversity; a comprehensive public education system that provides high-quality schooling so that the populace is provided with the tools to critically deconstruct systems of power; a culture that promotes creative self-expression and social diversity; and an economic system characterized by democratic decision-making.

Yet, in order to be intellectually honesty, one must not assume that reform is enough to establish socialism. It is not. The bourgeoisie is not going to allow the enacting of any progressive legislation that will abolish capitalist class relations; any reform that is actualized is going to actualize with the implicit (and sometimes explicit) permission of the ruling class. The rulers will not allow legislative change that takes away the power through which they rule - reform may address and tweak class relations, but it will not ever be able to the means through which they will be subject to a revolutionary re-constitution. Reforms that are enacted come into being with the support of the bourgeoisie itself, because their enactment de-radicalizes the working class - that is, the working class becomes complacent with a series of immediate political reforms (healthcare, education, infrastructure, social security and pension programs, etc) that improve its short-term standard of living, and thus looses sight of the greater socialist goal. The bourgeoisie has a vested interest in reforms because it drains the proletariat of revolutionary zeal, even if that de-revolutionizing forces them to capitulate to some working-class demands.

What should one do about reform, then? Should one support it because it has the potential to improve the living standards and economic conditions of the working class? Or should one reject it because it perpetuates capitalism and, contingently, systemic exploitation?

The answer is simple. One should do both. One should support the programmes that would bring about a legitimate, noticeable, and structural improvement of working-class living conditions, but one should not do so with the assumption that such reforms will bring about socialism. No parliament or congress is ever going to enact socialism. Fundamental economic change is not going to be enacted via a parliamentary route because parliaments, as the organized manager of bourgeois affairs, will never voluntary hand over the politico-economic decision-making power that they have which characterizes them as hegemonic. Any obtainment of meaningful power by the proletariat is going to be the result of prolonged, violent, progressive movements undertaken by the proletariat itself, not by the permission of the bourgeoisie. The rulers will never voluntarily step down from being rulers.

Yet reform does have the potential to advance the cause of the proletariat in some respects. It will not bring about a new mode of production, but progressive political parties that participate in parliaments have the opportunity of enacting social legislation that is conducive for the de-serialization of the proletariat - that is, reducing the fragmenting effects of identity politics by promoting social and financial parity, so that the proletariat will be able to focus on its class interests as opposed to demographic-specific ones.

Although Bernstein will always have a special place in my heart because he was one of the first socialists whose books I read, I must agree with Luxemburg. Her devastating critique of reform, and of the tendency of evolutionary socialism to directly detrimental to socialism as a whole, is something that I think that reformist-tactic socialists must read.

Luxemburg puts it well in the opening introduction to "Reform or Revolution":

"The daily struggle for reforms, for the amelioration of the condition of the workers within the framework of the existing social order, are for democratic institutions, offers to the social

democracy the only means of engaging in the proletarian class war and winning in the direction of the final goal - the conquest of political power and the suppression of wage-labor. Between social reforms and revolution there exists for the social democracy an indissoluble tie. The struggle for reforms is its means; the social revolution, it aims."

She also addresses an issue that I think has been systemic in the past: that political philosophy and critical-thinking have often been reserved by the revolutionary party, and any attempted dictatorship of the proletariat has degenerated into an élitist dictatorship of the intelligentsia. Indeed, socialism seems to have moved from being a movement of mass worker revolt to being an academic socialism of the intelligentsia. So long as socialist ideas are withheld from the general public, they will always be mental exercises for those in their ivory towers. Socialist ideas *must* be brought into mainstream discourse so as to expose the whole population to them if revolutionary consciousness is ever going to take root. She puts it better than I can in the introduction's closing.

"As long as theoretical knowledge remains the privilege of a handful of 'academics' in the Party, the latter will face the danger of going astray. Only when the great mass of workers takes the keen and dependable weapons of scientific socialism in their own hands will all the petty-bourgeois inclinations, all the opportunistic currents, come to naught."

The opening section of "Reform or Revolution" addresses something that I have been been saying for several years now: that the development of financial credit has has proven to be the means through which proletarian consciousness is suppressed. This is because cheap credit, loans, payment plans, and other ways of stretching out one's money have created an illusion of having more money than one actually does, which contingently prevents individuals from becoming aware of their real socio-economic position.

"The capacity of capitalism to adapt itself, says Bernstein, is manifested first in the disappearance of general economic crises, resulting from the development of the credit system, employer's organizations, wider means of communication, and informational services. It shows itself in the ... elevation of vast layers of the proletariat to the level of the middle class. It is furthermore proved, argues Bernstein, by the amelioration of the economic and political situation of the proletariat as a result of trade-union activity."

The "disappearance of general economic crises" may be true, because there has been a gradual improvement of the living conditions of the working class over the past several centuries; however, this "disappearance" has resulted in internal contradictions that occasionally explode into full-out financial meltdowns. The Great Depression, and the recessions of the 1970s and 2007, are examples of this. Yet this "elevation of vast layers of the proletariat to the middle class" is rooted in the belief that there *is* a middle class, which only exists as a manufactured illusion generated by credit, loan, and money-stretching schemes to convince proletarians that they are not really proletarians. If the working class is going to go from being a class in-itself to a class for-itself (that is, actually develops genuine proletarian class consciousness), then we socialists need to have open, frank, and honest discussions with everyday workers about the socio-economic position that they actually occupy.

On Social Intersectionality and Base-Superstructure Theory

What can we say about the base and superstructure? If we recognize that the superstructure (and the myriad social meta-narratives that constitute it) is but a sociologic reflection of the base (and its constituent relations of production at any specific anthropologic point in the historical dialectic), should it not also follow that classism would be carried over from the latter to the former? Would it not make sense that the oppressor-oppressed dynamic present in the current relations of production be carried over into the superstructure, establishing a sort of supra-narrative that is laced throughout all of the individual constitutive narratives, thus creating a *anthropo-sociologic class* to be the mirror image of the *politico-economic class*?

Does this dialectic relationship mean that there is both *economic class* (proletarian or bourgeoisie) and a *social class* (oppressed or oppressor)?

By this, it means that the numerous narratives in the superstructure (race, religion, gender, culture, sexuality, politics, etc) also have, within them, class relations that are expressive of one's position in production. That is, the intersectionality of one's positions amongst all of the social narratives that constitute the superstructure is the the purely sociologic representation of one's class in production.

Thus, numerous structuralist binaries have arisen amongst each of the narratives in an attempt to simplify sociologic class with directly diametric poles. Of course, there are most likely a variety of classes (a gradation, if you will) that are recycled amongst the two, given a particular political climate or economic moment.

Race is commonly broken down into "black" or "white", giving what is normally a simple biotic phenomena to have a profoundly politico-sociologic effect; thus, the historical-materialist process of history shows the anthropologic creation of "race" as a political factor came about shortly after the establishment of the "State" as a necessary organ of economic hegemony. The difference between race and "race" is that the former is an example of biotic evolution, the latter is a profoundly politico-sociologic term that has gained an increasingly heavy meaning and social context based upon anthropologic development. "Race", as it is currently discussed in political discourse, operates with the State-induced preconceived notion that there is any intrinsic difference amongst human beings; that is, it starts from a profoundly anti-egalitarian standpoint and unquestioningly accepts the structural boundaries of discourse. "Race", as a political term, arose after the creation of the State, and the battle to end "race"-ism is intimately tied up with the withering away, and eventual abolition, of the State.

It can be assumed that the fundamental "black"-or-"white"dichotomy that hovers over the capitalist plane occupies a space wherein non-binary individuals are not merely rejected by the political system but rather *not recognized* as part of the narrative at all. This is most likely in order to simplify the social antagonisms that are experienced in a given narrative. For example, "red", "yellow", and other colloquially described racial groupings are not factored into the overall equation in order to retain the structuralist simplicity of mere "black"-or-"white". This social anesthetization - this unconscious rejection of particular intra-serial group from the entire narrative - is most likely tied up in the anthropologic development of the contemporary State as a distinct politico-national entity. As the State secured totalitarian hegemony, so too did a profoundly politicized sociology replace one that had naturally developed amongst co-operative organisms.

The evolutionary migration of primitive *Homo sapiens* from the evolutionary cauldron of Africa-Mesopotamia westward across modern Europe, and eastward across the Middle and Far East, prompted cascading mutative distinctions based upon the environmental conditions that were present at that given point in time. And, given the smaller boundary westward of this area, exponential population growth and increasingly-developing communities created the need for a distinct political order (the "State" based upon productive class relations) that the Far East did. This is because the Far East had a far greater quantity of land necessary to explore before geographic boundaries were reached and population growth caused the rise of their own political orders. Thus, the political system in the east began later, and slower, than the west. As a result of this, the power systems in the west, being more developed, would have an infinitely more complex superstructure (specifically, in the aggregate number *of* constituent narratives, not necessarily the complexity of the class relations *within* each narrative). These factors - the smaller land mass, the contingently faster development of modern State relations, and the increasing complexity of the reflective superstructure - would give rise to the foundations of modern racial politics.

These are often illustrated in fascist (specifically, Naziist) theory by the fact that contemporary socio-cultural revolutions (the Enlightenment, the Renaissance, major scientific and mathematical discoveries, etc) have happened in the west which - with its contingently faster-developed political system - was wrapped up in the anthropologic evolution of the concept that we now refer to "racially" as "white".

The intersectionality of numerous factors - western economic development, reflective social development, etc - gave rise to a naturally-occurring evolutionarily biotic process being the space subject to intense narrative politicization.

What is it about the biotic white race (or, the "white" "race") that gives it any special characteristics? Nothing, other than the fact that "white" (in a profoundly politico-sociologic context) entity grew out of the conditions existent at a specific historical moment: a moment wrought with rapid economic development, subsequent rapid social-superstructure development, and thus the drive for absolutist simplicity in the new-found structuralist narrative binaries.

The "white" "race" is only superior to the "black" "race" in that the former has been given the position of occupying a social space reserved for the bourgeois amongst the social relations of production. With the need for simplification in antagonistic social-superstructure classes, the distinction of the white "race" as the superior "white" "race" came about only through the fact that white individuals were engaged in a specific cultural revolution at a specific time.

Thus do we see, upon deconstruction, how the capitalist relations of production are intimately caught up in its own anthropo-sociologic extension, political racism. Thus, we see racist nationalism (e.g., Naziism) as a distinctly necessary phase through which a society may have to pass, if the anthropologic and politico-economic conditions conducive for its development occur. It can be seen as one of the many "growing pains" of international capitalism, along with others (economic crises at the point of advent globalization, reactionary-feudal sentiment against the delayed bourgeois-democratic revolutions in the neo-colonized worlds, etc).

Race is not the only narrative which has been subject to a rigid, structuralist framework that oversees a purely-absolutist binary. As the "white" "race" (e.g., bourgeoisie) sits opposite the "black" "race" (e.g., proletariat), so do numerous other diametric contrasts. Examples of these can be easily seen in: in sexuality, "straight" opposite "gay"; in religion, the "saved" and "forgiven" opposite the "heretic" and "unforgiven"; in gender, "male" opposite "female"; in politics, "Left" or "Right"; in culture, "citizen" opposite "foreigner".

Thus, we see that the relationship that one has with production is given the privilege of simultaneously occupying a specific social space. The bourgeoisie coincides with the "white", "straight", "saved", "male", "conservative" "citizen". The proletarian represents the intersectionality of the "black", "gay", "unsaved", "female", "progressive" "foreigner". The oppressor-oppressed dynamic that exists between the bourgeois and proletarian classes in the economic arena is carried over into the social superstructure that reflects it.

It is quite obvious to see how heterosexuality was elevated above homosexuality. Not only is it easy to see how a naturally-occurring biotic phenomena that serves the direct propaganda of species could be rapidly politicized (that is, its direct relation to propagated "race"-ism), but one can see that its elevation to space of greater social supremacy correlates with the need to reinforce the developing capitalist relations of the family. The politicization of biotic heterosexuality into "straight", and the probably mutation-induced population control that is homosexuality into "gay", occurred at the anthropological point wherein it was necessary to enforce the idea of the capitalist nuclear "family". Thus the family became the "family", a distinct political unit, with the culmination of the the politicalization of "straight"-"gay", "white"-"black", and "male"-"female" binaries.

Heterosexuality has been given the politicized status of "straight" because, with organismal reproduction being a simple biotic process, it is merely a naturally occurring phenomena in nature, and natural biotic events are far more easily to politicize due to the fact that they are objectively normative (or, at least as "normative" as be without falling into nihilistic solipsism) and not a pseudo-philologic abstraction. It is far easier to politicize things that *exist* than to *create something* and give it a politico-sociologic connotation.

Because species propagation is a naturally-occurring objective reality, things that facilitate appropriate reproduction (that is, heterosexual relations) are more easily victim to the simple structuralist binary that reinforces capitalist family relations. This is because engaging in reproduction (as either parent organism) is a profoundly political act that ensures the possible creation of "others" (offspring, etc) who will require material sustenance, thus consciously inducing additional competition for finite material resources by increasing the aggregate population that seeks to use those resources.

In intersectionality of class amongst these three particular superstructure narrative - race, gender, and sexuality - form the basic foundation of what is, in contemporary political discourse, referred to as the "family". As each of these three social phenomena are the sociologic reflection of the given material conditions of a specific mode of production, it can be stated with a fair degree of certainty that a change in material conditions will yield a relatively parallel change in social conditions.

Does this suggests that reproductive child-rearing will loose its political character when the material conditions that constitute finite scarcity are overcome, thus rending population growth to be non-political act? Yes and no. We can say that, with the complete withering of the State, the class characteristics of numerous social power structures (such as the family meta-narrative) will contingently wither away, and the politics (that is, the class hegemony) of the family will gradually disappear until the "family" has been rendered only an apolitical unit characterized by the consenting and mutual association of love between individuals, regardless of their "race", "gender", or "sexuality".

As for "gender", it is easy to see how it (along with "sexuality") is politicized, as it, being rooted in biological normativity[92], is a natural target for hegemonic powers to take advantage of. In order to facilitate structural simplicity via binary absolutism, gender (and the wide spectrum of biotic sexes that organisms can be part of) has been reduced to an either-or, with the subject in question being labeled as *either* a male *or* a female. Thus, the politicalization of male into "male" and female into "female" has forcefully moved all human beings into one of these two absolutist camps, with non-binary genders (which occur naturally in nature) being violently rejected from the system and occupying a space of harsh, disenfranchising non-recognition. With socio-anthropologic developments and the rise of complex political communities, the concept of "male" and "female" have become tinged with increasingly powerful social presuppositions of masculinity and femininity, respectively. "Male" has since been associated with war, violence, protectionism, authoritarian structures, being the "domestic provider", and non-emotionalism. "Female" has become associated with pacifism, gentleness, emotional sensationalism, and being the "domestic keeper". Given anthropologic development, men and women have grown into deeply political "men" and "women".

---

[92] In an attempt to excuse myself from unconsciously subscribing to this State-induced structuralism, by "biological normativity" I mean individuals that participate in reproductive coitus by supplying testicular or ovule gametes; I mean male and female that occupy the space of viable embryologic activity. It can easily be seen how this *biotic* space an organism occupies can be radically different than its own *social* space.

Biologic males have been reduced to being a bourgeois-political "male", and biologic females have been reduced to merely proletarian-oppressed "female".

Individuals who identify as something other than "male" or "female" - be they transgender, transsexual, genderqueer, agender, post-gender, bigender, non-gender, etc - thus take residence in a unique social space. Like those who are neither "black" nor "white", those who are neither "male" nor "female" are generally subject to the unconscious neglect publicized (and indeed, propagated) by those who are hopelessly victim to State-defined boundaries of discourse. By this, I mean that those who have accepted, and function within, the socially "acceptable" boundaries that have been put forth by a State-created culture - that is, publicly-accepted and socially-perpetuated radical cis-normativity - are generally victim assuming that the either-or male-female binary represents the only two existent genders. To operate within one's *economic* class (bourgeoisie or proletarian) is systemic; to do so within one's *social* class (one of the cultural binaries in a given superstructural narrative) is done purely out of a induced sense of need, a forced participation in the structural binary as one of its two polar opposites through an educational culture that brings about a totalitarian-normative mindset. The binary is not real or normative - it is a sociologic perversion brought about by abusive and hegemonic power structures.

The economic base is deterministic, but the social superstructure is only influential. One cannot escape one's *economic* position unless the mode of production is fundamentally changed, but one can change one's *social* position[93] if one if able to break out of the State-provided framework of discourse. Rather than identify with the *opposite* binary option in order to challenge it (such as "black" individuals fighting for the same political rights as "white" individuals), one should occupy the intervening non-space that lies between the binary poles.

An example of this should be that those who care about the abolition of "gender" and "sexuality" as political constructs should work not towards "gender equality" or "same-sex rights", but rather should struggle for the conscious, total abolition of social-narrative binaries. One cannot escape one's economic class without fundamentally altering the relations of production, but one can challenge the relations of a given superstructural narrative by critically analyzing the narrative itself, and by consciously occupying the non-space between the binary poles.

The superstructural system has a vested interest in supporting those that oppose it. By having an opposition to a given structural narrative that is organized and vocal, the superstructure is able to institutionalize dissent by allowing to coalesce into a single, fused mass. Being "against" a social narrative reinforces the existence of the narrative itself, thus providing a situation of intense embourgeoisment wherein dissent is incorporated into the system. Much in the same way progressive labor unions have degenerated into a reactionary labor-aristocracy, so too does legitimate dissent fall victim to becoming an organ of the system itself.

---

[93] To a degree. The social "either-or" binary that exists in a given narrative will continue to exist so long as the mode of production that gave rise to it continues to as well. That being said, the system does support non-conformist activism because challenging structural boundaries reinforces the existence of those boundaries themselves. Those that challenge "gender" and "sexuality" through the gay rights movement's declaration of "same-sex" rights, for example, may be pushing the boundaries of social acceptance, but by doing so they reinforce the concept of "sex" as a political construct in the process. Rather than *abolish* "gender" and "sexuality", much of the LGBT liberation effort *strengthens* them.

An interesting example of this can include the fight for transgender rights and transsexual equality. Indeed, there are certainly individuals who's psychological profile does not match their biological one; the biotic phenomena that we call "the body" may not correlate with the State-induced sociologic role that one may identify with psychologically. Of course, this is natural, as gender and sexuality exist in a wide spectrum in nature. Yet, despite this, there are those individuals that are so hopeless indoctrinated by the system that they cling to superstructural-narrative interpretations of binary-challenging roles: religion decrying them as sinful, reactionary pseudo-science calling it a biotic abnormality, and so on. Yet despite the fact that these two opposite camps - the trans-advocates and the cis-supremacists - are politically diametric, they both serve the same purpose: to act as agents of the system that take inverted views of narrative-binaries, creating a complex network of dialectical support for the entire superstructure.

By being a cis-supremacist, one enforces the idea of being *either* "male" *or* "female", which the system enjoys for its radical simplicity, allowing the easy perpetuation of both the relations of production and of general capitalist hegemony. The either-or binary of absolute "gender" effortlessly facilitates the perpetuation of "gender"-based division of labor and of domestic relations, which both serve as some of the most fundamental building blocks of capitalist sociology. By being a trans-advocate, one argues that it is appropriate, acceptable, and even desirable (from a variety of perspectives - moral, secular, sociologic, medical, etc) for an individual of one "gender" to traverse the intervening non-space in the binary-narrative and situation one's self in the *opposite* "gender" pole. Trans-advocates preserve, sustain, and nurture the "gender" binary by giving one the option to switch "genders" - that is, to modify one's self (physically, sociologically, etc) so that the person in question can occupy the binary pole that is opposite their own. While cis-supremacists argue that one's gender and sexuality should match (indeed, by perfectly correlated with) the superstructure's "gender" and "sexual" narratives, trans-advocates assert that it is acceptable for one's gender and sexuality to *not* match either "gender" or "sexuality". By saying this, their argument dialectically synthesizes with that of their cis-supremacist opponents, into a culminating declaration of support for the narrative binary.

Cis-supremacists argue that the structural binary of "man" and "woman" is fixed and immutable; trans-advocates argue that one can move within the binary from *one pole* to *the other*. This is reductionist, but, by doing so - while asserting the right of individuals to be what they want to be (or, what they are, in the most fundamentally personal and sociologic sense) - they reinforce the binary narrative by stepping from one diametric pole to the other; that is, they capitulate to bourgeois hegemony by making their own self (biological, psychological etc) fall more in-line with the absolutist binary options of a particular narrative. By furthering transgenderism, the absolutist "gender" binary is reinforced through the acknowledgement of, and action upon, one's being in a particular bourgeois-defined space in the superstructural narrative. By being *trans*-gender, one is also *trans*-"gender", implying re-situating one's self in the diametric pole of the binary.

Rather than work for the legal and political right of an individual(s) to switch which binary pole they identify with, one should occupy the revolutionary non-space between them to challenge the premise of the binary itself. The comprehensive implications of this include the eventual abolition of "gender" and "sexuality" as a politico-sociologic construct, rendering all peoples (for all intents an purposes) to practice a sort of "pangender-pansexual"-ism, as it could be called today using contemporary feminist language, resulting in a mass post-gender eroticism; or, being the dialectical inverse, it has the potential to theoretically result in the universal practice of "agender-asexual"-ism based upon a non-sexual mass-Platonic dynamic.

Most likely, the abolition of "gender" and "sexuality" to mere gender and sexuality will result in the dialectic synthesis of the two, yielding individuals who are of numerous genders and sexualities yet whose labels do not retain a politico-sociologic character indicative of class relations. If effect, the de-politicalization of "gender" and "sexuality" will create a situation of proletarian liberation wherein individuals' given gender and sexuality (or, non-gender and non-sexuality) will be purely descriptive, apolitical qualitative terms, and will have no class character or be indicative of any position in the relations of production.

Challenging the structural binary that exists in each narrative is a deeply political, and profoundly revolutionary, act of sedition. To do so is to question and confront the social-narrative outgrowths of the capitalist mode of production. And, like any disease that requires that its symptoms and functionality be properly understood before it can be fully cured, so too will a proper understanding of superstructural narrative-binaries be needed before the capitalist base can be abolished.

Thus, the conscious rejection of the structuralist binary in a given superstructural narrative is only the first step in the revolutionary act of instigating its withering-away. In order for the narratives to be abolished proper, the mode of production needs to transcend capitalism and pass into socialism. Only when the means of production are held in common and operated in an egalitarian, democratic fashion that follows the principal of production-for-use as opposed to production-for-profit will the social superstructure loose its intensely politico-sociologic character. At that point, economic determinism will be but a relic of the past, and the voluntary, creative self-expression of individuals will replace bourgeois-induced sociologic roles.

Derrida puts it very well in his essay *Violence and Metaphysics* when he mentioned the "invasion of structuralism"; indeed, a majority (or even the totality) of the social superstructure is organized along structuralist lines, with absolutist binaries enforcing simplistic social relations to mirror one's position in productive relations. The "invasion" is over - at this point, it has transcended a mere entrance into social relations and the superstructure has become victim to an imperial occupation.

Violence is not necessarily a bad thing. Terrorism is, as Sartre said, the atomic weapon of the poor, and structural damage to the infrastructure of the oppressors can be a tremendous boon to the oppressed.

Death is not necessarily something that should ever be supported in and of itself. To kill another human being in cold blood shows a profound desensitization and soullessness; to use the death penalty is another. Capital punishment, in the hands of the bourgeois State, is a form of judicial coercion to induce conformity and ensure class hegemony through sensationalized "justice". Under a proletarian State, it is a tool used by the now-conscious working class to suppress reactionary criminals.

The "death penalty" is a tool of class hegemony. As the State withers away and looses its class characteristics, so too will the death penalty wither into an anachronistic, brutal power structure. Socialism will be classless, and those whose actions would have warranted death under capitalism will instead be subject to some form of imprisonment, an imprisonment whose goal is the radical alterity between criminal and society, contingent with a possibility for thorough education and re-integration into the socialist system.

It pains me to think that the proletarian revolution may need to be violent. I hate human suffering; there is nothing that grinds at my soul than seeing fellow human beings in pain. War, poverty, disease, famine - these are the things that we revolutions should be working to abolish. In our war against the structural foundations of capitalism, economic conditions that are not conducive to proletarian economic security may appear; during the violent revolution necessary to wipe the politico-economic slate clean, there may be people who are harmed in the process. Casualty and damage are unfortunate by-products of war, but the revolution is not meant to start a class war - it is the means of ending one, of ending a war that is waged day after day by the bourgeois against the proletarian.

What do I see when I look around me? I see so many people, casually sitting with one another, milling about and minding their own business. Some are doing homework; others are eating the food that they purchased at the miniature food court that our University sponsors. Every single one of them has a life. Every single one of them exists at the intersectionality of so many sociologic relations - from the stereotypical categorization of gender, ethnicity, sexuality, religion, and nationality to the privileged specificity of their own academic major and recreational hobbies.

Every single one of them is an individual. Every single one of them has made a million choices in their past, and every single one is going to make a million more today. Every single person is the culmination of a multitude of different social, economic, and political choices. Every single person is unique; there is not such thing as "average" or "the same" when it comes to human beings.

This is the freedom that man has - to do anything, to be anything, to make any choice at any time. Man has unlimited freedom and the unrestrained capacity to do anything that he wants at any time - or, the freedom to choose to do nothing, which is itself still a choice. It may be the most profoundly political choice, because an abstention from systemic participation has the potential to symbolize a rejection of all ambient reality. To do nothing is as radical as doing everything.

What does this say about Man? What does this say about the polity, when no Man can be like any other? If every person is unique and dynamic in a way unlike any other, what can be said about the legitimate feasibility of collectivism? Is not the polity antithetical to the individual? Does not any formation of social institutions through consensual social-contract participation result in the surrender of the Self in the name of creating the Group? The fact that the polity is "social" means that it is - in the most fundamental, syntactic way - at direct odds with the individual. When the Self begins to think of itself as having social definition based upon its relation to the political Group, then it has surrendered all liberty; there is no greater loss of Self than self-definition vis-à-vis the sociologic norms of the Group.

There cannot be a governmental Group and a personal Self. One only exists in the absence of the other; they are mutually exclusive. So long as social contract theory is upheld, the constituent individuals that form its sociologic collective will suffer radical dehumanization and a profound loss of personal identity. The social contract is a contract to destroy the Self in the name of creating the mass Group - in order to free man, there must be a complete abolition of the Group in every sphere of life. The Group must not survive. The Group must be destroyed so as to set the Self free and restore liberty to mankind.

But is this itself not a binary? Doesn't the act of forming a Group at the expense of negating the constituent Selfs generate an either-or binary wherein one is *either* a collective Group *or* an individual Self? And, if it is a binary, doesn't it mean that believing that it exists only means that we are falling prey to the simplicity of bourgeois sociology?

The human being, with all of its existential subjectivity, is far too complex and dynamic an organism to operate within the bounds of a radically reductionist either-or binary. Human beings are too creative, too expressive, too diverse, and too unique to allow every individual to fall into such a "this" or "that" category. To believe that superstructural binaries are legitimate expressions of humanity is an insult to the individuality of every human spirit. It is crude, reductionist, and anti-expressionist. Yet the collective-individual binary is something that must be addressed if those of us on the Left are to work towards the formation of a truly egalitarian sociology.

Perhaps we can overcome this binary by treating it the same way as the other superstructural narratives: by consciously occupying the revolutionary non-space between the binary polls in order to challenge the structural integrity of the whole system.

The revolutionary proletarian party occupies this non-space: the conscious, voluntary association of one's Self with other Selfs to constitute a heterogenous proletarian vanguard dedicated to the abolition of superstructural narratives is the means through which the binary, as a whole, can be structurally challenged and, eventually, deconstructed. That is, the revolutionary non-space between the "collective" and "individual" binary poles can be defined as the voluntary association of heterogenous, individually-unique de-serialized proletarians uniting as a class for-itself (and not in-itself) and actively working to abolish determinist social narrative via the building of a genuinely socialist mode of production. Only through the creation of a fundamentally new mode of production will economic relationships change; contingently, a chance in economic relationships will result in a profound change in sociologic relationships, including the de-politicalization of human-to-human association, thus negating the "collective"-"individual" binary and rendering it non-existent.

Like any and all binary systems, it will have fundamentally new characteristics and connotations when the capitalist base that gives it definition is changed in such a way that it is no longer capitalistic. Again, we come to the conclusion that the socialization of the means of production by the proletariat for-itself is the only way to effectively re-structure sociology so that it is conducive for the existential subjective to truly be free.

On Derrida's "Violence and Metaphysics"

Violence is absolutely necessary in the political process. Whether this violence manifests as politically metaphysic oppression (that is, conditions conducive for thought-control via mass media, the suppression of creative self-expression by intolerant morality, dissent-crushing undertones of social or racial supremacy in mainstream political discourse, etc) or explicit material destruction does not matter. There is one truism that runs through both: the violent engagement of one object on another only serves to show their respective structural integrities, and that violent challenge grants that structure definition, legitimacy, and meaning.

Things gain definition through conflict. There is violence around all of us every day - there is sociologic conflict as the moral and social values of the previous generations are clashing with those of the current one; there is military conflict around the world, testing the integrity, might, and will of domestic governments and their imperial colonizers; there is metaphysic violence when nation's cultures, and peoples' everyday behavior, promote the suppression of any voluntary, creative self-expression. Yet this violence is integral to the question of Being because its structural ontology is defined by the way that it interacts with conflict, regardless of its manifestation. Only through violent conflict do subjects, objects, and concepts gain any semblance of meaning and definition - as everything is politically and economically connected to everything else, each things gain definition through its engagement with everything else.

Because everything is connected and everything is violently interacting with everything else all the time, violence has a profoundly political characteristic because it serves the means through which all existential value is obtained. The gaining of existential value means the gaining of any value, because all value is determined by an existentially subjective subject. This means that the intentional integration of violence into political discourse is an attempt of de-stabilize means that, at some level, there is a challenge to the fundamental structuralism that constitutes the system and justifies its existence. This has profound implications, because it means that violence can be an effective and plausible means through which political agendas can be advanced.

Of course, violence must be integrated in some form or fashion into a revolutionary proletarian movement because it has the potential to strike at the core elements of the narratives that justify State hegemony. De-legitimizing those narratives by violently rendering them exposed to mass criticism can be a tool through which entire superstructures are politically deconstructed and contingently annihilated.

However, one should not take what I am saying and convolute it by thinking that I advocate violence for the sake of violence. I do not advocate for anything that is not directly conducive to the emancipation of the proletariat, and the improvement of all human relations as a whole; if anything, my views are rooted in peaceful co-operation and participatory democracy. I am simply pointing out the fact that violence has the potential to be used - and certainly, has been used - for political purposes. What I mean is that there are violent conflicts constantly raging between power structures that are competing for total hegemony, and that this violence is the means through which all things gain existential definition and social value. Nothing is more illustrative of this than the way wherein an individual psyche - what I have referred to as the "existential subjective" in other works - engages with the world each and every day, and comes to conclusions about world values via the accumulation of experiences.

Let us address the issue of the existential subjective operating within the confines of metaphysic violence.

Every single action that an individual does that engages them with the world is taking place at a time that is concurrent with the inter-violence of power structures that compete with one another for complete hegemony. *Dasein*'s being-in-the-world-ness takes place in a very unique context - a context wherein superstructural narratives all compete for both totalitarian institutionalization[94] and eternal perpetuation[95] in order to build a ruling meta-narrative. Yet because *Dasein*'s existential subjectivity and engagement with the world takes place amongst violently competing narratives that are reductionist and binary in nature, it's freedom is de-limited: the possible choices that it can make through which to gain existential definition are taking place in an arena of *either-or* and *this-or-that*. The direct sociologic choices that *Dasein* can make are limited and subject to operating in a reductionist framework established by hegemonic social narratives. It does not have the absolute freedom to do whatever it wants to gain existential definition, but is rather subject to operating within the confines of a totalitarian binary system whose own structural framework influence the outcome of the action *before the action is even made*. Sociologic oppression is manifest every day by violently controlling metaphysic choices, and the existential subjective will only be able to operate at its full capacity (that is, have the opportunity to gain existential definition via legitimately authentic, unrestrained, and voluntary actions and choices) when these behaviorally-determinist narratives are abolished. The conditions conducive for this abolition rest only in a revolutionary re-constitution of all economic (and contingently social) relations through the establishment of a genuinely socialist mode of production.

Binary totalitarianism violently limits *Dasein*'s existential subjectivity by forcing it to operate within the confines of politically-correct discourse. It does this in two ways. Firstly, by having the capitalist superstructure force sociologic conformitivity through a propagandistic campaign of "normalcy", "professionalism", and "political correctness".

---

[94] That is, the formation of a meta-narrative which is able to effectively dictate the structure and behavior of the social superstructure, and thus dictate all human sociology.

[95] By this, I mean that superstructural narratives are constantly fighting so as to establish conditions that are conducive for the given narrative (s) to be institutionalized indefinitely, and thus rendered radically normative

Secondly, it causes any discussion of *Dasein* or its existential subjectivity to only be able to be conducted in a manner wherein definition is gained by one's relation to either of the two binary poles. This has profound consequences, because it contingently means that any effective discussion about the nature of *Dasein*, its existential subjectivity, or the social narratives that violently de-limit the two is only able to take place in an arena wherein binary systems are already hegemonic. That is, no one can say anything about anything without already falling victim to the totalitarian system that we call "language".

Language is horrendously totalitarian in that every aspect of its structure only exists because binary systems have been institutionalized and made normative. Language is only able to exist because of binary totalitarianism. Things only gain meaning and definition by the relationship between their social position and one of the binary polls in a ruling narrative - and when numerous things gain meaning and definition, they are able to have reference. This reference is the basis of language, and helps illustrate why language is oppressive. Languages are only able to be formed on the basis of linguistic reference, and this reference only comes into being after a binary narrative is established This makes it impossible to do or say anything without already falling victim to operating within a rigidly authoritarian framework.

The only way through which *Dasein* and its existential subjectivity are able to truly gain definition is through the abolition of determinist narratives, but these narratives are fundamentally institutionalized in our day-to-day lives through both overt State support and the existence of language. Does this mean that advancing the cause of existential liberty will only be actualized by the contingent abolition of language, as language is the foundation for narrative hegemony? Yes and no - the answer is far too complex to say definitively one way or the other[96], but we have to make an attempt to deconstruct it if we are to have any insight into how to go about advancing the cause of human liberty.

It is impractical to ever think that language could be "abolished" in any legitimate way. Under no foreseeable circumstance will people wake up one day and universally decide to stop talking to one another because they believe it will expand their freedom. That would be ridiculous. However, we could do to language what is done to the State durning a genuinely Marxist revolution: create conditions that are conducive for the de-politicization, and thus self-negating de-legitimation, of language so that it looses its politically oppressive characteristics and becomes effectively classless. At first glance, this seems like a effective tactic, because the mechanism through which it can be done has already been laid out in other works: to change a sociologic construct, one has to fundamentally deconstruct and re-construct economic relations because, as has been discussed, any and all social change is merely a reflection of the *relations* of production under any given *mode* of production.

Thus, to go about changing language so that it is no longer socio-psychologically totalitarian, we would have to establish an entirely new sociology wherein it would not have those characteristics or connotations; and to establish such a sociology, we would not to construct a new mode of production. That is, the only way go about making language non-oppressive would be to systemically dismantle capitalism by changing property relations so that the means of production would be held

---

[96] And because declaring either "yes" or "no" would mean that we have, in the end, fallen into the binary trap wherein our answer is exclusively tied to a single pole. Having any answer or solution be located at a binary pole is the least definitive answer that one could give, because it in fact says nothing about the question at hand because, as we have already discussed,

in common by all[97], which would, by definition, result in the formation of a new mode of production contingently would generate an entirely alternative sociology. This sociology would be so different that language would have new characteristics, and the words used in day-to-day life would have different connotations than they do now.

While it is relatively impractical for us to debate what, exactly, would constitute this new sociology, it is reasonable to predict that fundamental changes in economic relationships would carry over into social ones - and that, given time, this change would become normative and eventually impact language. Thus do we see the rough framework in which we could start a campaign to de-totalitarianize language, although the fact that we now have an idea of *how* to go about doing so does not mean that there *will* be any movement to do so. A thorough understanding of Marxian economics shows that the only possible means through which a post-capitalist mode of production can be established is by a vanguard of de-serialized for-itself proletarians acting at a specific point in the historical dialectic when (given that net material scarcity has been globally overcome) both the objective and subjective conditions of mass revolution exist.

---

[97] The socialization of the means of production would be conducted *by* the proletariat *in the name of* all people. The global working class is the *only* socio-economic class that has the potential to successfully instigate a revolutionary dictatorship that would allow for the fundamental re-orientation of the economy. This re-orientation can only be done by the proletariat because of the unique characteristics that it has as a class in comparison to others that have existed in the over-arching historical dialectic, but will nonetheless result in a socialism enjoyed by *all* humanity.

Section Five
Early Works and Pre-College Essays

The Importance of Property

Many societies, be they based on Western capitalism or European social democracy, are confronted with the political paradox inherent in government: while its existence is necessary to maintain a stable and secure society, what natural authority does it have to intervene in citizens' lives to enforce that security? The concept of the social contract, postulated by the political philosopher Thomas Hobbes, states that people willingly group themselves into collective units and surrender various rights and prerogatives in order to construct a government that can provide that needed stability and security. However, in doing so, the people have also created a system of oppression, imbued with the authority to run against their individual will in order to execute actions for the betterment of the majority. While this contradictory system of inherent oppression and protection is a necessary evil so as to retain societal order, it raises a significant question: chiefly, does the government's power allow it to openly lay down its influence over social privileges, economic determinism, and property rights?

America was founded upon the firmest adherence to classical liberalism: individual autonomy, unwavering libertarianism, and inalienable self-determination. The modern-day resurgence of libertarianism, known among the prominent Austrian school of economics as *neoliberalism*, stands in direct contrast to the existing Keynesian and progressive system. Many of these progressives and American liberals espouse utilization of federal authority for the good of the majority, echoing the social contract and the desire to better the whole. However, this usage of governmental power often results in the intercession of personal matters and the exercising of the reserved right of eminent domain; that is, seizure of property by the state. The existence of government, while agreed to be a necessary evil, is, and always will be, an evil due to the fact that it innately retains the right to insert itself into one's personal affairs. This progressive concept of governmental involvement stands in stark opposition to neoliberalism: progressive politics dictate that the government has a higher authority than the individual, wherein neoliberals espouse the reverse. To contemporary neoliberalism, the individual is greater and more important than the government, and this realization that the administration answers to the person is exemplified in the exercising of the right to own property.

Property is, inherently, the most basic and fundamental right than an individual can have. With it, it signifies freedom from governmental oppression and the existence of an open society. To many schools of Marxism and radical leftism, property is viewed as theft and retention from the community; progressives further this by backing the government's power of eminent domain to seize private property and use it for the collective good. This, they say, is the epitome of human rights: equality, universal access, joint ownership, and non-discriminatory usage. However, this could not be farther from the truth: collective ownership and universalism is *not* the pinnacle of human rights - the right to property is the purest of human rights. The right for people to earn and build something for themselves, exclusive authority over their body and possessions, and the right to even *have* possessions - the existence of property is the measurement through which we can quantify how open and free a society is.

Left-wing collectivism and eminent domain is not the definition of human rights, but rather of thievery and interventionism. Personal property and property rights are the purest description of freedom.

How "free" where the people of eastern Europe and the Baltic states when under the thumb of Stalinism? Eminent domain, government repossession, and forced collectivization did not "free" them or grant them human rights, but rather put them under the control of government-induced monopolies and bureaucratic agencies. Their shift towards democratic governments and more neoliberal monetary policies since the fall of the Soviet Union show a desire for freedom, not a desire to remain in the chains of collectivism. Democracy and freedom are synonymous with neoliberalism and the right to property: the right to own property and have private possessions is an inherent right that stands side-by-side with freedom and self-determinism. Property is important in a free and open society because it is indicative that it *is* a free and open society.

The government should not have control over private property. Instead, it should remain true to the libertarian concept of the night watchman state, wherein government is reserved only for the regulation of police, judicial systems, the military, and other means of social protection and order. Its ability to seize and collectivize property, and thus insert itself into citizens' lives, is a dynamic representation of it overstepping it bounds.

In the United States, both the federal and state government utilize their endowed powers of eminent domain and economic retention, not for the good of the whole or even the majority, but rather for capital gain. This profit motive is the key trait to American capitalism. The seizure of land and property, and its turnover to corporations for the sake of profit and expansion, runs in direct opposition to the purpose of government or business. Government, in its oppression-protection paradox, exists to serve and better the community; business exists as an individual, or congregational, economic venture to better those that undertake it. Neither is constructed so as to damage or harm society, but the usage of eminent domain does so. Much land that the government seizes is either used for a project that does not better the majority, often resulting in a mismanaged and financial disaster, or is handed over to a corporation in the hopes that they can successfully complete the project and make profit.

Either way - seizure by the government for the government, or by the government for corporations - it is still thievery. If a society, after constructing a government to oversee it, allows it to run rampant and state blatant declarations of ownership over whatever piece of property it wants, then it has violated the social contract. Governments are, by their very nature, organic: they require sustenance (taxes), have appendages (agencies), give birth (opening new departments), and respond to stimuli (engaging in wars). And, like all organisms, the government can grow: by gradually expanding its powers and responsibilities through the inaction and laziness of its citizens, one may wake up one day to realize that the limited government of yesterday has become to overwhelming government of today. It may, if left unchecked, consume everything, perverting from the minarchist "night watchman" state to the collectivist "socialist" state - and history shows that governments prefer to grow rather than shrink.

The sole defender against this radical tyranny and complete government possession is private property. Historical observations will show that nations with an incredible amount of this governmental ownership and collective possession are remarkably undemocratic and horrendously oppressive. Again, the level of democracy and liberty present in Soviet Russia and communist-influenced Europe paint a picture of suppression. The progressive ideas of human rights and universal property are woefully absent from Maoist China: in a communist nation dominated by government property and with little personal possession, human rights are non-existent. If we can thus agree that collective ownership is proportional to human rights violations, than we must also accept that private ownership is proportional to human rights advocacy. The two are opposite and prove the point that the existence of the right to property is indicative of freedom.

Property rights are important in a free and open society because they are what *makes* that society inherently free and open. The freedom to begin an economic venture, to open a small business, to trade and barter, to compare services side-by-side, and to be free of the strong arm of governmental dictation: these are the characteristics of private property and freedom. You cannot have liberty and government, nor can you have democracy and statism; the cure for economic collapses are not to expand governmental authority and relinquish individual rights and hopes to the administration, but rather to return that authority, right, and hope to the individual. Free enterprise and economic determinism is what built the American economy, and its improvement will not come at the introduction of government, but rather its removal.

The right to own property is an inherent right to an individual, and when individuals band together to write the social contract and establish a government, they must not forget that relinquishing or forgetting that innate liberty will result in the death of *all* liberty. When the government can take your possessions, it has crossed a line and taken your freedom, too. Private property is important because property *is* freedom: freedom from control, from dependence, and from governmental oppression. Neoliberal policies and property rights must never be forgotten, lest we fall into the same pit of expanding statism and utopian collectivism that has, historically, proven to be the downfall of liberty. Rather than forget, we must remember: remember our inherent and human rights, and our right to free will and personal property.

The Alleviation of Poverty: Refocusing and Readjusting our Social Consciousness

"A nation that continues year after year to spend more money on military defense than on programs of social uplift is approaching spiritual doom."

This famous quote was spoken by Reverend Martin Luther King, Jr. during the tremulous civil rights period in the 1950s and 1960s. While the speaker passed away in 1968, the concepts and ideals for which he stood require strict adherence and remembrance today. During King's life and the pivotal age in which he lived, the concepts of civil liberties and classism were at the forefront of social consciousness. They were the defining concepts of the century: the idea that everyone, regardless of socio-economic status and inherent skin color, were equal human beings was considered radical. However, American progressivism and the passage of time has resulted in this revolutionary thought becoming permanently engrained in our society. Nowadays, it seems natural to think that every human being is equal; indeed, the "radical" concept of tolerance during King's life is perfectly accepted today. Yet although we have acknowledged the existence of classism and social and economic discrimination, there is little that we have done to alleviate it.

The United Nations International Children's Fund states that nearly twenty-two thousand children die each year due to extreme poverty and lack of adequate materials. These children come from a wide range of backgrounds - from the poor villages in inner Africa to the ghettos and slums of industrialized countries. Countless more live in substandard conditions, working in unsafe working environments and making insufficient funds, barely able to place food on the table for their family. Many nations around the world have taken steps to attempt to reduce poverty, from the wide social security programs in Scandinavia to the progressive childcare in France and the universal healthcare system in Canada. Yet the United States stands embarrassingly behind - the Census Bureau recently released a report stating that, in 2008, the number of Americans living in poverty had grown to 39.8 million, equal to nearly 13.2% of the citizenry.

Few wish to acknowledge that America is woefully inefficient at aiding those least fortunate in society. Globally, we have a weak social net and few nationalized social programs. The capitalist system in which we live is brutal on the poor, the ethnic, and the needy, and serves only to exalt the superrich. Few of us realize the drastic gap in income between the rich and the poor, and the corporations that control our government would leave us ignorant of just how fast that gap is widening. Rather than realize the desperate need that these people have, we turn our heads and focus on other things: sports, pop culture, and mass entertainment. We willingly ignore their plight and anesthetize ourselves to their condition - we would rather focus on our own lives and help ourselves rather than participate in a fair and redistributive system that would help them. In our culture of "me" and not "we", we engage in self-isolation and radical individualism and label all forms of collectivism and social unity as unpatriotic and utopian. So long as we glorify the principals of capitalism and self-determination rather than solidarity and charity, we will never be able to truly tackle the problem of poverty.

Removing poverty and eliminating radical destitution will not occur without an equally radical transformation in social thought. Our perception that the poor are poor by choice and by lack of initiative is the result of capitalist propaganda, wherein we are indoctrinated to believe that everyone has the opportunity to become the next Bill Gates if they simply try hard enough. Effort and motivation, they say, results in wealth and prosperity, and affluence is the product of hard work. This, however, is not truly the answer. It is what the corporatists would like us to believe; they would not want us to realize that there are those that are poor because they are victimized by the system in which they live. People do not understand that class mobility does not exist to the extent that we believe it does. Those that are born poor often remain in poverty, and it is easier to fall down the social ladder than it is to climb it.

As Martin Luther King, Jr. said, we cannot continue to neglect the poor by funding expansive military programs and expect the result to be a higher standard of living for all. We cannot assume that the construction of missile systems will heal the sick or feed the hungry, and that engaging in imperialist conflicts will better our citizens back home. Yes, we can make a difference and lessen poverty, but our society needs its perception altered so that we stop viewing the poor as dirty and lazy: we need to being to view them as equal human beings who are just as worthy of food and medicine as we are. Even more so than equality, we need to embrace the concept of equity and social justice. We need to be willing to remove the veil that society has constructed, a veil that covers our eyes and makes us believe that that system of extreme individualism and singularity is better than one in which we live in unity and fraternity.

Of course, a drastic shift in monetary and social policies need to take place in order to pull the poor out of their self-perpetuating situation. Commencement of universal healthcare, mass literacy and childcare programs, tighter social nets and comprehensive welfare networks - transforming our ignorance into compassion, and systematizing it into actual conduct, is what will help the poor. More so than enacting programs that throw taxpayer dollars at those stuck in extreme poverty in a hope that they improve, their true uplift and progression will not occur unless we ourselves willingly adopt a new social consciousness and perception.

Lincoln: Anti-Liberty and Necessary Imperialism

Perhaps more so than any other country, America was founded upon the principals of freedom and democracy. Wherein other nations exist as the contemporary heirs and continuations of empires and kingdoms, the United States is the singular country whose existence is the result of a societal revolution and breakaway. The British colonies' action of declaring their independence makes us unique: we are not the result of a monarchy evolving into a republic, or the progressivism of a nation to change its established government. This nation was born out of the desire for autonomy and self-determination, free from European statism.

Our fight for sovereignty and democracy marks our founding as distinct. George Washington, the Continental Congress, and the emerging government were all fierce advocates of libertarianism and the concept of being free from the strong arm of government that existed during the time of the autocratic English monarchy. The first years of the United States were remarkably free of governmental involvement; federalism was still in its infancy, and the nation had not grown to the point in which the state-country relationship had evolved so that the former was consumed by the expanding power of the latter. Individual liberty was at its zenith: judicial precedents, legislation, and executive orders had not yet been set down that restricted self-government and absolute freedom. The dawn of America could be considered a libertarian utopia and the 'proven' success of classical liberalism.

Yet the existence of world wars, political conflicts, and ideological schisms would all contribute to the perversion of America. We have been altered from that land of latitude and maximum freedom and shoved into an era of the corporatist police-state with boundaries set upon our civil rights. Time and progressivism has not proved to better us or our nation, but rather warp it into something that our Founding Fathers would decry.

Modern America prides itself on being the paragon of Western democracy, acting as the singular and last light in the darkness of emerging statism and collectivism. We desperately try to ignore the fact that our nation has changed; we hold fast to the concept that we are still the freest country on earth and the only place left where freedom and patriotism truly exist. We do not willingly acknowledge the fact that the government's control is rapidly expanding or that our civil rights are being constricted at an accelerating rate, but rather remind ourselves that we are still the home of the free and land of the brave.

We tell ourselves that we are free and democratic and that we advocate for democracy abroad, but we shut our eyes to our government's foreign policy. We ignore the American-sponsored dictators of Latin America, the generous donations given to Middle Eastern terrorists, and the intervention into the governments of other countries. We pray that our "democratic" country will live forever as the bastion of liberty while cringing away from the thought that our nation is involved in some of the most undemocratic actions conceivable.

Newly-founded American libertarianism gave birth to the free market and economic determinism. The free market gave rise to capitalism and personal profit, and even this mutated into corporatism and outright imperialism. Economic and social intervention is now the lifeblood of our government, and imperialism is the new patriotism that our country espouses.

Nothing serves as a greater example of our nation's undemocratic character and imperialist behavior than our actions during the American Civil War. The actions that President Lincoln took during that turbulent period runs against the freedom and separatism that we advocated for during our war of independence. Lincoln and the American government did what is expected of all leaders and governments: it fought for its existence and self-perpetuation, rather than give in to the wills of the populace that constructed it. It would rather expand and grow rather than shrink or dissolve.

The Civil War is a remarkable period in American history, in that it shows the ideological strife between two parties and the military action that they took place against one another. The War was not just a military conflict between two great powers: it was the manifestation of a philosophical movement and a resurgence of self-determination.

President Lincoln, while not having the same military experience as other presidents and members of the government, was thrown into the forefront of the War purely by his status as the commander-in-chief. His past experience was restricted to primarily political matters. He served in the House of Representatives in both Illinois and Washington, D.C. and as a lawyer; the little military knowledge that he had before the outbreak of the War was due to his captainship in the Illinois Militia during the Black Hawk War, in which he served as a soldier against the Sauk Native American tribe.

It is interesting to note that both Lincoln and Jefferson Davis, the President of the Confederacy and his political counterpart, were involved in the Black Hawk War. Davis' military background was more extensive, with his family serving in both the Revolutionary War and the War of 1812, and he himself escorting the Indian Chief Black Hawk to prison. However, despite having lesser experience, Lincoln proved to be a better commander: while he himself did not have the knowledge necessary to conduct a war, he surrounded himself with those that did. His cabinet consisted of leaders of the various factions of the Republican Party, and oversaw the appointment of top generals. Whenever the generals he appointed failed to capture key Confederate locales or their capital in Richmond, he would substitute them for another. In the early months of 1861, he appointed Ulysses S. Grant to take command of the Union army, which proved to be a wild success: Lee's military genius led him to win numerous battles, even culminating in the capture of Richmond.

Lincoln was able to successfully adapt to being a war president in that he was a deft politician. Able to act in a bipartisan manner and even reach out to the Democratic Party, he was able to garnish support for his war effort and became involved in power plays in several states. Davis was far less successful: he was overbearing, controlling, and meddlesome, and refused to accept advice from his military advisors. Taking it upon himself as President of the Confederate States to act as commander-in-chief, he utilized that power to the fullest and made several significant military decisions best left up to his generals. His personality flaws and temperament made him a failure of a leader, opening the way for Lincoln and his generals to step in and gain the upper hand in the War. Much of Lincoln's success in the Civil War could be attributed to the fact that he had knowledgeable advisors, was a shrewd politician, and was pitted against a weaker opponent.

Both Lincoln and Davis appealed to the European powers for support: while the Union was betting upon allied nations such as Britain and France to side with it, the Confederacy was taking diplomatic action and was appealing to those nations for military intervention. While neither country official recognized the Confederacy as an independent and sovereign power, it did show an interest in mediation; offering formal recognition would have resulted in almost certain war with the United States, and war could subsequently result in a loss of trade. As a result, much of Europe did not take part in the Civil War. However, Pope Pius IX created a controversy by writing a letter to Davis in which he labeled him "the Honorable President of the Confederate States of America". The Vatican never officially recognized the Confederacy as a nation, but it did sympathize with its fight for free will and independence.

The foreign policy of the Union and the Confederacy, while both factions of America, were just as mired in scandals and double-dealing as it is nowadays. Each faction appealed to the European nations and claimed that it was the "true" America - the Union arguing that it was the central American authority and established government, and the Confederacy arguing that it was just as legitimate as the Union and that it was merely exercising its right to secession and autonomy. The Trent Affair, in which the U.S. Navy seized two Confederates traveling on an English ship in 1861, could have potentially exploded into a war, but Lincoln released them, cleverly ending a potentially disastrous situation that could have pulled Britain into the conflict. Both the Union and Confederacy were allowed to work openly in the British territories, and Europe did its best to work with both American factions without picking a side between the two. This double-dealing is reminiscent of international diplomacy today, wherein the United States supports an Israeli state but not a Palestinian one, yet Israel respects both the United States and desires a peaceful Palestinian state as well.

Abraham Lincoln's actions during the war put him at odds with George Washington, and his own philosophies oppose the libertarianism inherent in the war for independence. Washington, and the movement for independence that he spearheaded, fiercely advocated for libertarianism and self-determination. His beliefs of state rights, and the intrinsic license that those states have to behave as they wish and reserve the right to secede, runs parallel to the ideology of the Confederacy. The Confederate states, due to the political climate at the time, wished to break away and establish their own nation and exercise that right to secession. The actions that the Union took to block them, and their desire to prevent secession and preserve the Union, could be argued to be little more than imperialism. Lincoln was undeniably a successful war president, but the driving philosophy and motive behind that war should remain in question.

The actions that Lincoln's government undertook during the Civil War and his behavior as a war president, while wildly successful, were ideologically opposed to the concept of American freedom. Self-determination, classical liberalism, and absolute freedom were the tenets on which the United States was founded, and every citizen in it was endowed with the right of individual autonomy. Each state was granted expansive rights by the Articles of Confederation, acting as little more than loosely-cooperative republics; the Constitution, however, solidified and expanded the federal government and gave birth to the concept of federalism. Under each document, however, the states were given the right to dictate their actions as they saw fit, and to dictate what laws and measures they desired within their borders, so long as it did not conflict with the endeavors of the collective nation. The fundamental right that the states reserved was the right to associate, or not to associate, with the Union, and to remove itself if it desired. The southern states, not agreeing with the political decisions that were taking place in the North and in

Washington, D.C., chose to apply that right and secede. The liberty for states to do so is in line with the libertarianism that was espoused at the founding of the nation, as it serves as an example of that fervent devotion to choice and free will. The states were, both philosophically and constitutionally, in the right as they chose to leave the Union.

The Union, under the leadership of President Lincoln, did not wish to recognize the Confederacy or the secessionist movement as legitimate. His goals, as president, was to protect and preserve the Union. He did so, forcibly, by engaging in the Civil War and working to retain the southern states and abolish their transitional government in Virginia. Lincoln's actions, while proving him to be a brilliant politician and open to military consul, echoed the same imperialism and possession that the English monarchy felt when the colonies attempted to leave Britain. As the English fought the colonies in an attempt to retain them, so did the Union fight the Confederacy in an effort to keep hold of it. The Civil War was not merely a conflict devoted to territories, trade, state boundaries, or even slave rights - it was the indication of an ideological schism and social realization that inherent American philosophy was changing as time passed. While the Union government, when fighting the British for independence, espoused liberty, choice, and autonomy, it supported opposing beliefs during the War: its perspective had changed to champion territorial retention, economic control, and a blatant declaration of ownership over areas that wished nothing more than their own right for freedom to be recognized. The Union had fallen into the same imperialist state that the English Crown was in during the Revolutionary War.

While Lincoln's actions proved to run against those of his predecessors, it does not diminish his capacity as a military leader. His rudimentary knowledge, when supplemented with the companionship of the key political and military figures of the time - such as Edwin Stanton, a military genius and the Secretary of War, and William Seward, his Secretary of State and an ardent abolitionist - lead him to run an administration that was far more prepared for a war than Davis' Confederate government. The ideology that the Lincoln administration and Union government espoused opposed the ideals of self-rule and individual prerogatives, but it does not change the fact that he was able to successfully slide from the role of state politician to war president and commander-in-chief.

With little prior experience, Lincoln was able to radically transform from a local representative in Illinois to the commander of a supraregional army and chief officer of the federal government. Forced into the heavy role by fate, Lincoln's mandate to become a circumstantial war president proved to be a sweeping success for the Union. At the advice of his competent advisors, he worked with his appointed generals to capture numerous Confederate locales and engage battalions of troops. He was also able to successfully tap into the industrialized resources of the northern state and mass produce materials necessary to spearhead his campaign. His growing support among Republican factions and the so-called "War Democrats" of the era led him to lead a unified and economically superior nation than the South. With a transitional government, bickering states, and agricultural economy, the South was woefully underprepared to engage in a war. Lincoln's rapid maturity into a war president during the erratic and uncertain first year of the Civil War gave him the upper hand. With a militarized government and productive manufacturing industry to support him, he was able to successfully step into the role that the Union needed in order to remain a cohesive country. In terms of military preparedness, the North was years ahead of the South, and Lincoln, while remorseful that Americans should have fight their own brothers, unapologetically fought to retain the government that Washington had established.

Ideologically, the South were naught but a series of minute republics that wished independence and freedom. They advocated for liberty from the North the same way that the English colonies had argued for separation from Britain. Constitutionally, they were exercising their right of association by removing themselves from an assembly that they did not support. The world would certainly be different nowadays if Lincoln had not lead the Union in the Civil War: there may have been a series of other secessions, breakaways, regional wars, and internal conflicts. The United States as we now it would not exist. Lincoln's actions during the War lead to the restoration and reconstruction of the Union, re-establishing the states as a singular unit. Philosophically speaking, the Union - regardless of who led and composed it - took on the same streak of imperialism that marred the English years before. Yet unlike that preceding period, it was good that there was no breakaway. Lincoln's rapid growth into a war president proved to be beneficial; it seems that, circumstantially, the Union's imperialist nature was advantageous to America as a whole, and his actions during the War kept us unified rather than fractured. His status as a successful war president are evident in the fact that the United States won the war and continues to exist today.

    Throughout the first year of the American Civil War, Abraham Lincoln proved to be a successful commander. He was able to fall back on his limited military experience when needed, but was aware of his personal limits: when necessary, he would call upon his advisors and generals, and was conscious enough of those boundaries that, unlike "President" Davis, he delegated overly significant decisions to those with the knowledge needed to make them. This two-sided trait - of both Union patriotism and a passion to lead, and the maturity to realize that he could not lead alone - put him farther ahead than his Confederate counterparts. His political cunning, renown oratory skills, and ability to mobilize support from various political groups proved him to be a rallying and inspiring figure. While political philosophy puts him at odds with the libertarianism championed by the Founding Fathers and the independence-seeking South, his circumstantial imperialism lead to the reunification of a broken nation. History proves that Lincoln was both a successful war president and American hero.

In Defense of the Progressive Presidency

The 2008 elections represented more than a turning point in American politics: it was more than the inauguration of a political majority into office, or the admittance of an President who stood as the ideological opposition to his predecessor. The election of Barack Obama promised a new era of politics, wherein ardent liberals and outspoken progressives would have as much say as the popular conservatives who denounced them as unpatriotic. Yet although the United States felt convinced that it was about to be ushered into a second Progressive Era and receive a contemporary wave of New Deals and social programs, it would fall drastically short of that dream.

As a self-described progressive and social democrat, following in the tradition of Eduard Bernstein's gradualism, I supported Obama after Hillary Clinton withdrew. I fully expected her to win the election, but with Obama's rapidly expanding fan base, it was wiser that one step down and the other absorb the now-leaderless backing, rather than split the Democratic vote and allow the Republican candidate to win. I also presumed Obama to act as Franklin Delano Roosevelt did while in office - by enacting sweeping reforms, streamlining government, and utilizing federal authority to confront many of the problems that we face nowadays. Yet as expectant and optimistic as I and many others were in 2008, we are in our third year of relative normalcy: wide socio-economic gaps, marriage inequality, and on-going wars still plague our nation. Obama did not spearhead the movement for single-payer and universal healthcare, nor has comprehensive immigration reform passed through our Congress. He has, in many respects, fallen short of the liberal dream that many of us on the American Left hold true to, with his primary successes being only near-universal health reform, enacted through a private insurance mandate, and withdrawal of combat troops from Afghanistan, but not the end of the so-called "war on terror". Our progressive hopes have not been lost: they have merely been placed in the wrong candidate. Even Clinton would surely have fallen into the same pit of corporatism and militarism that Obama has. The answer is not even one of the other utopian liberals, such as Dennis Kucinich or Al Gore. No, the real answer to America's problems lies in Senator Bernie Sanders.

Sanders, a self-described democratic socialist and chief leader in Vermont's universal healthcare movement, made national news when he spent just under nine hours filibustering a vote on extending the disastrous Bush-era tax cuts. A man who stands to the left of progressivism, Sanders is the longest-serving Independent member of Congress, due primarily to the fact that there is no legitimate socialist party for him to join; he did, however, establish and chair the Congressional Progressive Caucus. He does more than idealistically praise European liberalism: he has proposed numerous bills to Congress, including two for single-payer healthcare, and lead the American Left in a recent fight to audit the Federal Reserve.

Sanders, staunchly and ideologically opposed to big business and corporate involvement in government, would do more than raise false hopes. He is not objected to using federal power to fix national crises, nor inserting executive authority into areas wherein the private industry has drastically failed. While having already stated that he is not going to run for the presidency in 2012, the elevation of Senator Sanders to President Sanders would be more than a step in the right direction for American economics - it would be a rekindling of the American dream and the restoration of progressive hope.

Radical Westernism:
Imperialism, Consumerism, and the Abuse of the American System

The Errors of Democracy

Progressivism is more than a political ideological or a cultural phenomenon: societal change and evolution is a natural, social trend. With the advent of new philosophies, inspiring political figures, and governmental revolutions, communities inevitably adapt to mirror the new social outlook that the majority adopts. Social consciousness, as it changes, is also reflected in the governing body, as it's exercising and creating of public policy moves to match the new developments. This concept of social perspective and echoed government action is the key tenant of progressivism and, ultimately, the determining factor in the improvement or detriment of a society.

Communities often evolve at a pace that corresponds to their form of government, and the leading ideology that it espouses. Primitive, agricultural areas undergo little, if any, change, bound to their current state by time-honored traditions and customs; religious states openly condemn social change, working fervently to maintain their dogmatic hold; and democracies and republics may attempt to stave off modernism, but will eventually cave to the collective will of the citizens. Yet while the government is designed so as to be a mouth of that collective will and act on its behalf, that will itself can be openly nefarious. If the majority of a public is woefully ignorant, intolerant, or apathetic, the government may take actions that run contrary to the greater good.

Espousing the critical and adverse opinions of the majority, even if they *are* the majority, is, be definition, democratic. A system that prides itself on holding true to the principals of democracy - that is, wherein the government, should one exist, act on the dictations of the plurality - does not have to be good. Democracy is not, inherently, a superior system. Via the democratic process, some of the worst governments and decrees have been established. Some of these include the election of fascist parties in Hitler's Germany or Mussolini's Italy; others include the wide-spread acceptance of racial segregation and the preaching of social division. While looking back at these moments can show their unjust nature and blatant malevolence, one must always remember that some of the worst atrocities and most hateful bigotry has been the majority will and, therefore, acted upon by the government. The democratic process, while preached as sacred by Western civilizations, has proven to give birth to some of the most evil moments in history.

Yet it is not democracy that causes evil - its potential for social corruption is due to the two main cogs that build its tyrannical machine: government's existence and human nature.

The existence of governments is something expected: all Westerners - that is, those in industrialized nations with representative governments - expect to see government in their lives. They give it little thought and assume that it is natural, that it is necessary in life. People often assume that government is needed in order to have a secure country and a stable social order. Without it, they say, there will be little more than anarchy, riots, and chaos. When people rarely give thought as to what would happen *without* a government, they do not look at what happens when there *is* a government, and do not take that time to examine and dissect its origin an purpose.

People are naturally social animals. The social contract, a theory that attempts to explains government, states that people willingly group themselves into collective units and surrender various rights and prerogatives in order to construct a government that can provide needed stability and security. However, in doing so, the people have also created a system of oppression, imbued with the authority to run against their individual will in order to execute actions for the betterment of the majority. While this contradictory system of inherent oppression and protection is a necessary evil so as to retain societal order, it raises a significant question: chiefly, if the government is made so as to protect people and act upon the majority will, what happens when the majority's beliefs and interest run against those of the minority? If a democratic government is designed to do what the majority tells it to do, what happens when that majority wants things that, years down the road, it may look back and consider "evil"? What is a government to do when the actions that the populace's social consciousness desires would harm the minority - that is, its own citizens?

This is the intrinsic problem with government: that if you are not part of the majority, your views will not be expressed and your ideas will be actively ignored and suppressed. This "tyranny of the majority", as it is called, is the reason that democracy can prove to be an ineffective system. The majority will can be to elect Nazis to power, or place a fascist as a head-of-state, even though those actions can bring about harm to the minority. As it seems impossible that one could construct a government that could act in a completely fair and faultless manner, a democracy is, idealistically, the most fair and tolerant system possible - yet because it expresses the plurality's will, it is also one of the most abusive systems. Democracy is an imperfect and oppressive system because government is inherently imperfect and oppressive.

Human nature is the second of the two reasons that democracy can result in evil. Humans are, by their disposition, static. There is a sense of comfort in routine and habit, and knowing what lies ahead is a source of ease. Having simple explanations and plans for society, be they due to religious teachings or time-tested secular wisdom, allows everyone to have a pleasant spot in their community and know what is culturally expected of them. Human beings enjoy conventional and consistent social niches (which may be directly related to biotic evolution, with comfort found in ecological niches, and economic niches may be a direct extension and coping mechanism of industrialization). Change, however, can throw off these expected patterns, and new thoughts can pose as a serious threat to the traditional community. The social norms, when assaulted by new concepts, often pushes back and attempts to legitimize and protect its existence. This reactionary tactic of conservatism condemning modernism and fighting to remain in its comfortable stasis is what makes democracy ineffective.

Human nature innately resentful of change. This deep-rooted desire to remove all contemporary social changes, when channeled through the oppressive mouthpiece that is government, serves as the mechanism through which persecution and misery are born.

When the majority condemns change and the minority supports it, the democratic government will do what is expected of it: act on behalf of the majority, and use its power to suppress minority thought. The actions of the government are, expectedly, to attack those that deviate from social norms; this persecution is often enacted through the refusal to grant equal rights and civil liberties, in an attempt to leave the conventional majority in power, legitimize its comfortable stasis, and preserve the traditional order. Attempted social preservation, via the inherently oppressive system that is government, is tyranny on the different.

Cultural Reaffirmation

When confronted with an element of change, society will attempt to justify its existence and structure by openly reaffirming its principals. When various social changes attempt to penetrate that cultural cocoon and alter and adjust it, that civilization will work to make its established order indisputable and pronounced: restating a society's cultural beliefs and expected social order gives it legitimacy and a sanctioned existence. Humans - naturally inclined towards being in collective groups and espousing traditionalist systems - intrinsically desire to create conservative governments. This innate trend towards conservatism makes it instinctively opposite and hostile to any form of modernism and social change; indeed, this "natural complex" outright denounces nonconformism and individualism, if it runs against the complex's established cultural order.

The natural complex's outright reaffirmation is of great importance: the fact that is *openly* reaffirms its principals - that is, those that make up and run the government do - is what creates social radicalism and fringe behavior. A society, when exposed to change, attempts to suppress that change by redirecting the social consciousness to the way that things were before the change was introduced and remind it of its comfortable stasis. The cultural cocoon protects the natural complex from alteration, and the complex, at the same time, demonizes change while exalting traditionalism.

The United States of America is unique in that its cultural cocoon is reinforced with the unrelenting presence of religious orthodoxy and ever-present, if willingly ignored, social intolerance. America was founded upon fierce support of classical liberalism: unwavering libertarianism and inalienable self-determinism. Both its constitution and government espouse absolute liberty and steadfast freedom, all laced with the opportunism necessary to improve one's life. However, the natural complex of America does not truly support any of these things. The social pressure of normalcy, supported by organized religion and the existence of openly hateful institutions, runs in opposition to what the nation supposedly encourages. This contradictory system of liberty-advocacy and culturally-enforced conformism has corrupted many pieces of America: chiefly, the free market.

The free market is an system that is based upon willing association, mutual exchange, and the freedom to undergo an economic venture should one choose to do so. This absolute liberty is a key tenant of libertarianism, one of the primary political philosophies that lead to the country's founding. After its construction and actualization, the natural complex accepted it, and the cultural cocoon protected it. The American system, it seemed, would hold the supposedly sacrosanct right of economic liberalism close to its heart and support it with the same level of advocacy that it did during its own construction.

Yet the natural complex's backing of the free market would come to change at the introduction of alternative thought; that is, the conceptualization that the system could be run differently would lead the natural complex to openly reaffirm the market's support and existence. The ideas of nationalization and collectivization, or placing the markets under the authority of the government, would be met with open denouncement by those who believed in the virtues of the free market. The market would receive government-sanctioned freedom and immunity to collectivization; decrees and dictions, often in the form of deregulation, would take place, granting the free market the power needed to fight the ideology of change. Yet just as the change would have altered the market, so does the natural complex's official support.

Whether assailed by concepts of change and modernization, or reinforced by the ideas of convention and traditionalism, the item in question is, by the mere fact that it is denounced or encouraged, forever altered. Both negative and positive arguments still impact the item.

Both progressivism's desire to change the free market and conservatism's aspiration to reaffirm it will, and do, affect it. Reaffirmation results in exaltation. The right to participate in the free market is a right that is considered holy in America; private enterprise is what separates it from overwhelmingly large and tyrannical governments, or so the natural complex says. The focus the America has on this one right does more than emphasize it: it singularizes and separates it from the other liberties that citizens can partake in, making it seem unique and in need of unwavering defense. American obsession with free enterprise has not protected it from the alleged horrors of government regulation: the constant fixation and reaffirmation of the free market has exalted and deified it into something that, as a culture, America worships. The free market has transformed from a libertarian concept to a revered idol; the market has become something that is glorified to such an extent that it has been warped and perverted.

The natural complex's tendency to stave off change by reaffirming its cultural principals is exemplified in America's constant proclamation of the wonders of the free market. Constantly asserted, the market has been placed on a pedestal, and the right to enterprise is treated as if it is wholly separate and completely divine.

This incessant advocacy has, unfortunately, come at a great cost: the deification of the free market has resulted in its death, its perversion into something that is no longer recognizable. The death of the market came at the moment that politicians, citizens, and businessmen began to view it as a profit-making system. The end of the free market came when it was glorified into capitalism: the birth of capitalism was only able when America, as a nation, singularized enterprise to such an extent that it was viewed and acted upon differently. This singularization and affirmation, in the end, resulted in as much radical change as the progressive change itself would have caused it was allowed to have been introduced. The free market, and by extension, liberty, was struck down at the moment of conceptualization of profit: that is, enterprise died the moment capitalism was born.

Governmental Refocus

The natural complex in America would lead its people to believe that "free market capitalism" is the greatest system on earth: that they are the synonymous, equal terms. To respect the free market, it says, is to respect capitalism. American, and the natural complex that composes it, states that the free market and capitalism are the same thing, and the two words are used interchangeable to describe the for-profit system that turns the national economy. However, the belief that they are the same is a woefully ignorant belief - they are completely different and irreconcilable.

The free market, as stated above, is a libertarian concept of willing association and mutual exchange. This exchange is defined in the trade between two people, each trading services or goods with one another, because they believe that what the other is intrinsically more valuable than they have. There is no net gain or loss between these two individuals: each person is giving the other their service or good in exchange for the other's service or good, in the belief that they are each getting the better end of the trade. These two individuals, after seeking each other out and willingly trading, each believe that they have benefited.

Capitalism, conversely, exists when one is able to objectively state that one party has received a better outcome than the other; that is, when one gains and the other looses. Quantifying that one of the individuals has made a profit is what defines capitalism. This is the key difference between capitalism and the free market: while the latter exists as a system in which the one making the gain is subjective, the former is in existence when the gain is objective.

Existence of gaining at another's expense, and obtaining a service, item, or good by taking it from them another and leaving them without, is capitalism. It is not a system of financial exchange or individuals associating with one another: capitalism is a form of legalized thievery and social oppression. The removal of something from the ownership of another, potentially to their detriment and possibly harming them, is what defines a capitalist system.

The deification of the free market has twisted it into capitalism: the thorough singularization of the right to enterprise has molded it into a right to profit, and the American government no longer simply espouses the free market. Nowadays, the federal government speaks of the glory of capitalism, openly describing the transformation. This culturally-accepted form of stealing and suppressing has become the foundation on which the United States has come to rest.

The natural complex's tendency to push back at cultural change and reaffirm its own inherent traditionalism has resulted in the reaffirmation of the free market, and thus the creation of capitalism. This system of economic worship and continued glorification has taken a libertarian concept and twisted it into cultural radicalism. Indeed, this sanctioned radicalism has spread like a cancer to all of the places that have or do support the idea of a "free market". Economic liberalism in Europe, recently tolerant towards the free market in the past generations, has become likewise infected with materialist tendencies. In fact, capitalism has become the new patriotism that many countries espouse.

Capitalism, or the conceptualization of gaining at the loss of another, has destroyed much of America; Europe, fortunately, has tempered capitalism with systematized compassion and established comprehensive welfare programs that protect the citizenry and point social consciousness towards solidarity and charity, not extreme singularity and for-profit self-determinism. Up until this point, the United States is the only nation that is currently still exalting capitalism *without* realizing how brutal it is on the poor, the minorities, and the needy. Profit and individualism, considered the finest points of the "American free market", have savagely crushed many industries - ranging from healthcare and education to housing and agriculture.

The healthcare system, often labeled as "broken" by many in the government so as to be able to pass their own ideological agenda through the legislature and alter it as they see fit, broke the moment that the practice of capitalism was applied to it. The moment that someone conceptualized being able to make profits and material gains off of the sickness, injury, and potential death of another human being is the moment that the system broke. Application of capitalist principals has spoiled it; putting money before human welfare destroyed it. The health insurance industry is nothing more than the physical manifestation of capitalist greed: the existence of an organization that serves only to collect money from those that are not currently receiving care, and then refuse to cover all of the services and procedures required when they do need them, only places a wedge between an individual and proper health and serves as a medium through which wealth is obtained.

Government regulations and interference have not broken American healthcare - capitalism has. The system will not be fixed until the citizenry - or the government composed of them - willingly stop applying capitalist principals and the socially-accepted doctrine of greed to their own welfare and well-being, and remove the insurance companies that stand between them and their health. No reform or change in the system, so long as it retains insurance companies, will ever "fix" the perceived "break". Only the forceful abolition of private healthcare insurance will restore it to the system of compassion and healing that it is supposed to be. A purely public, collective, charitable network of citizens working to take care of each other in the name of mutual aid and solidarity will work; that is, enacting a massive government takeover of the entire healthcare industry on the behalf of the people, and constructing a universal single-payer system, unadulterated with the taint of capitalism, that covers all individuals from birth to death. Seizing the healthcare industry back from the relentless grip of those who desire nothing more than to make a profit off of those in it is what will restore the system. Deregulation is not the answer, bur massive regulation and absolute governmental control is.

The same goes for any other sector of the national economy: introduction of the profit motive and legalized greed into an institution will corrupt and destroy that institution. The belief that capitalism is but a synonym for the free market and that capitalist tenants will improve "broken" systems is not merely wrong - it is evil. The simple thought of using patients' healthcare, children's education, the poor's housing, or the nation's agriculture and food as a means through which one can make personal, material gains is unethical and runs contrary to the greater good. The few should not invoke capitalism to try and make profits off of the many; the government should immediately step in on behalf of the many and curtail the actions of the few.

Yet this concept of exploiting governmental power, for either the real or perceived good of the community, seems contradictory. It runs against the social contract, which states that government's existence and efforts are inherently oppressive, and proves that democracy can be the voice of that oppression. If governmental influence truly is wrong, then why should it be applied to industrial matters? If government takes control of medicine, food, education, and housing, should that not be considered to be a blatant example of oppression?

The answer is no. This seems to be in opposition to all that has been postulated before this. Government is an abusive, tyrannical, and cruel institution by definition, and legitimizing its existence via democracy only gives it the power to enact that abuse on the orders of the majority. But that is, intrinsically, what makes nationalization of key industries different than governmental oppression: the fact that it is not being done for the majority, but the whole.

Democracy exists to serve the majority, and government exists to give its citizens a secure and ordered society. They both do have their faults: overwhelming, innate traits that make them both corrupt. But the nationalization of business, production, and industry is not a democratic action, for it does not serve either the majority or the minority; nor it is governmental oppression, for it is done for the direct and clear benefit of the whole community.

Government, allowing the private companies to apply capitalism to its citizens' healthcare, is oppressive. Taking it from them on behalf of all people is liberating.

The problem with American economics is that the government, due to its nefarious tendencies, would willingly go along with the natural complex's constant reaffirmation of the free market and deify it into a fanatically materialist system that worships money, and places income and affluence above human health and well-being. The government's oppression is enacted by allowing private industries to destroy the lives of its people, and for it to work for the people, it must have a massive and fundamental restructuring; it must nationalize key industries and take care of the whole, not apply democracy and care for simple majority.

Governmental oppression will always exist so long as their is a government, but that government is a necessary evil so as to keep society ordered and safe. The only way to reduce that oppression, and allow the people to be as free as possible, is to throw off the immortalized systems of democracy and capitalism, and willingly look at both of them and see that they are far more oppressive than any collectivized government could be.

Oppression comes when a government, democracy, and capitalism all coexist. True liberation will only come when all of them are abolished, but in order to live in a safe and stable community, the people should remove these idealistic and utopian concepts and instead be willing to live under a minimalist government that works for their collective will, not the majority will. Realistic liberation will come when three things are done: government is shrunk, democracy is abolished, and capitalism is returned to its rightful state as a free and open market. The government should concern itself with the welfare and prosperity of the collective, not the profit and desires of the majority.

Absolute Liberty

How is it, one can say, that the government can work for the good of everyone and take back the free market from the clutches of capitalism, when shrinking government itself would impede this process? How can the people assume that the government has the vested power in it to take back all healthcare and education from for-profit institutions, when the people also call for the minimization of government itself? A small, limited government cannot effectively run a nation-wide healthcare program or make all education publicly available if its power is small and limited.

The solution to reconciling minimalist government will nationalized industries and expanded liberty is simple: leave the government's power only over the industries which it is meant to nationalize.

The government should take immediately take over key, basic needs in society and leave the rest to the people themselves to do through a re-empowered "free" market. If the market can exist without the constant exaltation of the right to enterprise, then it will exist in such a way that association, competition, and trade will cover all of the industries and actions that the government cannot. An economy liberated from capitalism, and one that pushes for a pure free market without sanctioned greed, will work for the people. As a means of trade for subjectively-defined superior goods and services, the free market can give people their desired *wants*; the government should concern itself with fundamental *needs*.

Government should collectivize primary institutions and leave the rest to the market. It must create a comprehensive, publicly-funded, universal healthcare system wherein every citizen cares for every citizen; absolute, total seizure of all agriculture, food, and water businesses, so not as to leave nutrition and sustenance vulnerable; creation of simple, comfortable homes so that all of the citizenry have a place to be safe from exposure, and place in which they can exercise their innate right to privacy; community-funded and all-inclusive education programs to teach the populace and ensure their chance at future success; and the natural resources that a nation has, so as to secure its usage for the benefit of the community

These things - health, housing, education, food, and energy - should be what the government confines itself too. Of course, consistent with the social contract, the government exists so as to make society secure and ordered. Therefore, it should also concern itself with military defense, but in such a manner that it *is* purely defense and a means to protect the community from foreign attack, not a tool with which to enforce capitalist expansion and imperialist conquest.

Perhaps more so than anything else, the government should completely remove itself form social matters. If a society truly wants to be liberated and experience freedom, than it must abolish government in every sector of the economy and their lives except those just mentioned. Definitions of marriages, prohibition of narcotics, censorship of speech, regulations of reproduction, and forced military service - each of these need to instantly eliminated. The government needs to remove itself from the lives of its citizens and discontinue all practices that constrict, define, or control social behaviors. Any and all attempts by the government to do so are oppressive - individuals in society must have the right to do whatever it is that they wish, so long as they do not hurt anyone else in the populace. Their decisions, whether or not they are moral, just, or right, is another matter; personal ethics and cultural principals aside, a person should have the right to engage in whatever action they desire, so long as it does not harm anyone else.

Restraints on behavior are often due to the cultural cocoon, or the social norms, expectations, and cultural tone that the society has. In the United States the social authoritarianism that the people are forced to live under does much the same with social liberties as it does with economic ones: singularize certain rights and scrutinize and obsess over them to such an extent that, in the end, are are radically different than the rights that were originally constructed. This cultural obsession that America has over its rights - and a wildly misplaced and ignorant fear of non-traditionalism, born out of anti-liberal McCarthyism and the relentless grip of religious orthodoxy - is such that it seems unlikely that any true minimization of the government and liberation of social freedoms will come to pass. The right to religious freedom, for example, has been reaffirmed and repeated to such an extent that it is no longer the right that one would expect, as the right to enterprise became the right to profit. The "right to religion", reaffirmed by the partisan and historically incorrect fact that the country was founded as Judeo-Christian nation, has become the "right to live in a free, moral society". The American Right, in a desire to legitimize and quantify their status as churchgoers and win over the religious electorate, has restated this debunked belief to such an extent that the majority of citizens do believe that America has an association with conservative religion. Conservative religion, however, is often the organ through which the natural complex strikes back at change, and is the tool with which to aggressively put down attempts at universal equality and social modernization; it has, realistically and unfortunately, an element of intolerance. The United States has such an ingrain streak of intolerance in it that true social freedoms will never manifest unless a massive shift in social consciousness occurs.

The tremendous mental refocus that America needs will have to encompass several things: a rejection of materialist capitalism for a pure and free market; a willingness to stand together in collective solidarity, rather than majoritarian democracy; a complete minimization of the government and its removal from *all* matters other than a small number of key industries; and the a social perspective based on tolerance and equality, not dogmatic bias.

Yet, with the American consciousness the way that it is, it is not willing to adopt this perspective. It is trapped in an endless cycle of consumerism and imperialism: that is, radical Westernism, a system of misplaced values that places religious dogma, materialist economics, and a fervent deviation from libertarianism to static conservatism. And, throughout the years, radical Westernism has branched out into more than a prejudiced culture or a poorly functioning economic system: the extreme views held by modern America have permeated into imperialist foreign policy and blatant corporatism. Radical Westernism holds, in fact, truer to statism, fascism, and government interventionism that is does to the libertarianism and minarchism that the country's founders espoused.

The Modern Imperialist-Consumer

The materialist and fanatically traditionalist system that is radical Westernism, most easily exemplified in America, has two key elements to it: imperialism, as demonstrated in the foreign policy of interventionism and nation-building, in the name of "national security"; and consumerism, wherein members of society are judged as valuable only when they are able to effectively produce wealth and purchase superior products. These two elements have become the pinnacle of capitalist thought - the belief that material production and consumption makes a person inherently valuable, and the concept of entering a foreign nation to tap into their potential resources to churn the capitalist machine. Regrettably, capitalism and traditionalism - and their imperial and consumerist extensions - have been so reaffirmed and restated that they have become permanently etched into the American psyche. Imperialism and foreign conflict, America believes, is natural and right, and expansive military might grants the right to act as the world moderator and police force. The wonders of "free market capitalism", too, are now readily accepted, even though those being brutalized by the too-big-too-fail corporations in it and the endless consumerist cycle refuse to believe that removal of private industry could ever be good.

Continuous reaffirmation is propaganda, and the United States has self-indoctrinated itself into believing its own propaganda.

American citizens have become little more than imperialist-consumers: individuals who regard "free market capitalism", interventionist and nation-building foreign policy, and materialism as normal part of their lives. As imperialist-consumers, Americans love the concept of attacking those in foreign nations for actual or perceived offenses, or working fiercely to promote democracy and build an allied nation. They also love money, wherein many citizens base important life decisions and actions on finances, not their true desires or wishes. They have become mindless, willing slaves to capitalism.

Imperialist-consumers, blinded by the veil of capitalist worship, make up an overwhelming majority of the American populace. They are so prevalent, in fact, that they are both the citizens and their governmental representatives. The representatives, being imperialist-consumers, use the oppressive mouthpiece of a democratic government to pass their own pro-capitalist and anti-modernist ideology. The American government is unique from all others that it is unapologetically in line with the behaviors and beliefs of the imperialist-consumers that make it up: the United States openly uses its power to pass capitalist agendas, preserve its intolerant traditionalism, and suppress any dissenting thought.

The concept of the "thought police" are common in dystopian nations - a specialized police force in charge of enforcing the dominant political party or leader's ideology, and crush any difference of opinion. The United States claims that such totalitarian behavior is unjust and evil, and reminiscent of authoritarian countries such as the Soviet Union under Stalin or the Third Reich under Hitler. Yet while the United States may claim to stand in opposition to fascist ideology and condemn state-sanctioned secret police, its actions do not. The radical advocacy of capitalism by imperialist-consumers is a form of cultural police, an intangible but ever-present social atmosphere that shuns those that wish to dismantle capitalism, labeling *them* the radicals, and alienates the non-conformists, decrying that their actions are an immoral "alternative lifestyle". The United States may not have an organized secret police to actively advocate its capitalist doctrine, but the culture of imperialist-consumers does so. This "police culture" enforces societal norms and suppresses dissent more effectively than any organized police force could.

The American government and the imperialist-consumers have twisted the libertarianism that the country's founders espoused and into a perverted form of statist conservatism: a paradoxical system in which conservatives, while calling government evil, openly use its power for the benefit of corporations and to instigate foreign conflicts. The passage of laws that restrict freedoms and privacy, the usage of federal authority to enforce traditionalism, and the anti-liberal sentiment that runs through American politics - the government of imperialist-consumers relentlessly pushes forth its agenda, edged upon by the support of the police culture.

American imperialist-consumers have no qualms with using federal power for their gain, and to enforce their own philosophy. The empowerment of the military-industrial complex is present in the ever-expanding "defense" budgets passed by the legislature, with which funding foreign invasions and missile systems are built; the passage of anti-privacy laws, wiretapping rights, and racial profiling only imposes statist control; and refusal by the government to grant equal rights to all demographics shows the harsh bias of religious orthodoxy. Unfortunately, there is no mass opposition movement in America against radical Westernism: these schemes and plans will constantly come to fruition became the imperialist-consumers are so indoctrinated by the police culture and consistent reaffirmation. Radical Westernism has become so overtly materialist and statist that it has warped into a degenerating neo-fascist state.

The concepts of libertarianism, minimalist government, and free markets died generations ago: they grew into statist conservatism, capitalist worship, and an imperialist-consumer society. Even nowadays, it continues to change. The United States of America has become an openly authoritarian state that blatantly invades other countries for their resources, and preaches orthodoxy and social segregation; its anti-liberal and pro-capitalist structure make it something that any European fascist would be proud of.

America, while not a fascist state, is well on its way to becoming one.

The primary reason for this is its because the free market, singularized and glorified, has become profit-idolizing capitalism, with the police culture and the imperialist-consumers supporting its existence - and, with that unwavering support and the approval of the government, individuals with money have risen to power. Money, presently, is the means with which we quantify a person or institution's value, and those that have a great deal of money rise above the rest. This elevation of businesses and profit-earning institutions to near godhood has taken capitalism - already perverted and destructive in its own right - and laced it with elements of corporatism. Corporatism, or the existence of overwhelmingly large corporations and their direct influence in government, has become a stable part of the American economy. Large, private corporations enter deals with the government over weaponry, natural resources, and commercial rights and are involved in interventionism. They donate incalculable amounts of money to political candidates that would deregulate them and allow them to run free; they have a parasitic relationship with the government and the two are intimately connected.

Big business and government have, quite literally, become molded together into one entity. This disturbing realization, when coupled with the fact that the government pushes fiercely for traditional values and refuses to acknowledge modernism or individualism, have given it a distinct authoritarian slant.

The evolution of the free market into capitalism, and capitalism into outright corporatism, as well as the incessant desire to preserve traditionalism through the refusal to grant universal, equal rights, makes the government markedly leaning towards fascism. Certain elements, such as the belief in racial segregation and genetic purity, are not present; but others, such as racial profiling and anti-immigration sentiments, could very well evolve into them. The participation in never-ending wars, the status as the world moderator and police force, and the perception that warfare and interventionism are patriotic are all on their way to becoming the open veneration of war itself. And the American trend of anti-communism, born out of McCarthyism, has grown to encompass all left-wing thought, swelling into hatred for socialism, progressivism, and liberalism, be they real or perceived elements of them. These traits: corporatism, anti-immigration, revered warfare, and left-wing hostility are all prevalent and active in American society.

These features are but the ingredients in America's evolution into a neo-fascist state. Actions must be taken by the citizenry in order to curtail this degeneration, or else this objective theorization will become manifest. These actions cannot be small pockets of dissenting opinion and a gradual re-shifting of American consciousness - they must be a massive, societal reaction against the expanding powers of the natural complex. The change cannot be gradual or slow; it must be immediate and rapid.

A National Solution

For all of the problems that the United States faces, they are each tied by a single, common thread: economics. Unfortunately, money has become the root of evil in America, and is widely viewed as the lifeblood that keeps the nation moving. In order to restore the country to the minarchist state that it should be and regain liberty, there is one solution: a total transformation of the American economy. As America has come to rest on a capitalist foundation, the community needs to remove that foundation and replacing it with a new one.

Removal of capitalism will do multiple things: first off, it will put an end to material worship, and take all power from the corporations; end the viscous cycle that imperialist-consumers are trapped in; dissolve majoritarian democracy; refocus government and place its authority is key industries; and liberate individuals and grant them social freedoms.

The powerful corporations that influence the government and dominate society derive their power from the cultural police and the societal belief that money and capitalism are superior to anything else. By eradicating capitalism, the social perception that money is power will fade, and the too-powerful companies and business that influence the government would be taken out, leaving the government to do what the people say, not what the corporations want. Corporatism's existence is a travesty, wherein capitalism and profit are placed above all else. A conspicuous transition from revering capitalism to restoring the free market will come about via a shift in social awareness.

This shift in awareness and understanding will not only refocus the collective consciousness on the free market, but the end to the ceaseless self-imposed slavery to capitalism that imperialist-consumers are in. Capitalist worship is self-induced imperialist-consumer behavior. A nation, ceasing to obsess over the wonders of the "free market capitalist system", will be able to give true economic liberty and determinism to its people.

A complete dissolution of democracy is also needed: while many countries, ideologies, and individuals fervently espouse democracy and democratization abroad via nation-building, democracy is, as stated before, nothing more than a tyranny of the majority. This tyranny overlooks the dissenting views of the minority and refuses to acknowledge or act upon their will or welfare, caring only for the plurality. Many state that democracy is a superior, wonderful system, and condemn the abuse inflicted by socialist and communist governments. Yet while such governments do, and have, had a track of human rights violations, at least they were working towards establishing a collective, fair, and equal society; they may have ended up as a dystopia, but they at least willing to open their eyes to the horrors of deregulated capitalism and have tried to do something about it. Democracy, socialism, and communism all need to be ignored and forgotten, and the United States needs to work towards a system that advocates solidarity, charity, and equality, yet without any elements of majoritarianism or revolutionism. The transition from capitalism to equality must be peaceful, and the system that replaces it must take the interests of the entire community into consideration, not just the majority.

Leaving capitalism behind, the government must withdraw all of its expansionistic tendrils and interventionism, both domestic and abroad. The government needs to remove itself from all activities and drastically shrink - every element of it needs to dissolve except those capable of providing healthcare, education, housing, food, energy, and defense. These six key industries is all that government should have any power over, and that power should be complete and unrivaled. It should not concern itself with economic regulation, as a truly free market will be self-regulated through competition and trade; it should not attempt to interfere with the market or affect the rate of currencies, as market fluctuations and demands will act as the regulators of currency value. The government should also not deal with land ownership or property limits, as all natural terrain is in existence for the collective use of the community, and the free market may only stake a claim to land and acreage so long as it does not harm the public.

The government's sole involvement should be fiercely restricted to these six industries: any other influence should be immediately revoked. Any attempt to control people's lives, dictate what they can or cannot do with their body, or control their actions is both inappropriate and a gross violation of power. Free association, drug usage, marriage, reproduction, and open speech - these things, among many others, are given, human rights that all people have and should not be subject to governmental involvement.

The dissolution of capitalism will come about with an equal, collective society that can practice true liberty, with its members caring for each other through solidarity and compassion. A solution to the nation's problem is a change in the level of government spending, regulation or deregulation, or passing or repealing laws. The solutions that all nations need is the absolute, unapologetic destruction of capitalism. The people must be willing to open their eyes and look past the veil of propaganda that they surrounded with; they must be willing to recognize that America is on the definitive road to fascism and must immediately turn around.

Radical Westernism must be destroyed, and it will only come about at the eradication of capitalism; capitalism, in turn, can only be eradicated when the people stand up and refuse to participate in an abusive, increasingly corrupt system. The people, having singularized and radicalized the free market into capitalism, are the only thing that can revert it back to its natural state, and they must do so immediately. The beginning of an American empire and fascist regime is close at hand and it must be stopped.

The only solution to America's problems is the action of its people, and that action must come soon, lest the nation slide into the same pit of overtly racist fascism that consumed Europe in the first half of the twentieth century. The people need to rise up and place well-being before profit, equality before majoritarianism, and community interests before those of corporations. The people, unwillingly and unknowingly, created the swelling cancer that is capitalism, and only they can remove it. Only the people, and a massive change in social consciousness, will be able to restore the United States to the country of liberty and equality that it was meant to be.

"Right to Work" not right for NH

New Hampshire has a long libertarian tradition and a strong support for its motto, "Live Free or Die". Since its conception, our state has been a safe haven for lovers of liberty and those who wish to escape the strong arm of government. We love the concept of being able to life our lives as we wish, with everyone holding strong to the idea of live-and-let-live. Our state is renown by numerous statistics for being a safe place to raise a family and a place of close-knit communities. Yet this seems to be changing: our advocacy for freedom and dependability appears to be taking a turn for the worse.

    The New Hampshire government has often remained at a distance, doing its best to protect our citizenry and attempting to stay out of our private affairs at the same time. Since the admittance of William O'Brien to the position of Speaker of the House, our conventional perspectives of Concord have drastically shifted. He has taken it upon himself to establish his personal doctrine, working to repeal marriage equality and restrict college voting rights. His latest escapade includes this so-called "right to work" bill. Has he forgotten the national attention that Wisconsin received when their government tried to dismantle the rights of labor unions? Or has he been oblivious to the recent court cases that have voted in favor of those workers? It seems that O'Brien, and his willingness to go against standard congressional procedures, is doing everything that he can to ram through another ideological bill.

    Let's take a moment to compare the environment that workers were in in 1910 and those that they had in 2010. Over the space of a century, what did labor unions accomplish? Child labor laws were far less rigid, the workplace was less safe, and there was less of a chance for bargaining for better hours, wages, and benefits. Without the advocacy of unions, we would still be trapped in the early phases of the 20th century, wherein wage-laborers has no defense against the power of the industrial complex. Unions have served as an integral piece of what has make the American markets so great.

Every worker should reserve the right to take part in an occupation that does not have a union that mandates membership for employment. However, O'Brien's "right to work" bill stretches farther than that. It removes the right of those unions to bargain with the employer. If your union wants to negotiate with its employer for an employment contract and better healthcare, it will be unable to; if you want to utilize union resources to improve your workplace, you will not have that opportunity.

There are those who hold anti-union stances because they believe that unions are little more than institutions that take care of slackers. Yet regardless of whatever public entity you have, there will always be those that abuse it. Human beings are not inherently altruistic; there will be those who will use it for their advantage. But this does not discount the fact that unions have been instrumental in bettering the work environment. We need to remember the improvements that have happened over the years to protect laborers due to employee-employer bargaining.

I pray that our state representatives and senators remember the progress that labor unions have made, and side with the working class by voting against O'Brien's "right to work" legislation. This bill is not right for workers anywhere, especially in our state that respects minimal government and individual liberty.

The Realpolitik of Socialism

"People speak of socialism. Perhaps they should speak of socialisms."
- Michael Harrington

Nowadays, the term socialism means almost nothing. It has been used by such a number of differing people to describe different things in different time periods that the word itself has been completely devoid of all meaning. The political parties throughout industrialized Europe, the government-run economies of China and the former Soviet Union, the Communist Party-led massacres throughout Asia, and the dictators in Latin and Central America - each of these have been associated with the word socialism, yet none of them come close to its original definition.

Even here in the United States, where socialist organizations and groups that like to declare themselves as "socialist" have never amassed a particularly powerful presence, the word has been used as a rhetorical cudgel in politics to describe things so dirty that to be associated with it is political suicide. All too easily conservative politicians and commentators refer to progressives as socialists, even though neither camp is particularly qualified to understand it.

This represents a problem for those of us that want to understand what socialism is. Not the biased description that a would-be authoritarian regime has proclaimed, either; to understand the meaning and practice of socialism would be much harder than simply listening to the totalitarian Party élites.

The first thought that comes to mind at the word *Marxism* is a parade through the streets, with military-grade vehicles flying enormous blood-red flags adorned with the face of the nation's glorious leader. Images of North Korean-style dictatorships saturate the meaning of the word. But is that truly what Marxism represents? Is it an ideology of systemic oppression, of dictatorial power? Is the Western world's branding of Marxism as evil and anti-liberty warranted, or is it merely the product of a long-term propaganda war?

Marxism is, first and foremost, a philosophy of freedom. It may pursue liberation differently than constitutional republics traditionally have but it, in the end, is yet another political movement about liberty. And not some romanticized notion of liberty, either, as all-too-often expressed by the world's various patriots: the foundation of Marxism is a thorough analysis of the nature of capitalism, the laws of the economy, and the trends of history. It is objective, not an emotionalist appeal to some would-be utopia, free from the long arm of government intervention. No. Marxism is not an applicable political program; it is not a bulleted list of reforms that political parties petition congresses and parliaments to enact. Is is less of a ideology that can be passed and brought about through governmental legislation or action.

Marxism is a tool. Like the magnifying glasses and microscopes used by scientists of every discipline, Marxism is a tool with which we can analyze the power structures and economic systems that make up our world today. It is a way of studying the world, not a way of living in it; it a tool that we to see the world, not a way to rule it.

When non-Marxists look at the world, they analyze it many different ways. They may look at the religion of a culture to try to understand it. They may take a sociological point of view. They may study its language, art, and music. Or they may study its politics and government structure.

When Marxist looks at the world, though, he or she does focus on a single, specific facet of what constitutes the entire society. Culture are dynamic, organic, ever-changing, and complex. To limit ourselves to analyzing the world through one specific lens is both a disservice to us and the culture that we are trying to understand.

All of these things - religion, sociology, language, art, politics, and so on - are each narratives of society - they are one small piece of it. Marxists view society *as a whole*, not as a narrative. We recognize that all of them, when strung together, complement each other and build off one another until a truly bold culture is made. This culture, this collection of narratives that we have before us and which we can find in any society that has every existed throughout history, is what we Marxists call the superstructure. If we want to truly understand the world, we cannot pick a single piece of the superstructure to look at.

But if we can't break down the superstructure into its constituent pieces and analyze them, then how do we go about understanding the world around us? What on earth can we possibly do to unravel the mystery about what makes the world turn and history to continue to progress? The answer is right in front us of. We all remember the joking maxim that money is the root of all evil. It's more than just a simple turn of phrase, however. The root of all evil is the almighty dollar: everything in our capitalist society revolves around money. Thus we see that, instead of analyzing a society based on its *superstructure*, we need to view the *base* that acts as the foundation on which the superstructure stands.

The base in the political economy - the dynamic web of economic relations that, when viewed in its totality, constitute an economic system. The base is what needs to be scrutinized, not the superstructure.

Lenin expanded upon the theories that Marx and Engels penned in the *Manifesto* (as well as their other writings) by conceptualizing and coining the idea of a having a political party be the spearhead of the revolution[98]. This vanguard party, he called it, would be composed of the proletarians who *had* developed class consciousness and who would act as the élite responsible for educating and organizing the remainder of the proletariat for the revolution. The Leninist vanguard party (incarnated in Russia as the Bolshevik faction of the Russian Social Democratic Labor Party, of which Lenin eventually assumed control) would lead and direct the revolution. It would practice democratic centralism, wherein the party would debate what policy to advocate and how to go about performing the

---

[98] Lenin is not the only one to deal with the idea of a vanguard party. Amedeo Bordiga, an Italian communist, came to many of the same conclusions, although it was Lenin who put the ideas of vanguardism into practice. The result, as we now know, was the Communist Party dictating the actions of the Soviet Union.

revolution, but, once that policy is decided, the entire party would adhere to it and would not tolerate any dissent. Democratic centralism has been criticized as being inherently non-democratic, but Leninists defend it as being an effective method for coordinating mass-proletarian action against a retaliating bourgeois class.

The dictatorship of the proletariat, too, would be replaced with a "dictatorship of the party", for lack of a better analogy. Rather than have the proletariat seize control of, and centralize ownership of, the means of production and the State, the vanguard party would do so in their name. With the vanguard in control of the State and all production, it would be able to marshal and direct all national resources towards instigating sympathetic socialist revolutions in surrounding countries, and to wage war against the bourgeois, bourgeois-sympathizing, and anti-revolutionary groups that may seek to quell the new proletarian system.

Lenin theorized that the proletariat would never obtain the class consciousness necessary to spark a truly proletarian revolution. He argued that the best that the working class would develop would be trade union consciousness, that workers would group together into trade unions and labor unions to push for better rights, conditions, and benefits in the work place. The proletariat, Lenin said, would fight for specific, momentary reforms rather than try to abolish the entire oppressive capitalist system; once they got the small reform that they wanted, they would stop pushing for change. As an example to illustrate this, we can look at two specific examples:
the lack of proletarian revolutions, and the stopgap of social democracy.

No capitalist nation has ever had a socialist revolution. Why this is, and whether nor not it will happen and when, are fiercely debated topics amongst the Marxist community. Marx did not predict a revolution in feudal Russia or agrarian China - he postulated that they would happen in advanced, industrialized countries instead. The fact that such countries - most notably North America and Europe - had there workers eventually grouping into trade unions instead of rising up together *en masse* to replace capitalism with a proletarian-based system. It's working class was forming workers *unions*, not workers *governments*. Countries that have robust and influential trade unions, such as Germany or France, have not formed socialist or proletarian governments - they are very much industrial and capitalist, and will continue to be so for the the imaginable future.

Both Germany and France, however, contain elements of social democratic politics, wherein the government has intervened and granted its citizens universal healthcare, social security, and pro-active social policies. Or have the bourgeoisie granted them to the proletariat so as to keep them complacent enough that they will not revolt against the system? That is the question that needs to be asked about progressive nations - not about how much "progress" and "equality" it has accomplished, but rather how much the bourgeoisie has tricked the proletariat by dangling the carrot of reform in front of them to keep them just comfortable enough. This stopgap measure of the proletarian complacency quells the working class' revolutionary tendencies and keeps them as part of the capitalist system.

Unfortunately, the primary premise of Leninism - the establishment of a revolutionary vanguard party so as to work around trade union consciousness, and to use that vanguard party to centralize the means of production against the bourgeois - proves to be its historical undoing. As Marx himself pointed out, socialism must be brought about by the proletariat itself in an advanced capitalist country. It runs in opposition to the historical dialectic, which states that history has a natural course. Lenin's vanguardism circumvents that course by attempting to surgically insert the party into the historical process and induce a revolution when the time for one hasn't come about. This is the underlying problem with vanguardism: that one can never be sure if the revolution is taking place in the right historical moment, or if it should be delayed until the means of production are more sophisticated.

When Russia and China both underwent their vanguard-led revolutions, they took place in backwards villages; they were still trapped in feudalism and agrarianism. Neither of them had entered modernity and developed sophisticated productive processes. They were, quite literally, not ready for socialism. Vanguardism, however, attempts to insert itself into the historical process and instigate a party-led revolution - as we can see from looking back in history, neither Russia nor China were ready for such an event. What resulted was not socialism in any sense of the word, but rather a party-led regime whose attempt to centralize the means of production so as to induce the industrialization necessary for socialism ended in sheer totalitarianism.

The government-run production in the Soviet Union was not socialist. Indeed, we know that socialism requires a society to pass through capitalism beforehand. Despite what Soviet sympathizers and self-described "socialists" may say about the achievements of the Soviet Union, it was in no way socialist. DSA founder Michael Harrington justifiably referred to the USSR as "bureaucratic collectivism". However, the term generally accepted on both the Left and Right to describe the Soviet Union is *state capitalism*. State capitalism refers to any nation where production, distribution, and allocation - in effect, total control of the means of production - are under the control of the State. Government ownership of the means of production allows it to influence the rate at which production and industrialization occurs, and places in absolute control of the economy.

As his Bolsheviks assumed leadership and established the USSR, Lenin became starkly aware of what an enormous task lay before him in turning feudal Russia into a socialist utopia. He recognized that the country was not developed enough to step fully into socialism. Therefore he advocated state capitalism in the form of his New Economic Plan (NEP), which placed only the "commanding heights of the economy" - that is, the most powerful and influential sectors of the Russian economy - under direct government ownership. Over time, this ownership expanded to encompass most, if not all, industry. With the Soviet Union able to dictate the direction that they economy took, they tried to find an alternative, non-free market approach to sufficient industrialization. The government's forced production lead to the mismanagement of resources, poor allocation of produced materials, and wide-spread famines.

We cannot merely look at the Soviet Union's state capitalism as destructive to its people, although its relentless, government-ordered production did lead to incalculable deaths. It also led to Russia going from a feudal-agrarian society still in the clutches of an autocratic monarchy to being an industrial superpower with an economy dynamic enough to challenge the United States as the world's leader.

State capitalism, for all its faults and authoritarianism, did allow Russia to develop sophisticated means of production. Who knows if it would have been able to accomplish, if it and the United States had not entered the Cold War and its economy collapsed? Perhaps it would have found a way to obtain the prerequisites for socialism that differed from the US' free market capitalism. Perhaps it really would have allowed Russia to develop rapid, powerful, planned production that could have completely overcome all forms of scarcity.

If the revolution would have occurred in a mature capitalist country, the outcome would have been entirely different. Even if the revolution would be lead by a vanguardist organization, the means of production are much more likely to be sophisticated and diverse enough to overcome scarcity and allow the society to transition into socialism. As we have discussed before, the hyper-active and poorly planned usage of the modern means of production have expectedly induced a Marxian crisis of overproduction. The result of a modern day proletarian revolution or vanguardist revolution would certainly have different results than they did in the Soviet Union, and the potential need for any modicum of state capitalism would probably be very rare, temporary, and restricted to small, specific sectors of the economy.

Keynesian vs Austrian: Two Names for Bourgeois Exploitation

As much as they would like you to think otherwise, the economic approaches of the progressive Democrats and the conservative Republicans are one and the same. The rhetoric that the American Left (although there is certainly nothing legitimately left-wing about it) and the Right may sound wildly different - they'll both evoke romanticized notions of personal liberty and economic prosperity, with wealth being created in such abundance that no citizen will ever be victim to scarcity or market volatility ever again.

The Keynesians think that the utilization of government funds to stimulate the economy will lead to greater wealth for all. Priming the pump, they say, will cause money to flow easier, circulate faster, and reach all parties. What they're doing, though, isn't providing defibrillation to a seized-up economy: it's setting the foundation for a state-run economy vis-à-vis massive government subsidies. As economic stimuli, subsidies, and bailouts become more common and more needed to prop up the government-dependent economy, the market shifts to one of increasingly public ownership. This doesn't liberate the proletariat from the exploitation inherent in private property, though; transferring property from the private to public sphere doesn't change the fact that it is still *capitalist* property. Keynesianism sets the stage for a host of terrible possibilities: state capitalism and private centralization of all the means of production; fascism, hiding behind the veil of patriotism and the fetishization of private property; or outright corporate rule, codified into law by the monopoly-run nation.

Those that decry Keynesianism as socialistic for its usage of public funds clearly have an inadequate understanding of socialism - pure socialism, unadulterated by the taint of the Western propaganda machine. Keynesian economics empower the State apparatus by granting it greater economic control - and socialism, if it is anything, is vehemently opposed to the State.

The Austrians take an approach that is directly opposite that of the Keynesians. Rather than declare government intervention to be the answer, they presuppose that all economic decisions should be made by *private* entities instead. Thus we see that the public-private dichotomy, with which many Western capitalists view as being synonymous with oppression-liberation, shown again. Keynesians and Austrians do not focus on anything more superficial than whether or not property should be public or private; they do not have the insight necessary to see that the probably inherent in the *existence of property*, not whether or not it is public or private.

The Austrians, though, passionately evangelize about the perfect competition and universal equality that would be present in a deregulated and governmentless market with alarming purism. Their approach is a fundamentalist one, one that bears no room for compromise or for any modicum of regulation to protect the weakest of citizens from the harsh edges of the market. And when their approaches fail - as they are certainly doomed to, as the "free" market is only the embryo of monopolies and of state capitalism - they will laugh and brush away the criticism, saying that the market was not deregulated enough, that capitalism was not pure enough, or that there were too many elements of government involvement that tainted the natural wonders of the "free" market.

Their unwillingness to acknowledge economic logic is astounding. They will spin webs of emotionalist rhetoric, speaking endless about how they, and they alone, understand liberty, and how the application of their liberty will result in abundant wealth for all. Their misunderstanding is not only comical, but downright dangerous - Austrian ideology spawn not only economic blindness, but also a viscous and unpredictable market-place that serves as an economic synonym for Darwin's jungle. Only the strongest will survive, and if their survival and growth is dependent upon crushing the lesser ones beneath then, then so be it. In a deregulated market, there are no rules other than this: the strongest will flourish, and the weakest will be cast aside like scraps as food as the corporate powers consume the small business in their never-ending quest for profit.

In the end, does it matter whether we act as Austrians or Keynesians? Whether or not we set the foundation for outright corporate rule by deregulating the market, or if we expand the public sector and redistribute the wealth via economic stimuli, will not make any difference. Focusing on, and expanding, private or public property will not solve our problems, nor will it create a sustainable economy geared in the interests of the working class. Doing so will only perpetuate capitalism, and that means that both ideologies are tools of the bourgeoisie. If we are going to abolish the capitalist mode of production and replace it with an alternative, then we need to look at the *real* causes of capitalist failure and end these shallow, politicized arguments.

Made in the USA
Lexington, KY
11 March 2014